Louis Massignon

The Crucible of Compassion

Louis Massignon

The Crucible of Compassion

MARY LOUISE GUDE

University of Notre Dame Press
Notre Dame and London

Library of Congress Cataloging-in-Publication Data

Gude, Mary Louise, 1939–
    Louis Massignon : the crucible of compassion / by Mary Louise Gude.
    p. cm.
    ISBN 0-268-01308-X (hardcover : alk. paper)
    1. Massignon, Louis, 1883–1962.   2. Orientalists—France—
Biography.   3. Scholars, Muslim—France—Biography.   I. Title.
BP49.5.M3G83   1995
297'.092—dc20
    [B]   95-18778
                                                                          CIP

*The paper used in this publication meets the minimum requirements of the
American National Standard for Information Sciences—Permanence of
Paper for Printed Library Materials, ANSI Z39.48-1984*

Contents

Acknowledgments

This book became a reality thanks to the insights and unfailing generosity of many persons. My work and life have been enriched by their friendship and support. Frank Bowman was crucial to the inception of this project: he challenged me to write a biography of Louis Massignon for an American audience and later critiqued successive versions of the manuscript. Others who read the manuscript and made invaluable suggestions include David Burrell, C.S.C., Sidney Griffith, and Herbert Mason. John Dunne, C.S.C., who years ago introduced me to the study of Hallaj, discussed Massignon with me on many a Sunday evening. Access to unpublished or out-of-print materials became possible thanks to Roger Arnaldez, Patrick Gaffney, C.S.C., Jacques Keryell, and François de Laboulaye. Finally, a word of thanks goes to Eugene Gorski, C.S.C., who listened and encouraged every step of the way, and to Ann Rice, a most patient and perspicacious editor.

Introduction

This account of Louis Massignon's life introduces a rich and complex story to an American audience in the hope that more complete studies will follow. Although it is by no means a definitive biography, it will provide access to the life of a world-renowned scholar of Islam who was also a Christian mystic, a man whose academic career is inseparable from his personal commitment to the Muslim world. The work of Louis Massignon is well-known to students of Islam or of French history in the twentieth century. However, aside from his monumental four-volume *Passion de Hallaj* and several essays, all translated by Herbert Mason, little else by or about him has yet been published in English. In the last fifteen years useful works about various aspects of his life and work have appeared in France, but these are limited because primary sources remain scattered and unevenly available. By necessity then, while this biography uses Massignon's own writings and some primary materials, it also relies extensively on secondary sources such as the testimony of those who knew him personally. Because in some instances little material for a given period was available, a given source was used more extensively than might otherwise have been the case. Although gleaned piecemeal from a variety of documents, nevertheless a compelling image of the man emerges. However elusive that image, the glimpse provided by monographs, personal tributes, and reminiscences reveal an extraordinary human being whose life spanned an extraordinary period.

Louis Massignon (1883–1962) dominated the field of Islamic

studies in the first half of the twentieth century, and his career, begun in 1900, spanned more than sixty years. Yet distinguished as that career was, today his name would probably be known only within the scholarly world were it not for a life whose range defies easy categories. The era in which he lived was itself remarkable; Massignon's generation saw a world undone and another, more frightening one, arise from its ashes. Their youth ended in the conflagration of one world war; their careers and countries were almost shattered by the second one; and their final years were accompanied by the disintegration of colonial empires and the beginning of the cold war.

As a university professor, Massignon could have been only minimally involved in the shifting events of his time. However, such was not the case, in part because at the turn of the century, when he came of age, scholars and universities expanded their role in French society. Thus, by reason of his spectacular intellectual gifts, he was well placed not only to shape Islamic studies in France for two generations, but to make his voice heard well beyond his discipline. In this he was not alone, although the positions he took often marginalized him; during this period French intellectuals within and outside the academy made their presence felt in the larger society.

As controversial as the voice of Massignon sometimes was, both admirers and detractors agree that he was a genius. Superbly educated by some of the best teachers of the time, he could converse knowledgeably about topics as disparate as European literature, medieval Baghdad, Celtic and Japanese folk traditions, or contemporary Middle East politics. His learning was prodigious, so prodigious in fact, that listeners often came away with their minds reeling from the dense erudition of his celebrated monologues.

Initially trained as a philologist, Massignon spoke ten languages and read many more. The unique stamp of his scholarship, namely his effort to comprehend Islam on its own terms, can be traced to this grounding in language, where a given culture expresses itself most intimately. Through his focus on Semitic languages, particularly Arabic, the man and the scholar became one; the experience of reading the Qur'an and texts of the Muslim mystics fused a deeply personal quest for God with professional aspirations. This led, on the one hand, to his dramatic religious conversion in May 1908 and, on the other hand, to his monumental doctoral dissertation on the tenth-century Sufi martyr Al-Hallaj. The decision to study Islam from within and to understand it on its own terms resulted not from preconceived method; rather it expressed the direct link between Islam and his own life. Through Islam he had rediscovered his Christian roots and pledged himself both to a passionate search for God and to the welfare of Muslims throughout the world. Hallaj became not merely a topic for study; the Sufi challenged him to live heroically, and Massignon met that challenge with single-minded passion until the end.

The biography of Hallaj reconstituted the entire social and political milieu of the period and would have sufficed to assure Massignon's academic renown, but his interests were more far-reaching. His research covered the entire range of Islamic studies, from history to literature, from theology to philosophy, from archeology to contemporary issues, and he published in all those areas. However, by personal affinity, the development of Muslim mysticism remained Massignon's subject of predilection. Many judge that his most lasting scholarly contributions were made in this area. At his death Massignon was working on a second edition of the *Hallaj*, and he had published literally hundreds of articles. Whatever their immediate focus, the impetus for writing them remained the same, to further understanding between Islam and the West, and between Muslims and Christians. This goal, pursued in all areas of his life, bore fruit most strikingly perhaps in the deliberations of the Second Vatican Council. More than any other single person, Massignon was responsible for modifying the Church's stance toward Islam, a change he did not live to see.

Both tenacious and implacable, Massignon irritated some, who considered his demands for social justice unreasonable, his anger excessive, and the solutions he proposed, naïve. Yet all concur that Massignon was no ideologue and that his positions evolved along with the convulsions of the century. The agnostic became the Christian mystic; the young military officer became the disciple of Gandhi; the venerated scholar became increasingly an outspoken defender of the disenfranchised. And if the years have underscored that some aspects of Massignon's thinking reflect the prevailing political and theological currents of his time, they have likewise confirmed other insights as prophetic. He foresaw the potential impact of religious fundamentalism on the development of Muslim countries, decried the situation of the Palestinians vis-à-vis Israel, and predicted that the refugee camps would yield only a harvest of violence. He saw that an increasingly interdependent world would survive its racial, ethnic, and religious differences only by understanding, respecting and ultimately welcoming the stranger, the other. For Massignon this conviction went well beyond political necessity. The commitment to sacred hospitality, as he termed it, was grounded in his deep faith in the transcendent other, the God who in Jesus asked for hospitality and died on a cross. That commitment ultimately defined and consumed his life.

ONE

Beginnings

A period of intellectual and cultural ferment marked the 1880s in France as the society moved ineluctably toward industrialization and the twentieth century. The works of artists and writers reflected either nostalgia for a world rapidly disappearing or enthusiasm for the emerging new order. The painting of the salon artists was challenged and ultimately supplanted by the Impressionists. Yet the sculptures of Auguste Rodin were often considered too radical for official commissions. The Symbolist poets rebelled against the positivism of Auguste Taine even as Zola illustrated the theories of naturalism in his novels.

If in retrospect the age was illumined by the outpouring of literary and artistic genius from a rising generation, the turmoil perceived at the time produced uncertainty and tension in all segments of society. The government sought to restore confidence in the nation following the 1870 defeat at the hands of the Germans, and its strategy included colonial expansion; to Algeria, conquered in 1830, was added Tunisia, which became a protectorate in 1881. The Catholic Church was beleagured from within by the "modernists," who taught a developmental unfolding of dogma, and from without by increasing hostility from the government. Finally, the Dreyfus affair had laid bare profound societal divisions. Conservatives, usually Catholic, often anti-Semitic, tended to be nostalgic for the monarchy and opposed the policies of the newly formed Third Republic, while those who had fought to rehabilitate Dreyfus supported the republic and tended to be agnostic.

Into this contradictory and shifting world Louis Fernand Jules

1

Massignon was born July 25, 1883, joined by a sister, Henriette, five years later. The chateau of Agnes Sorel, favorite of Charles VII, once stood on the site of his birthplace, a home in Nogent-sur-Marne, a suburban area southeast of Paris near the park of Vincennes. The Massignon family traced its history back to 1603, to the Vexin, a region on the Oise River northwest of Paris. In the village of Arronville a family of "massons," small tradespeople, provided the earliest record. The ancestors of Massignon's mother, Marie Hovyn, had originally been weavers from Flanders. Massignon's father, Fernand, was the grandson of peasants who had cultivated the land for five generations. They had lived in Labbeville from around 1628, moving eventually to Paris to escape the upheaval following the revolution.[1]

Fernand Massignon (1855–1922) was born and died in Paris, but by his son's testimony, never lost touch with the land and his peasant roots; "he remained permeable to the spell of simple agricultural life, to the sense of a pure mystery hidden behind Nature's naive cruelty."[2] The elder Massignon was educated as a doctor, but his passion was art, and he abandoned medicine to became a sculptor, medalist and engraver, under the pseudonym Pierre Roche, the name of his maternal grandfather.[3] A student and friend of both the officially favored Jules Dalou and the more controversial Auguste Rodin, Roche also frequented the Impressionists. He was a well-respected figure in the Paris art world of his time, best known for his experimentation with various materials, from wrought iron to paper. His sculpture still adorns certain Parisian buildings and gardens, including the Luxembourg. Influenced by the art of Japan, as were many of the Impressionists, he derived from the simple lines and heavy paper of Japanese prints, a technique which combined his skills as sculptor and engraver. He made "modeled etchings" by first setting them on plaster molds and then coloring them. A further refinement involved inserting the color in the mold itself so that color and form were imprinted simultaneously on the paper. These "*gypsographies*" as Roche named them were exhibited in Paris and later in Japan (1922), a fact his son recalled when he himself traveled to Japan in 1959.[4]

Either at home or in his studio, rue Vaneau, the artwork of Pierre Roche nurtured the imagination and intuition of his son. It prepared the latter as a young man to see haunting beauty in the desert and the Middle East. And if he continued to evolve intellectually throughout his life, the ability to do so was undoubtedly influenced by his father's wide-ranging interests and openness to the world. Reporting on an exhibit at the Galliera Museum, Roche noted that critics "insisted on the important role the Galliera exhibits were called upon to play in the renewal of the industrial arts." He talked about how "the contrast between Past and Present was instructive for the artist, and how the engaging mixture of tradition and innovation conferred an attractive novelty on these exhibits and the unique place they occupied among the creations of the city of Paris."[5] The elder Massignon was actively involved in his son's education; his intellectual vigor, passion for travel, and artistic sensibility shaped those same qualities in the young Louis.

The family lived comfortably, first in the rue Solferino and then in the rue de l'Université, not far from the Invalides. Both streets were situated in the seventh *arrondissement* of Paris, then the most affluent residential area of the city. Because his family was financially secure and intellectually privileged, myriad opportunities existed for the child to explore. When Louis was fourteen, a trip to Italy with his parents was carefully prepared beforehand by an intensive study of its language, history, and art.[6] In the summer of 1898, when Massignon was fifteen, he traveled by himself through Germany and Austria. At seventeen, in 1901, he encountered the world of Islam for the first time, when he went alone to Algiers. However, family connections had introduced him to North Africa long before. Fernand Massignon had traveled in Algeria, and Louis as an old man mentioned the influence of his mother's godfather, Ferdinand-Désiré Quesnoy, who had served there as a military doctor.[7] By age twelve Louis was subscribing to the *Bulletin du comité de l'Afrique française* (and he remained a subscriber until the outbreak of World War II).[8]

As a *lycéen* from 1893 to 1899, Massignon pursued the baccalaureat, first at the Lycée Montaigne and then the Lycée Louis-le-Grand. There he was educated not only by some of the most renowned teachers of his time but also through the uniquely enriching friendship of Henri Maspero, son of the celebrated Egyptologist, Gaston Maspero. They met in 1896 when both were thirteen. That year, since Henri as a supervised day student was obliged to eat at school, their time together was limited. But the following year "we were able to see each other more easily, by quickly finishing our homework and using our free period to satisfy together our rage to read and understand."[9] The two made a conscious decision to scrutinize and in some sense " 'justify' all the other human cultures overseas, those scorned and trampled by our Greco-Roman hegemony." Together they prepared voluminous notebooks containing historical notes on the Middle East, the Orient, Africa, Oceania, and America before Columbus.[10] Massignon's interest in Middle Eastern studies began in the elder Maspero's library, and the boys' friendship had a decisive influence on the development of that interest. The two received special permission to work in the library of the Ecole des langues orientales, where Massignon would later earn a *diplôme* in classical and spoken Arabic. Even their leisure activity reflected the all-consuming interest in learning. Together they explored the basement areas of the Sorbonne, a practice which once caused them to stumble into the middle of an ampitheater, interrupting a class. Years later Massignon reminded Maspero of the incident in a letter about the marriage of his sister, Henriette Massignon: "Her husband, Pierre Girard, works in physiology (blood circulation) in the physical chemistry laboratory of Dastre (Sorbonne) above the underground passageways we used to explore back then."[11]

The correspondence between Louis and Henri began in 1901, a year after Massignon matriculated at the Sorbonne; it reveals the giftedness and the intellectual curiosity of the two young students, "absorbed in turn with Greek and classical literature, mathematics, history and archaeology, science, physiology, language, politics."[12] The two remained lifelong friends, Maspero becoming a Sinologist and colleague of Massignon at the Collège de France.

Letters of those school years confirm that Massignon's interest in languages and philology began early. In February 1901, while studying for the baccalaureat in mathematics, Massignon regretted that he was unable "to read much in the realms of history and philology, whose aroma we used to bask in together. However, I can tell you that I've gone through Ujfalvy in the Oriental Languages section, and that I find it altogether clear, scientific and precise, although a little long (in the phonetics)."[13] Three years before he "had compiled for himself a lexicon of the Germanic roots of the English noun, a feat characteristic of his scientific curiosity and his methodology of research throughout his life."[14]

If evidence of the future intellectual is manifest in these early years, traces can be found as well of the religious sensitivity that would so characterize the man. The family's religious tradition was Catholic, although only Marie Massignon practiced her faith. This disparity of belief within the home, which reflected tensions of the wider society, certainly influenced Massignon's own development. Fernand Massignon was an agnostic who had joined the newly formed League of the Rights of Man during the Dreyfus period. Yet as an artist and lover of nature, he was hardly imbued with the accepted positivism of the age. According to his son, the mystery inherent in the rhythms of nature allowed his father in spite of his agnosticism to accept that miraculous incidents did indeed occur. Foremost among these was the case of Joan of Arc, which Louis Massignon recalled when he visited Japan in 1959 and expressed in his own inimitable English:

> He had ceased to believe in God, but he confided [*sic*] in the miraculous birth of France in the fifteenth century, in the virginal apparitions among trees witnessed by Joan of Arc, after her candle offerings to Our Lady of Bermont in the forest; and had made a solitary silent pilgrimage in 1889 to Domremy.[15]

Fernand Massignon's veneration was also founded on the role of the Maid of Orleans in French history and her steadfast defense of her mission in the face of opposition by Church authorities. His son noted that a small image of Joan, an *églomisation* remained always on his father's studio table.[16] When asked about his own devotion to the saint, Massignon replied that it went back "forever, as with Saint Louis. Just as my father taught me to love Joan, my mother 'imposed' on me the name of Louis."[17]

The name Louis was officially conferred at his baptism, September 4, 1883, at the Church of Saint Saturnin in Nogent-sur-Marne, when the infant was a little over a month old; the ceremony had been delayed because of his father's misgivings about religious doctrine and practice. However, his mother's influence prevailed, and Louis Massignon had what could be described as a devout and very traditional Catholic childhood; he studied catechism at the Church of Saint Clotilde and sometimes served mass for Louis Poulin (1862–1924), the priest who oversaw his religious formation. As a boy of eleven in 1894, Massignon received his first communion and was confirmed. On that occasion, Marie Massignon, ever solicitous for her son's religious formation, had copied out from Bossuet, Fénelon, and Saint Francis de Sales, daily meditation texts for each day of the year. However the mother's faith was certainly countered by the father's skepticism, and the sensitive young boy was in some sense caught between the two, because no choice he might make about religious belief would please both his parents. Eventually the growing agnosticism of the period coupled with the thirst for discovery nurtured by his father, shifted the balance. The boy began to distance himself from the Catholic faith of his childhood. This disaffection proved a source of great anguish for his devout mother; she sent him to Lourdes in 1900, but to no avail.

Yet, fragments of Massignon's own writings and those of friends who knew him well revealed an early spiritual restlessness and longing, together with a desire to confront head-on and somehow understand the mystery of life's meaning. Very early this desire seems to have been linked with North Africa, Massignon's earliest contact with the Muslim world, a world which at the end of the nineteenth century was synonymous in the European mind with a realm of exotic escape. "As a very young child I had been attracted by desperate escapes out of a production-minded and Taylorized Europe."[18]

He was referring to nineteenth-century French explorers such as Camille Douls, who, leaving behind an increasingly industrialized society, undertook risky expeditions among native peoples. In a letter Massignon described how he had come to love Arabic; he states that "as a very young child I had dreamed about 'Africa and the desert' as countries where one could finally do battle—face to face— with neither veil nor armor, against danger and death."[19] The precociously intelligent boy seemed first to perceive North Africa as a land where imagination and the world somehow coincided. By entering it he could transcend the evident dilemma posed by the differing religious views of his parents. In this new and different world the thrill of intellectual discovery converged with the perception of surrounding mystery.

Yet for all his life-long involvement with the Muslim world and however far afield travel would ultimately take him, Massignon remained ever a Frenchman and was deeply rooted in the land of his birth. His setting in France rotated between Paris and Brittany all his life. He lived with his parents until his marriage in 1914, and the same seventh arrondissement always remained his home in Paris. Around 1901 Fernand Massignon bought property in Brittany: a home near Pordic in an area called Ville Evêque and a family burial chapel in the cemetery of Pordic. The Massignons spent summer vacations at their comfortable stone house overlooking the bay of Saint-Brieuc on the northern Breton coast. When the property no longer belonged to the family, Massignon rented a house at nearby Binic and until his death continued to spend summer vacations in Brittany with his own family.

As a young person, the ocean near his country home roused in him the same sense of mystery evoked later by the desert. He told his friend and editor, Vincent Monteil, that the ocean had provided a setting for his youthful questions and longings during his final years at the lycée: "He told me that before his year of philosophy, wandering after nightfall on the Breton beach of Binic, he remained stirred up, haunted by the impossible dilemma of death; either to cease thinking or to think indefinitely."[20] The image of the sea as limitless expanse would remain forever powerful for him and like the desert would come to signify the mystery of transcendence.

The son of an artist, Massignon responded throughout his life to such images and their ability to suggest ineffable meaning beyond themselves. Long before his conversion he perceived intimations of the sacred through art. During the trip to Italy with his parents, he walked into the Church of San Donato de Murano (on the isle of Merano in the Venetian lagoon) and was immediately overwhelmed by a sense that the immense mosaic veil of Mary was falling toward him from the altar.[21] Indeed, it could be said that Fernand Massignon, meticulously concerned about forming his gifted son's intellect, ultimately exerted his greatest influence through the legacy he bequeathed as an artist. That gift indirectly prepared Massignon for his dramatic conversion. Art hinted to the son that the meaning of existence transcended all immediate perceptions of the world as conveyed by the five senses.

The father's work also introduced Massignon to literary and artistic personalities of the time, thereby expanding the boy's perspective beyond that of his privileged *bourgeois* background. This was nowhere more true than in the case of Pierre Roche's friendship with Joris Karl Huysmans (1848–1907), the novelist of the French "decadance," celebrated not only for his writing but also for his conversion and return to Catholicism in 1891, which were documented in three later novels, *En Route, La Cathédrale, L'Oblat,* and the posthumously published *Là-Haut.* The intellectual and spiritual journey recounted there traces his attempt to find moorings in an age of profound transition. The lessons of such an itinerary would not be lost on Louis Massignon.

Huysmans was the only Christian friend of Pierre Roche, and the artist sometimes visited the novelist in Paris or later at the latter's semi-monastic retreat at Ligugé, a village in Poitou near the Benedictine abbey of Saint-Martin. There the writer had constructed a home for his life as a Benedictine oblate. Roche and Huysmans possessed a common friend in a young religious artist, Charles-Marie Dulac, who had introduced the two. Roche created the frontispiece for *La Cathédrale*, a novel in which Dulac is highly praised. Both Huysmans and Roche watched over the young artist during his last illness and at his death in December 1898. Dulac willed a crucifix to Roche, which according to Massignon his agnostic father did not keep.[22] The following spring Roche helped organize an exhibit of the deceased artist's work. In January 1900, he went to see Huysmans at Ligugé and later that year sent his son to visit, armed with a letter of introduction for his old friend.[23]

Massignon arrived from Béarn on the afternoon train October 27 and spent six hours with Huysmans "listening to the strange confession of the new convert and struck by it only to the extent of being astonished."[24] Among the topics touched upon was Huysmans' forthcoming biography of Saint Lydwine of Schiedam, whose life exemplified the writer's belief that one could atone for the sins of others by offering up one's sufferings on their behalf. If this notion of mystical substitution made little impression at the time on the seventeen-year-old boy, it later became one of the cornerstones of his Catholic faith. And the deathbed sufferings of the writer would be perceived by Massignon as crucial in effecting his own conversion. On the other hand, Gustave Boucher, the friend of Huysmans who after the visit accompanied Massignon on the train to Poitiers, created a very negative impression, which the latter personally recalled for Huysmans' biographer, Robert Baldick.[25]

The autumn of 1900 left little time to muse about the significance of Huysmans' conversion. Having obtained the baccalaureat in philosophy, Massignon was beginning his studies at the Sorbonne and studying for his baccalaureat in mathematics. He received it in 1901, the same year he made the initial contact with Muslim culture by traveling alone to Algiers at his father's urging. Religious preoccupations seemed remote, yet traces of them can be found in this period. It was during this trip to Algeria that Massignon first encountered the beauty of the desert, which nourished him throughout life. In a letter to Paul Claudel he stated that "it was there that I was truly born," referring not only to his later, May 1908 conversion in Mesopotamia but also to his earlier experience in Algeria at

seventeen. The reference to the latter is contained in a single, paren-
thetical mention of the oasis of El-Kantara, situated on the edge of
the Sahara. In both 1901 and 1908, the birth in question "three years
ago (just as nine years ago at El-Kantara)" involved being "pulled
out of myself by the beauty I entered. Do you think that there is before God in the realm of plastic beauty on our earth, beauty more
remarkable, more persuasive and more rhythmical than the desert?"[26]

The impact of the desert on the formation of Massignon cannot
be overestimated. His delight in its beauty was matched only by his
first-hand experience of its unrelenting rigor, which, by challenging
him to the very core of his existence, pared away all distraction and
pulled him beyond himself. Over the years he reiterated this fact in
different contexts, for example in 1921 before the Société de sociologie of Paris:

> There is a certain school of Arab culture which is important not
> only for the philologist, a certain pedagogy after one's fifteenth
> year, around the age of twenty, which has been experienced by
> many men of my generation. That is what I want to mention in
> closing; something newer, fresher and younger, much younger
> than that Anglo-Saxon culture the cinema has sated us with for
> four years, or than the Germanic culture whose manuals have glut-
> ted us since 1870. There [the desert] one finds a lesson in the
> stripping of self which the desert alone gives. I experienced it per-
> sonally, and I cannot forget it, because it was precisely in Arab
> milieux and by speaking only Arabic that I was able to understand
> it, like a certain number of contemporaries, whether officers, scien-
> tists, laymen or religious, assigned to missions in North Africa,
> Chad, Mauritania or in Arabia. All of them were people who strug-
> gled in the desert and who understood the strong discipline of this
> school of the desert.[27]

The beauty and harshness of the desert also secretly fostered
Massignon's religious yearnings; its stark contours spoke of a reality
beyond human experience. So did a *gypsographie* created by his agnostic father for Huysmans. Massignon recalled the image of Saint

Christine the Admirable, exhibited in 1902 at the Salon du Champ de Mars. He was profoundly affected by this image of the medieval Flemish mystic who offered her sufferings for others in mystical substitution:

> It was twenty years ago, around my twentieth year—far removed from the faith of my childhood. In the works of art I glanced at, among all those images of beauty, profane or profaned, tempting or suspect, which crowded in on the threshold of my imagination, suddenly this image appeared, adorned with a unique glory, the glory of sanctity.[28]

The works of the mystics, Eckhart, Ruysbroeck, and John of the Cross, were studied by Massignon as he prepared his *mémoire* for the *Licence ès lettres*, conferred in July 1902.[29] The eminent philologist and literary historian, Ferdinand Brunot, was his director. Both the topic: love, specifically the vocabulary of love in *L'Astrée* (the early seventeenth-century, pastoral novel of Honoré d'Urfé), and the linguistic approach of the study prefigure the focus of an entire career. In Book 9, part II, the shepherd Silvandre defends true love to the fickle Hylas before other inhabitants of Forez; love is born from an act of the will which propels it to that which the understanding judges to be good. In perfect love then, the reason must theoretically consider the beloved to be the summit of perfection. However, Silvandre admits that it is actually impossible for reason to know if the beloved is perfect; in fact, rather than being guided by the understanding, the will imposes a judgment based on natural impulse that the loved object is perfect.[30] The will guides the human lover toward the beloved in both *L'Astrée* and mystical writing. The same paradigm, albeit with one critical difference, can be found in the mystical writing studied by Massignon. In the latter, where God is the beloved, the will is first propelled toward divine union, not by impulse, but by divine initiative. Through the lexicon and syntax of the Arab mystics, Massignon would study and embrace the desire which had nurtured their own quest for God.

Having completed his *licence*, Massignon entered the army in

September 1902 as a *dispensé*, a rubric by which young men enlist-
ing early served less than the three required years of military service.
Maspero and Massignon were separated, the former sent to Chartres
and the latter to Rouen. A picture of military life emerges from their
continued correspondence. Music and reading constituted the chief
diversions, but fatigue took its toll: "I am trying to keep up with the
many varied questions we used to study, but everything sinks beneath the physical fatigue, and I hardly have the force, once free, except to eat and sleep." Massignon also mentions "the curious life of
the peasants who came with the class. Some are more unhappy than
we are."[31]

However, he had peers as well from his own student milieu, including the novelist Roger Martin du Gard (1881–1958), and the
soldier-writer Ernest Psichari (1883–1914), who would later recount
how he had rediscovered his Catholic faith in the desert. There was
also his roommate in Rouen, Jean-Richard Bloch (1884–1947), the
Marxist writer and essayist. Writing in 1955, eight years after the latter's death, Massignon evoked their days together in the Rouen barracks and under a tent in Mailly when Bloch was "still passionately
Jewish and I insufficiently Christian."[32] Roger Martin du Gard provides a glimpse of the nineteen-year-old Massignon: "a tall awkward
boy, with a pale complexion, clear, bright eyes, and a very gentle
smile, a bit constrained. Among those noisy recruits, he had a distracted look, which he kept, moreover, during our ten months of
service."[33] Together the members of this highly elite group amused
themselves by endlessly commenting on the mores of the professional soldiers and by presenting the "soirées Mailly," organized by
Martin du Gard. When evenings of music and song were successful
they began undertaking small plays. On August 12, 1903, shortly
before his tour of duty was completed, the group put on a play
by Tristan Bernard entitled *Allez Messieurs!* Massignon played
"Maurice"; Bloch, the role of "Bar," and Martin du Gard, "a second
witness."[34]

Massignon's spiritual sensitivity continues to reveal itself in the
Maspero letters. The latter is happy in Chartres, and his friend com-

ments: "I am happy that Chartres has charmed you. I look in vain in the churches of Rouen for the ambiance of purity, of devotion even, in which one bathes there." The rigorous physical regimen, the November cold and lonely weekends combined to give Massignon a sense of his need for others. "I am beginning to understand under this tough regime, the word 'solidarity' or charity (ad libitum), without which boredom would have long ago sent me elsewhere. Just think a little of what exercise would be, done all alone."[35] However, during these months of military service the last vestiges of formal religious belief seemingly "slipped away like a worn-out coat; [Massignon] read sometimes in the evening the little office of the Blessed Virgin in Greek, but his last prayer was situated somewhere between Lhuitre, Domrémy, and Metz in the summer of 1903."[36]

The name of Huysmans returns in the long list of varied works read during this period. Along with Karl Marx's *Das Kapital* and Thomas de Quincey's *Confessions of an Opium Eater*, Massignon read *L'Oblat*, Huysmans' semi-fictional account of his stay at Ligugé and the third novel in his Catholic trilogy. He characterized it to Maspero as possessing "a very open feeling, much interesting information" but thought it was "overall less original than his first works."[37] In that same letter of January 30, 1903, he also mentioned dabbling a little in Arabic.

Choice of a research area came up in the letter of May 23 because both men were to continue their studies in view of a university career. The decision was a logical one since the professor's role in French society had been enhanced by recent academic reforms and the increasing importance accorded to science. Along with a wider public and better salaries for professors came a proliferation of new reviews in which to publish and the prestige of being among a burgeoning group called "intellectuals." The latter would exert influence well beyond academic circles, as the career of Louis Massignon amply illustrates. The choice of an academic career ideally positioned him for making his voice heard in the wider society. In the May 23 letter he asks Maspero "Does Chinese still interest you, and have you decided to 'Sino' it?" His own decision is not mentioned, but given his long-standing fascination with North Africa, it was predictable. At the end of the summer, with military service behind him, Massignon began his *Diplôme d'études supérieures* and chose as the subject of his *mémoire*, Leo Africanus.

This sixteenth-century geographer of Morocco, whose real name was Al-Hasan Ibn Muhammad Al-Fa'si, bridged Islamic and Western cultures as Massignon would later do. Born in Grenada, he grew up in Fez, was captured by Mediterranean pirates, taken to Rome and baptized by Leo X (hence his European name). There he taught Arabic and wrote *Descrittione dell' Africa* in Italian, a work consulted by European explorers until the nineteenth century. Massignon's study, like his earlier *mémoire* on *L'Astrée*, prefigured research interests of a lifetime. First it traced the history of the much translated *Descrittione* and attempted through philological methods to reconstitute its original state. Then, using Leo's work as a base, Massignon provided an exhaustive description of sixteenth-century Morocco, which extended well beyond geography to include facts about religious and social customs, political divisions, and economic practices of the period.

The project demanded language expertise and firsthand knowledge of the area. Preparing to visit North Africa by studying both Arabic and Hebrew, Massignon outlined to Maspero, in a letter September 3, his thoughts about the languages' structure. As with so much else, his later work is foreshadowed in his early fascination with the unique elements of Semitic languages. However, for those familiar with the elliptic and staccato prose of his adult years, a style which seemingly reflected the structure of Arabic, this youthful critique of Arabic's abrupt syntax marks the departure point of a long and complex evolution in both his thinking and his writing:

> Very curious really the special logic of these races. No syntax of subordination. Sentences linked simply by 'and' or by nothing at all; they are incapable of solidly coordinating a group of ideas; there are simple, tiny and rapid ejaculations which they express without a connector. And so, rather than the nuances we introduce

in the meaning of our verbs through periphrases or particles — they prefer notes within the verb itself, through changes in vocalization (*piel, hiphil*), which clearly isolate the simple verb from its derived meanings.[38]

In 1904, Massignon headed for North Africa again, accompanied by a friend, Pierre Sainte, a sculptor whose suicide in 1921, he would feel keenly. This time the destination was Morocco, the land described by Leo Africanus, and the city of Fez, where the latter had lived. The venture was risky for an inexperienced twenty-year-old heading his own caravan, because the area beyond the coast was barely known to Europeans and the routes were unsafe. Nominally ruled by a sultan, the country was in fact controlled by feudal chieftans, and it was the sole area of North Africa not under European domination (Libya belonged to the Ottoman Turks, and both Algeria and Tunisia, to the French). Nevertheless, the fascination which the region had earlier exerted on the child captivated the young man. Travel by horseback revealed "Morocco in the fifteen hundreds, the same steppe filled with game, splashed with flowers, the same olive groves framing the villages, the identical traditions and the charm of the covered streets of Fez."[39] After his conversion Massignon recalled the expedition in a letter to Claudel; he placed it within the context of his emotional outlook at the time, that of a young man seeking an "elsewhere" in which to reconcile his need for autonomy with a longing for wholeness and beauty, since he felt the task impossible in his own environment. The trip also allowed him to fulfill that imperious need to endure extreme physical rigor in order to feel truly alive:

> And one fine day, when years of stupid intellectualism, prolonged after my ten months as a *dispensé* . . . had completely poisoned and dried me up, I could see nothing of beauty around me; in the first months of my twentieth year, I felt myself suffocating altogether, and I left for Africa. January 1904, Algiers where I led a very violent life; Teniet el Haad (the great forest of cedars where I galloped on horseback in the middle of the snow); and April 1904, my grand

excursion on horseback from Tangiers to Fez, full of physical energy and a certain intellectual equilibrium. An unconscious agnosticism, unfortunately, and which was only to be cured, laid bare, cauterized, in Mesopotamia, in May 1908, as you know.[40]

The Moroccan expedition, was remembered by Massignon for an episode which tested his love of physical danger. In April, on the road from Tangiers to Fez, Massignon realized that his caravan was heading back to Tangiers instead of proceeding forward. In his characteristically elliptic prose Massignon explained what happened, "Caravan attacked, betrayed by my Arab interpreter, I vowed to learn Arabic (I'm still learning it), I stopped drinking wine." Friends to whom he recounted the tale elaborated, saying that his guides had become drunk. Then Massignon "with revolver in hand, smashed their wine bottles and ordered them on to complete the journey." He stationed himself in the last carriage for the duration of the trip in order to insure that his orders were obeyed.[41]

Upon his return to Paris, Massignon successfully defended his work on Leo Africanus and obtained in June 1904 the *Diplôme d'études supérieures* in history and geography. The next three years were largely taken up with intense intellectual preparation for an academic career. By now well known as a very promising young scholar, he returned in April 1905 to Algiers and presented his work on Leo Africanus to the fourteenth international congress of Orientalists. There he met two celebrated Islamists, Ignace Goldziher, a Hungarian who would mentor his early professional career, and Asin Palacios, a Spaniard who became a friend and whose work would engage them throughout their careers in keen critical debates.

However, in spite of this precocious celebrity, neither Massignon nor Henri Maspero ever became *agrégés* in history. In that same spring of 1905, agnostics though they were, the two young men signed a letter written by a group of historians in protest against a pamphlet which treated Joan of Arc as a charlatan and a prostitute. It was perhaps Massignon's first gesture of public protest and, like many that followed, it proved costly. When the two young men took the examination for the *agrégation* in history, a degree allowing them to teach at the secondary or university level, they both were failed because of their action. Henri Maspero abandoned the project altogether, but Massignon persisted and failed again the following year. The episode would be a deciding factor in Gaston Maspero's later decision to suggest they leave Paris so as to make them less visible for a time.[42]

Massignon continued meanwhile to broaden and deepen his knowledge of the language and culture of the Islamic world and the Middle East. Remembering his inability to communicate effectively during the Morocco trip, he worked seriously to learn Arabic. In 1906 he obtained his *diplôme* in classical and spoken Arabic at the Ecole des langues orientales after first failing the *agrégation*. (Ironically, from 1946 until he retired in 1954 from the Collège de France, Massignon was president of the jury which awarded the *agrégation* in Arabic.) That same year, 1906, the *mémoire* on Leo Africanus was published in Algiers, under the title *Tableau géographique du Maroc dans les quinze premières années du xvie siècle, d'après Léon l'Africain.*

As a student in the section of religious sciences in the Ecole Pratique des Hautes Etudes, Massignon came under the tutelage of Hartwig Derenbourg (1844–1908), an eminent Jewish Islamist who, with his father, pioneered Orientalism as a scholarly discipline in France. It was Derenbourg who introduced Massignon to the Arab mystics, a topic which at the time held no conscious religious significance for the young scholar. He began reading them the way he had studied the Qur'an; both were repositories of classical Arabic and therefore subjects for Semitic philology. However, through his work Massignon made a discovery with far-reaching consequences for the direction of his future research:

> It was through Semitic philology that I was led to examine true mystical texts closely. Going from Hebrew to Arabic in order to study the Qur'an, I was surprised to see with what increasing clarity, the Semitic languages, Arabic above all, tended to distinguish religious

revelation from poetic inspiration, prayer from poetry, mysticism from literature, through their mode of verbal presentation.[43]

This insight, gleaned from the study of language, formed the basis of Massignon's analysis of Sufi mysticism and of his lifelong research of the area. Hartwig Derenbourg later encouraged his student's choice of Hallaj for the topic of his doctoral thesis.[44] At the time the tenth-century Sufi mystic was relatively unknown. In gratitude Massignon later dedicated to Derenbourg the preface of his second, required doctoral thesis, the *thèse complémentaire* on the lexicon of Muslim mysticism.

Massignon also studied the sociology of Islam under the professor whose chair he would one day occupy at the Collège de France, Alfred Le Chatelier (1855–1929), a man with firsthand experience of French rule in the Maghreb. As an army officer the latter had founded a town in the Algerian Sahara, Ouargla, and as an academic used a variety of surveys and investigations to aid the government in dealing with its North African colonies. Whereas warmth characterized the relationship between Massignon and Derenbourg, contact with Le Chatelier was more difficult, undoubtedly because, in the case of the latter, both the material and approach were less congenial to Massignon's own more intuitive temperament. However, both through his background and his methodology, Le Chatelier fostered his student's interest in contemporary Islam and taught him the skills necessary to study it. The apprenticeship bore fruit in countless reports and analyses over the years.

The research in Morocco had also put Massignon in contact with an earlier explorer of the region, Charles de Foucauld (1858–1916), who, like Huysmans, was to exert a powerful influence on Massignon. In 1886 Foucauld, a former soldier, had rediscovered Christianity, again like Huysmans, and then felt impelled to live out his life in complete imitation of the poor Christ, first as a Trappist and later as a quasi-beggar at the gate of a Poor Clare convent in Nazareth. At the time of Massignon's 1904 stay in Morocco, Foucauld was living as a hermit in Algeria. But twenty years before, in 1883, he had made a year-long journey across Morocco disguised as a Russian rabbi and later published accounts of his adventure.[45] Preparing for his 1904 expedition, Massignon had come across *Reconnaissance au Maroc* and found it invaluable; he cites Foucauld as an essential source.

Massignon commented years later that like himself "Foucauld had undertaken his 'reconnaissance' in Morocco, driven by the secular rage to understand," and he drew parallels with his own experience as a young man.[46] In a conference at the Sorbonne in March 1959, Massignon recounted how he had first contacted Foucauld. To thank the hermit he had decided to send him a copy of the *Tableau géographique* and asked Count Henri de Castries, another explorer who had rediscovered his faith in the desert, if Foucauld were still alive. Castries responded yes but added that he had spoiled his life and was living as a priest near Beni-Abbes, an oasis in southern Algeria, close to Morocco. Massignon persisted in his request and Castries agreed to confide the book to Hubert Lyautey (1854–1934), the general who later conquered Morocco, created it as a protectorate, and enjoyed a reputation for enlightened governance in the Maghreb. Lyautey did transmit the book to Foucauld along with Massignon's formal letter of thanks. The hermit responded politely but added one sentence which was to have a lifelong impact on the young man. After praising the quality of Massignon's documentation, Foucauld added, "I offer to God for you my poor and unworthy prayers, begging him to bless you, to bless your work and your whole life."[47] Massignon summarized his own feelings about this exchange of letters, "I had lost all faith, but this poor man's alms, I accepted. Then forgot."[48] His career was unfolding rapidly, and in the kaleidescope of events and places seemingly little time existed for reflecting on this modest note.

However, Massignon could not help but notice that his own love of the desert's beauty, discovered at seventeen, echoed that of both Charles de Foucauld and Henri de Castries. And in both men the desert had awakened religious awe. Massignon knew their work; he later cited the one religious passage in Foucauld's *Reconnaissance au Maroc*, which described the then explorer's trek across the desert in 1883:

> The moon, shining in the middle of a cloudless sky, throws off a gentle brightness; the air is soft, not a breath stirs. In this profound calm, in the midst of this fairylike nature, I reach my first rest-stop in the Sahara. One understands in contemplating nights like this, the Arab belief in a mysterious night, *laylat al-qadr*, when the heavens open, the angels descend to earth, the waters of the sea become gentle and all inanimate nature bends low to adore its Creator.[49]

In 1896, at age twenty-five, Henri de Castries had published an account of his own introduction to North Africa. The rigid constraints of European military dress had made him feel ridiculous when his guides knelt in the desert to pray, "How in harmony they were with that magnificent scenery, those men majestically draped in their woolen robes."[50] He felt "attracted more and more to the beauties of Islam. It seemed to me that for the first time in this nomadic life of the desert, I had really seen men render homage to the divinity."[51] However consciously Massignon had rejected faith, his own response to the beauty of his Algerian surroundings was not unique; it echoed those of his predecessors and carried the same religious overtones.

With his *diplôme* in Arabic completed, Massignon rather predictably wished to spend a year in an area where the language was spoken. Named a member of the Institut français d'archéologie orientale of Cairo in October 1906, he would be reunited there with his childhood companion Henri Maspero and the latter's parents. Gaston Maspero was director of the Institut and Henri was preparing a topic in Egyptology for his *diplôme* before definitively opting for China as a research area. Encouraged by the elder Maspero, Massignon intended to pursue a topic in Egyptian archeology: "Because of my research on the topography of Fez, Gaston Maspero had asked me to complete, through the study of Darb al-Ahmar, the grand survey of the historical topography of Cairo, which he had given from 1887 on, to the Arabist members of the Institute he had founded there."[52]

Ultimately, however, an encounter on board ship proved to be the most significant moment of the year in Cairo. Sailing from Marseille, Massignon met a young Spanish aristocrat and Islamist, Luis de Cuadra, son of the Marquis de Guadalmina. Luis, age twenty-nine, was returning to Cairo, "where he had quit Christianity for Islam so as to continue adoring God without remorse for his life, in the manner of Omar Khayyam."[53] Until this meeting, the record of Massignon's attachments as a young adult remains vague. One finds mention that in 1904 he began a two-year liaison with an actress named Jeanne, and his journal (November 22, 1906) reflects that during his first months in Cairo he missed her greatly.[54] Whatever she meant to him, her memory faded when Luis de Cuadra entered his life.

The homosexual nature of this involvement is well known because Massignon, whose fierce reticence on some subjects was matched only by his compelling need to discuss others, was always explicit about its nature. Whether it was rebellion, love, or a way to understand the world of the Middle East, the relationship marked him forever. After his conversion, Massignon struggled with and ultimately rejected its homosexual expression, but the bond with Cuadra remained. Only the latter's suicide in 1921 ended weekly letters to the Spaniard, and his memory accompanied Massignon until the end. The fact that the correspondence was evidently destroyed probably matters little; those who knew Massignon well have remarked, "for his friends he made hardly any mystery about the most secret things."[55] While one cannot assess the degree to which Massignon's homosexual experiences as a young man influenced him, by his own admission their impact was profound and must be considered in any attempt to understand his adult life.

The lifestyle which Massignon said he had pursued two years earlier in Morocco continued during the year in Egypt. In Cairo and Luxor he embraced Arab life, dress, and customs to better understand the culture, a choice facilitated by the mentoring of Luis de

Cuadra. Massignon recalled that it was he "who first took me by moonlit nights to the Qarafa" the old cemetery of Cairo.[56] The first-hand experience with a living culture gradually lessened Massignon's interest in the archeological pursuits suggested by Gaston Maspero but paved the way for him to discover and embrace his life's work as a student of Islamic culture and history. There his expertise in archeology would be secondary but would prove invaluable because he could buttress his historical arguments with data which had quite literally existed for centuries.

However, this gradual shift of intellectual focus did not fill the spiritual void which had been slowly deepening since Massignon's last years as a *lycéen*. Indeed, the intensity with which he pursued the discovery of Islam suggests a hint of desperation, as if the endeavor could fill the perception of emptiness. He summarized the period 1906–8 in the Sorbonne talk about Charles de Foucauld: "Two years of work in Arab linguistics and of moral crisis: in Egypt, archeological work with, on the side, violent escapades, disguised as a *fellah*, an outlaw milieu, the rage to understand and conquer Islam at any price."[57] Massignon felt that his own attitude paralleled that of the young Foucauld when the latter, as yet an unbeliever, explored North Africa:

> I tried myself, twice, in my secular rage to understand, to "penetrate" Islam: in Upper-Egypt, then in Iraq. The failure of the first effort resulted from the fact that, although well prepared from a linguistic point of view, I had through boredom sought out an unhealthy hospitality: the false asceticism of physical degradation and the perverse abandon to the getup of a *fellah* who snuffs out fleas on his chest, even as his unblinking eyes are haunted by flies.[58]

In the midst of this intense existence, fragmented between precise intellectual work and a freewheeling lifestyle, Massignon continued his habit of reading widely and deeply. He scanned Arab historians, encyclopedists, jurists, and philosophers. During his Cairo stay, the *Munquidh* of Ghazali and the *Pensées* of Pascal became his bedside reading. Echoes of the love poetry in *L'Astrée,* which

Massignon had studied in his *mémoire,* could be found in the Arab and Persian mystics.[59] Because of his linguistic sophistication and passion for Arabic, his whole being responded to the unique qualities of their abrupt syntax: "I had been surprised by certain sayings of Muslim mystics which, by their atemporal quality, penetrated one's life like arrows."[60]

The effect of somehow inserting timelessness in time served as a dramatic counterpoint to the life Massignon was leading. Because the relationship with Cuadra occasioned moral conflict for him, albeit perhaps unconsciously, it was fraught with anguish and allowed him no sustained moments of self-transcendence in the experience of love. The writings he discovered from the mystics spoke of another reality which, while embodying love, was far removed from the one causing him so much pain. Through the Arab mystics he made a discovery which transformed his life, a discovery that reconciled him to himself and his past, even as it linked his profound but diffuse religious aspirations with both his intellectual preoccupations and his academic background. The encounter was decisive for Massignon "on the verge of my apprenticeship in spoken and written Arabic."[61]

The name of the tenth-century Sufi mystic, Husayn Ibn Mansur al-Hallaj, had undoubtedly come to Massignon's attention while he was studying Leo Africanus, whose work mentions early Sufis. The name certainly recurred in his reading that winter. However, Hallaj emerged as the integrating figure of his life only one day in March 1907; a verse of the latter caught Massignon's attention in the *Memorial of the Saints* by Attar: "Two moments of adoration suffice in love, but the preliminary ablution must be made in blood."[62] The introduction to *Parole donnée* mentions Luis de Cuadra as the one who pointed out the verse, an attribution which was seemingly not denied by Massignon when years later he recalled his emotion upon reading the fragment of Hallaj:

> A brief allusion to him [Hallaj] in the margin of Khayyam's "quatrains" held out by an ambiguous hand [*une main équivoque*], a

simple maxim of his, in Arabic, glimpsed in the Persian 'memorial' of Attar, and the meaning of sin was given back to me, and then the piercing desire for the purity read on the threshold of a cruel Egyptian spring.[63]

Massignon could not throw off the image of the martyred Hallaj. It insinuated itself in those hungry recesses of his being which for years had been unconsciously seeking a meaning for his life. In a 1912 letter to Claudel, he recalled that the figure of Hallaj haunted him. (Unfortunately the comment is edited in the Claudel-Massignon letters). "I will never forget that springtime of 1907 [. . .] I saw bending towards me in the midst of all those past figures of Islam, this crucified effigy, a striking double of the Master whom I had loved when young."[64]

Hallaj, although the object of popular devotion for centuries, was at best a marginal figure for traditional Muslims and at worst a heretic because of his doctrine. Born in southern Iran around 857, Hallaj moved with his family to Wasit (in present-day Iraq) as a child. There like all Muslim children he learned the Qur'an by heart and was schooled in Arabic. Very early he felt drawn to a direct and intimate knowledge of God. At twenty, he went to Basra and received the Sufi garb but soon clashed with other Sufis because, unlike them, he did not keep secret his experience of God but openly preached that through love one could know divine union. After a first pilgrimage to Mecca, in 895, he abandoned the Sufi habit and traveled through the Arab colonies of Iran preaching his doctrine. Then around 903, along with 400 disciples he made a second pilgrimage to Mecca where he was accused by his former Sufi friends of practicing magic and sorcery. During an even longer trip he spread his message beyond the limits of the Islamic world and reached India. He returned to Mecca in 906 on his third and last pilgrimage and stayed two years. By this time Hallaj was proclaiming that the road to Mecca was not necessarily a material one. It could be traveled in the human heart when one understood that the desire for God drew one to Him more surely than any pilgrimage: "Hallaj understood that our desire for God must mentally destroy in us the image of the Temple in order to find the One who created it, and to destroy the temple of our body so as to be united to the One who came there to speak to men."[65] Hallaj then returned for the last time to Baghdad in 908 and proclaimed that he desired to die condemned and disgraced by Islamic law, in order to be united with God and save others.

During this period he supposedly uttered his celebrated affirmation: "Ana'l Haqq: I am the Truth," or the equivalent of "My 'I' is God." The declaration seemingly verged on blasphemy because it equated him with God. "For all later Muslim tradition, this saying stands for Hallaj; it is the mark of his spiritual vocation, the cause of his condemnation, the glory of his martyrdom."[66] Suspected to have been involved in a political plot, Hallaj escaped the city in 910. In 913 he was retaken, brought back to Baghdad and interned for nine years in the palace prison. For much of this period Hallaj continued to write and receive visitors. Finally, after a second trial of seven months, begun in 921, he was sentenced to death for heresy. Executed March 22, 922 after a series of tortures, including crucifixion, Hallaj was almost immediately venerated as a saint by many groups of Persian and Turkish mystics.

One can only speculate why Massignon was initally so drawn to Hallaj. On the one hand, the attraction was undoubtedly linked to the fascination North Africa had held for him since childhood. Seen first as the faraway land where life could match the richness of imagination, North Africa became the place where Massignon had achieved independence as an adult. The Muslim culture he had discovered there suggested mysterious richness and nurtured his impassioned sensitivity. It had likewise provided material which engaged his intellect and allowed him to use his education as a scholar. Thus, his own temperament and gifts primed him to respond to a historical Muslim figure whose heroic doctrine was transmitted in exquisite poetry. On the other hand, the story of Hallaj recalled to Massignon that of Jesus but separated the latter from both the promptings remembered from a devoutly Catholic mother and the accretions of a post-Tridentine Church. Stripped of accessory elements, the stories of both Jesus and Hallaj revealed to him a stark but dazzling message which responded to his deepest longings: God offers intimate union with himself, and through total self-renunciation, the heroic few render such union accessible for the many. At the same time because Hallaj was a Muslim, Massignon could respond wholeheartedly to his story without fear of being challenged to reexamine the faith of his childhood.

By the end of April, Massignon had decided to make the biography of Hallaj the topic of his doctoral dissertation, but as yet he ignored the profound motivations for the choice. He later remembered having first taken on the project "as a whim, marginal to my professional work then."[67] Writing to his father at the end of April, he ascribed it to capriciousness and omitted any reference to the religious significance of Hallaj's life:

> In a spirit of contrariness I have set to work rather assiduously, not on the archeological work Gaston Maspero spoke of (I'm doing it with growing distaste), but on the critical study of the martyrdom of a Baghdad mystic of the tenth century, about whom have been spun innumerable stupidities. He was in reality a very beautiful figure and the story of his martyrdom has an intense quality, a tragic aura which enthralls me. I want to do my doctoral dissertation about him.[68]

Indeed, Hallaj is described to his father in such a way that the latter could be reminded of his son's defense of Joan of Arc in 1905, when Louis and Henri Maspero signed the letter which cost them their *agrégation* in history. Fernand Massignon had taught his son to respect Joan for her courage, and Hallaj presented another heroic figure, calumniated as was she, and unjustly put to death by religious leaders. Neither father nor son could guess that the choice of a dissertation topic would become a lifelong commitment.

TWO

Conversion

Massignon returned to Paris in June and in July spoke with a friend of his father, General Léon de Beylié, an archeologist who had written the preface to the book on Leo Africanus. The general proposed to him an archeological mission in Mesopotamia, then part of the Ottoman Empire, to visit areas rich in historical sites but unknown to Westerners because of the insecurity of the region. Such areas included the upper Tigris and the territory crossed by the lower course of both the Tigris and Euphrates. The mission was approved by the French government, and the ministry of public instruction requested the necessary approval from the Ottoman authorities.

The need for such approval indicates the degree of tension existing in the area at the time. The Ottoman Empire, "the sick man of Europe," was on the verge of collapse from internal corruption, the opportunism of the European powers, and ethnic conflict within its boundaries. In Mesopotamia itself the Arab tribes had revolted in the deserts to the south and west. The Kurds were fighting in the northeast, and a state of war existed along the eastern border with Persia. The central government was a virtual dictatorship. In 1878 Sultan Abdul Hamid II rescinded the constitution and parliament he had authorized in 1876. Reform-minded elements within the army and the government had created the secret "Union and Progress" movement and were preparing the coup which materialized in July 1908. At the time Massignon began his assignment, Nazim Bey, the minister of justice and head of a reform commission appointed by the sultan, was touring the provinces of the empire in an attempt to convince the power elite that the sultan was sincerely pushing for reform. His tour of Mesopotamia coincided with Massignon's own. Thus, an explosive political climate multiplied the risks posed by the feuding Bedouin in the region.

Massignon did not inform the general of his secret desire to study Hallaj, but the fact that Baghdad had been the scene not only of Hallaj's preaching but also of his martyrdom made the project almost mysteriously compelling.[1] Massignon set sail from Marseille on the *Luristan,* November 7, 1907. The ship passed through the Suez Canal, traversed the Red Sea, navigated around the Arabian peninsula and through the straits of Hormuz, arriving in Basra, December 8. Massignon spent a week there and on December 15 sailed up the Tigris on the steamer the *Bloss Lynch.* On the evening of December 19, he reached Baghdad.

Massignon liked the city because it was less European than Cairo, and he could continue to experience Islam on its own terms. The French consul, Gustave Rouet, looked after him, a fact much appreciated by Pierre Roche, who wrote Rouet in gratitude. The consul introduced Massignon to both the European colony and the educated Muslim elite of Baghdad. Among the latter, significant friendships were formed with Hajj 'Ali Alussy and his cousin, Muhammad Shukri Alussy, archeologists and epigraphists who had authored works on the historical topography of Baghdad. Massignon later cited them in his own work on Hallaj.[2] Hajj 'Ali Alussy, like his father before him, was overseer of the Mirjaniya, the famous fourteenth-century mosque madrasah (school) of Baghdad and of its rich library of manuscripts. Gustave Rouet also put Massignon in touch with Ra'uf Chadirchi, the young adjunct secretary general to the Wali of Baghdad and member of a well-known family in the city. Both Hajj 'Ali and Ra'uf Chadirchi were active members of "Union and Progress."

The Alussy family rented a house to Massignon near theirs in the Muslim neighborhood of Hayderkhaneh, where no Westerner lived. The necessary permission was obtained from Turkish officials for him to live in an all-Muslim neighborhood, and the Alussy family promised to answer for his behavior. Massignon, pleased with his living situation, wrote in January to Henri Maspero: "Here I'm taking Arab roots, that is to say that I've found people to my liking, well intentioned and rather educated, with whom to talk, when the normal dose of solitude has been overdone—near whom to live, far from the European colony—may Allah scatter it, as the Abyssinian army did in the war of the Elephant. Amen."[3]

At first the Alussys were wary of this newcomer and suspicious of his desire to live in their area. They thought he might prefer it because, far from watchful European eyes, he would not have to explain either his Arab dress or commerce with young men. Massignon told of an exchange between Hajj 'Ali and himself shortly after he moved into the house, an exchange evidently preceded by much discussion about him in the Alussy household:

> "What is he looking for with us?" I told him "my life." There were in fact things which were objectionable in it. So they said to each other, "Is it because of that?" . . . Thus my day had come, one of the really beautiful ones of my life, this day when I basked in eternal love; it was the day he suspected I had come to live among Muslims in order to satisfy some of my passions. I could say nothing: he was my father . . . He was my host. I simply looked at him; he paled. We saw each other again several days later. He didn't doubt me anymore.[4]

Hajj 'Ali, drawing on his own Islamic faith, had recognized the young, defenseless Frenchman as his guest, and Massignon had silently committed himself not to embarrass the family by his behavior. Massignon never forgot that mute dialogue in which only their eyes had spoken; it signified a primordial example of Muslim hospitality and ultimately for him an experience of the divine. In the experience of a shared moment he and Hajj 'Ali had each become the guest and protector of the other, and in that mutuality the love of God was shown.

Through their unending kindness and ongoing conversations, the Alussy family indirectly prepared Massignon for the conversion which was shortly to disrupt and refashion his life. He was impressed that they had extended friendship in spite of his interest in Hallaj, because for the Alussys, Hallaj was a problematic figure in Islam. Devout, traditional Hanbali Muslims, they believed that God was essentially unknowable and that the gap between humanity and God could be bridged only by faith; hence Hallaj's claim of union with God was spurious. Yet during their frequent talks on religious differences, Hajj 'Ali Alussy never tried to manipulate the young Frenchman, "But I was his guest. He took me as I was and tried to make me reach my destiny."[5] Massignon described one of the exchanges in which the Alussys confronted his agnosticism with their own belief, and it is clear that for Massignon, even as an unbeliever, faith in God was inseparable from the love of God:

> They tried to make me believe in God: "Faith is due in justice only to God, alone immutable." "And love?" "Prostituted to no matter what creature." "But if he wishes us to love him?" "Something supererogatory, a private delicacy: what he requires, it's faith." I felt myself different from them. Another day, Hajj 'Ali wrung from me a confidence: "I am sad, I'm thinking of someone in Egypt. If I'm forcing myself to be chaste here, I, an unbeliever, it's to keep the word I promised you, so that this house will not be sullied, where you have made me, your guest, welcome in a neighborhood exclusively Muslim until now." "You are flesh, you are too hard on yourself." "You, what do you do?" "I try not to scandalize, and when I fall, I pray to God in secret at the canonical hour." This idea of a purifying prayer without contrition dumbfounds me.[6]

The conversations were amiable and Massignon cherished the interest of Hajj 'Ali, "I had come and perched on the corner of his roof, like a bizarre bird from somewhere. Well, he did not try to tame me. But he nourished me at a time when there was no other place where I could drink something very pure, which was the Muslim doctrine, the way he understood it with all his heart."[7]

Less than a year had passed since Massignon had come across the phrase of Hallaj which prompted him to study the Sufi mystic in earnest. If during this period Hallaj held no conscious religious significance for Massignon, a curious incident he recounted years later suggests the persistence of his longing for the Absolute:

> In Baghdad a long time ago at the end of winter, a timid young hand once held out to me "Haqqi" doves in a basket. (They nest in the minaret of the Suq al-Ghazl, from where in 922 they dispersed the ashes of Hallaj, the mystical martyr of Islam; the popular legend says that these doves coo "Haqq," in memory of this dying man's cry "Ana'l Haqq," "I am the Truth.") Rather harshly I had responded: "your doves are mute."[8]

During these months Massignon, totally integrated into Arab ways, worked intensely both on his archeological assignment and on research for his dissertation on Hallaj. Every day, encumbered by heavy equipment, he went off on horseback to map out areas of Baghdad and collect inscriptions of ancient monuments. The Alussys gave him invaluable help in uncovering documents about Hallaj; in thanks, he would one day dedicate his thesis to them. Massignon studied Turkish with Ra'uf Chadirchi and became fascinated with Arab music, which called to mind French folk music. He had two *'udth*, lutes specific to Baghdad, made for himself by his friend Habib Effendi, the most famous lute maker of the city. Totally absorbed in his work and the culture around him, he understandably provoked both criticism and curiosity. The young European in Arab dress, weighed down with technical equipment, was a bizarre figure in a world where tourists had not yet penetrated. Moreover, given the political situation, such singularity exposed him to danger.

The French consul had requested that the Turkish police keep Massignon under protective surveillance because he was the first Westerner to live in a Muslim neighborhood. General de Beylié was dismayed at his lifestyle and the fact that by the end of February he had not yet explored any areas beyond Baghdad :

> If the young Massignon is satisfied with what he's doing, I myself am infinitely less so. It appears from the letters I have received from

the consul in Baghdad and Monsieur Violet, an architect, that
M. Massignon has not yet left Baghdad. He has bought or rented
an Arab house in an obscure neighborhood, walks around in *ba-
bouches* [slippers] and with a fez, which is totally ridiculous, and
lives like an Arab.[9]

In the same letter de Beylié allows that according to Rouet, the consul, Massignon "is likeable and a worker but he broods and listens to
no advice." The young scholar's lingering sojourn in Baghdad constituted a major mistake in de Beylié's eyes because the general had
devised the Mesopotamia project in order to beat out two German
archeologists, Friedrich Sarre and Ernst Herzfeld. "I see only one
thing, it's that we engaged this young man for Samarra so as to cut
the grass from under the feet of the Germans and that he has not
fulfilled the first part of his program."

Understandably, Massignon was regarded with suspicion and
perhaps jealousy by the two German archeologists, whom he met
thanks to the German consul. He had sensed their wariness and attempted to win them over by inviting them to tea at home in his
Arab neighborhood and explaining his willingness to give them free
rein in Samarra. North of Baghdad, the city interested both them
and General de Beylié because of its important ruins dating from the
days of the Abbasid caliphate. However, the gesture proved fruitless.[10] One day in late January, Massignon was completing a topographical summary on the banks of the Tigris near the "tomb" of
Hallaj when he heard a chorus chanting that he was a spy. Ra'uf
Chadirchi, hearing of the incident, revealed that the two Germans
had indeed denounced him as a spy to the wali of Baghdad.

Under pressure to complete his assignment, Massignon prepared to undertake the exploration mandated for the region around
Baghdad. He was forced to revise the original plan. The German
archeologists, having failed to obtain the requisite Ottoman permission, could not go north to Samarra. The route to the east was
blocked because of the Ottoman-Persian conflict. Massignon decided "to begin by doing what was most pressing, to go as soon as

spring began to the edge of the desert and then back up to Baghdad along the banks of the Tigris."[11] He would head first in a southwest direction to investigate previously unexplored ruins and then swing around towards the east in the direction of Wasit before returning north to Baghdad.

Ra'uf Chadirchi alerted the Ottoman authorities about Massignon's itinerary, while Rouet helped put together a small caravan and requested a military escort from the wali of Basra. The latter responded cautiously because his region was unsafe; troops were busy suppressing sporadic anti-Turk uprisings of the Muntafiq, an Arab tribe. They were situated in the province of the same name, in the southeast between the Tigris and the Euphrates. Rouet was obliged to repeat the request, this time to the wali of Baghdad. The caravan eventually included three domestics, two of whom had worked for Massignon in Hayderkhaneh; servants who cared for the saddle horses and pack mules; and finally, thanks to the Alussys, four *zaptiyes* (policemen on horseback) under the command of an officer.

Louis Massignon left Baghdad March 22, 1908; he stood on the threshold of a new life. Before departing he had been persuaded by the Alussys to allow his name to be engraved on a small piece of crystal, a seal with religious significance, because beneath his name would be found the word *abduhu,* meaning "his servant." The gift would be ready upon his return. "My amiable incredulity made me acquiesce, as when Foucauld had proposed to me . . . his prayer, in 1906."[12] Promised to Massignon before he left and received after he rediscovered faith, the crystal would always recall for him not only the Alussys but also those weeks in the spring of 1908 which transformed his life.

The first part of the journey was tranquil enough. To shield themselves from the relentless sun, the group traveled only at night, between 10 and 11 P.M. and 9 or 10 the next morning. Days of rest were interspersed at least every four days. With the spring rains oases were flooded, and the Euphrates had overflowed its banks, necessitating detours in many places.

The caravan reached Karbala, a Shi'ite holy place one hundred kilometers south of Baghdad.[13] Massignon, ever alive to beauty in his surroundings, described the town's hold on him:

> Short rest in Karbala, an important site of Alid Islam. How to forget the pomegranate flowers bursting under the palms of the oasis, the horseback rides towards Imam Hurr, the penitent deserter of Arab honor, and the tombs of Wadi as-Salam, and by night, the unpetaled roses in the copper tubs at the doorways of the Imams, and at dawn, the cry of the milk boy . . . [14]

The caravan then headed westward to the oasis of Shithathah. Massignon examined the ruins in the surrounding area and became the first Westerner to explore the immense fortified castle of Ukhaydir, situated in the middle of the desert, south of Shithathah. During his first visit on March 31, he was attacked by a group of Bedouin, an episode he recounted with youthful bravado in a letter to Rouet:

> You will perhaps not be upset to learn that my *'iqal* and my *'aba* merited my receiving a dozen shots at 250 meters, all around my horse and the horses of my escort, the first time I was at Al-Ukhaydir. No wounded: What would have happened if I'd had on the respectable "colonial helmet"? Allah is the most wise.[15]

Massignon finished his observations of Ukhaydir during a second visit, April 3. By April 5 he had returned to Karbala, where he telegraphed Rouet, asking the latter to inform his father that he was fine; then he headed south to another center of Shi'ite pilgrimage, Najaf.[16] Rouet was understandably not amused when the *kaimakam* of Najaf[17] delivered Massignon's letter describing the March 31 Bedouin attack; he responded immediately:

> Thank you for your letter of April 3, which followed your excursion to Shithathah. I'm not at all surprised that dressed as an Arab, Muslim, Jew or Christian, you have been attacked; the contrary would have surprised me greatly. Upon receiving your letter and being unable to request that he force you to wear a hat, I asked the Wali to give strictest orders to the authorities of Karbala and Najaf not

to let you undertake any excursion without being provided a serious escort.[18]

Properly contrite for having caused his protector such anxiety, Massignon responded with thanks for the telegram assuring his parents he was safe and apologies for having taken so lightly the danger incurred at Ukhaydir:

> The little scuffle at Ukhaydir was a simple hors d'oeuvre, and I am sorry that my letter caused you the inconvenience of the action you told me about. I informed you about it from the simple desire that my account be complete and because I insisted you be directly informed.[19]

Using Najaf as a base, Massignon visited Kufah and, on April 14, Khawarnaq, a village south of both cities which is not shown on modern maps. Because of the rising waters of the Euphrates and a renewed anti-Turk uprising near Wasit, in the Muntafiq region, he revised his original plan of heading due east to Wasit and instead crossed the Euphrates at Kufah, went north to Kifl (the supposed tomb of Ezechiel), and then to Al Hillah, April 19. Having circumvented the uprisings, the caravan reached the right bank of the Tigris and Bughayla (An Nu'maniyah) on April 27; there it was supposed to rest two days. By this time Massignon was behind schedule and had in a little over a month logged almost 450 miles in the desert, alone except for the members of his caravan and occasional meetings with other archeologists in the larger towns. This unbeliever, obsessed with the martyred tenth-century Sufi mystic Hallaj, was living in virtual solitude with the unresolved contradictions of his life. At age seventeen the stark beauty of the desert had awakened in Massignon a longing for transcendence. Evoked by the desert once again that same longing contrasted sharply with his feelings of moral malaise, compounded by fatigue and loneliness.

In Bughayla the next day, April 28, an incident indirectly set in motion the events which culminated in Massignon's conversion. It began with an argument with Weli, one of the domestics. "In the evening, having overheard my escorts' reflections, attributing to me effeminate manners, I questioned Weli, who said that he himself had preferred these rumors."[20] When Massignon responded angrily, Weli retorted by leaving the caravan and taking with him the purse he held in order to meet daily expenses. The next evening the caravan without Weli headed westward toward Kut and arrived there the morning of the thirtieth. Massignon went to see the *kaimakam*, not only to apprise the Ottoman official of his itinerary and Ra'uf Chadirchi of his arrival, but also because of his concern about the incident with Weli two days before. The *kaimakam* urged Massignon to press charges of theft against Weli and another domestic, Djabbouri, as an accomplice. Massignon did so, and both were arrested.

Since he now had no funds because of the theft, Massignon had recourse to two Chaldean Christians, the Tessi brothers, who were supposed to cash for him a letter of exchange drawn on the Ottoman bank. They nervously refused and cast doubts on the identity of the young European in *keffie* and *'iqal*, saying "I was a dead man. They could give me nothing. This refusal, evidently inspired, prevented me from continuing my trip to Wasit."[21] To generate some cash Massignon sold the pair six guns Weli had made him buy in Karbala. The decision to deny Massignon help in his situation evidently resulted from the *kaimakam*'s suspicions about the real motives for Massignon's presence in the region.

That evening when Massignon returned to thank the *kaimakam* for having the two domestics arrested, he received a cool reception. The Turkish official expressed doubts about his identity and asked why, upon his arrival, Massignon had had recourse to Ra'uf Chadirchi instead of the French consul. When Massignon explained that Chadirchi had cleared the original itinerary, someone murmured in the background, "Why does he trust Ra'uf Chadirchi since in fact Ra'uf Chadirchi . . . ?" Snickering over Massignon's episode with Weli, the *kaimakam* and his aides left, muttering that "I should thank Abdul Hamid." Continuing unrest prevented the trip to Wasit, and now an overland return to Baghdad was impossible because even with the sale of the guns, Massignon did not have enough money. The *kaimakam* had the Tessis advance him the price of a steamer ticket back to Baghdad.

It is unclear whether the officials of Kut knew of Chadirchi's adherence to the movement "Union and Progress" and therefore suspected Massignon's complicity, but their comments suggest that, for whatever reasons, Chadirchi had in part effected the changed attitude of the *kaimakam* toward Massignon and that the latter's safety now rested only on the original assurances from the Ottoman government, requested prior to his arrival in Iraq. These assurances contained conditions. When Rouet had first written to the walis, requesting military escorts for Massignon, uprisings by the Muntafiq were disrupting the region near Kut. The wali of Basra had replied that the expedition was untimely because the military was occupied with local problems. Rouet made the same request of the wali of Baghdad and then further specified that if travel from Kut to Wasit were impossible because of political conditions, the *kaimakam* of Kut should be instructed to refuse Massignon a military escort. It is unclear if Massignon himself knew of this caveat, but the *kaimakam* did. To this knowledge was added Massignon's suspicious appearance in Arab dress and the fact that earlier in April, south of Kut, an assassination attempt had been made on the life of Nazim Bey, the Ottoman minister of justice. Finally a letter from the *kaimakam* to Chadirchi indicates that Massignon did not appear in his right mind during his April 30 visit. "M. Massignon came to see me yesterday [April 30] at my place. From the way he was speaking I understood that he didn't have all his wits."[22] It would seem that the *kaimakam* had therefore used Massignon's misadventure with his domestics as warrant to remove the strangely dressed young European from the area. In this way Massignon's safety was assured as well as that of Arab friends like Chadirchi who were planning the July revolt.

Massignon himself officially attributed his unexpected return to Baghdad to the political upheavals in the region: "On May first, the region of Wasit remaining troubled, I resigned myself to retreat back to Baghdad . . . "[23] He did not say then but later affirmed that he had been caught in a trap and that Ra'uf Chadirchi had been partially responsible:

> True friendship born in danger must be able to stand fast in the hour of testing: to be loyal for two at any price, when the other grows faint, which sometimes happens. It's the only realistic solution in the true battle for life; I had the experience twenty-five years ago in a little adventure on the edge of this desert. Captured thanks to a trap known to one of my Arab friends, a Turkish official who was at the same time a conspirator, I remained obstinately faithful to the word we had exchanged before my departure. I held fast, and he ended up by rallying.[24]

Exhausted, without resources and unable to piece together the elements which had caused the abrupt termination of his expedition, Massignon sent his escort by land back to Baghdad while "brokenhearted" he boarded the Turkish steamer, the *Burhaniye* for the trip up river. May first was a Friday that year. He was the only European on board; the other four or five first-class passengers were all Muslims, and among them Massignon recognized one of the advisors of the *kaimakam* of Kut. Since the boat was small, first-class passengers were lodged in the salon, while the others remained on the bridge. Massignon arranged himself in the corner of the salon on a cot, while the others played cards: "I found myself stared at brutally, less for being suspect of espionage than for loose morals, probably because of the tales of Weli to his jailers."[25] In the presence of the Turkish and Iraqi passengers, Massignon felt suspect and isolated:

> They questioned me about things I had not done. What interest did that have? They had already devised a system for interpreting my life, and anyhow, I judged myself guilty on many grounds they did not know about, so I didn't have to plead innocent. In the first place, is one able to plead innocent?[26]

Massignon wrote that later in the day an officer told him he would be dead before morning because he knew Massignon had participated in the assassination attempt against Nazim Bey, that he had penetrated the forbidden region of the Muntafiq and that he was a spy traveling under a false name. Massignon kept silent, "terrified by the spirit of untruth and gratuitous hatred that gripped this man." However, the perception that his situation was dangerous suggested to him a fleeting prayer in Arabic.[27] "It was in Arabic that I made my first prayer to Him (I was living in the desert, alone with the Arabs for three months) 'Allah, Allah, *as'ad du'fi'* (God, God! help my weakness!)"[28]

Articulated in Arabic, this prayer assumed great significance for Massignon after his conversion. Arabic was the language of Hallaj and of the aphorism which had first attracted Massignon to the mystic. He had discovered through Arabic "that sort of communicable consciousness of the *true* which language should communicate to us." On the other hand, Massignon's stays in Arab countries had engendered moral conflict because of the life he was leading. "The problem for me was that I used the language of my sin, the language of the desperate life I had led, searching among strangers for something I did not know . . ."[29] In retrospect the brief prayer signaled the first step in reconciling his longing for the absolute with the reality of his life.

After the prayer in Arabic and according to his unpublished summary of 1922, Massignon went to the captain and surrendered his revolver. He explained that he had been involved not in any espionage but in archeological research. The captain, whom Massignon later discovered to be the uncle of Ra'uf Chadirchi, appeared very concerned and promised his help. Massignon then recalled returning to his bed. He fell asleep, his imagination "still haunted by impure desires" and his ears filled with a chorus of voices stating that he would be shot at dawn as a spy and that "a Christian should kill himself rather than endure such shame."[30]

Captain Hamid's two versions of what happened on the *Burhaniye* between May 1 and May 5, when it arrived in Baghdad, differ from Massignon's 1922 unpublished summary of the conversion experience. They also vary somewhat from each other. However, in both it is clear that the captain became progressively more anxious about Massignon's erratic behavior and that the measures he took to deal with it were motivated by concern for the young man's welfare. Massignon's as yet uncertain mastery of spoken Arabic made him difficult to understand and contributed to the captain's perception that he was not lucid. Both Hamid reports agree that Massignon complained about his treatment at the hands of the other passengers. Massignon placed this episode during his first night on board, May 1; for Captain Hamid in his first report, it occurred May 2. The doctor, Assad Efendi, who later cared for Massignon on board reported that nothing unusual occurred Friday, "To tell the truth, that day and the next day, Saturday, he provoked no incident of any importance."[31] While the accounts vary as to when the significant sequence of events began and mention some incidents rather than others, they complement rather than contradict each other.

Massignon does not mention two small *cartes de visite* on which he wrote messages to the captain in classical Arabic and Iraqi dialect; Captain Hamid later turned them over to Rouet. The cards reflect that later exchanges occurred with the captain the same night, whether May 1 or 2. Since during their first encounter the captain had not responded satisfactorily in Massignon's eyes to concerns about his safety, Massignon evidently wondered if indeed he would be executed. If that were to be the case, he himself wanted to give the signal to fire. When the captain did not respond to the first card, Massignon penned a second one, but that one was also ignored. Then, according to Hamid's version, Massignon returned to the captain's cabin, seized a revolver, pointed it first at the captain and then at his own head. The captain secured the gun and in order to watch over Massignon had him placed under observation.

Massignon recorded awakening the next day, May 2, in the salon, only to discover he was being kept under surveillance and confined to the area of his bed. Food was brought which he ate. Then, either in defiance of his captors or already affected by the malaria which manifested itself shortly thereafter, he requested two cigarettes, which, according to his version, "I swallowed in succes-

sion, both lit, without hurting myself and in spite of the protes-
tations of my guardian." That evening he noticed while returning
under guard from the toilet that the boat had run aground next to a
coal barge along the banks of the Tigris. This fact, never mentioned
by Captain Hamid, was confirmed in the written report of Doctor
Assad Efendi. The boat had stopped near the ruins of Ctesiphon and
the huge palace, the Taq. Massignon decided to flee: "I believed the
moment had come to escape . . . persuaded that if I stayed on board
I would be mutilated or killed in reprisal. I bolted, overturning
everything and was only retaken by a group of determined men."[32]

Upon his return to ship, Massignon was tied and placed on a
divan in the captain's cabin. Towards dawn, May 3 or 4, insensed at
the apparent hopelessness of his situation, he tensed his body and
managed to roll off the divan; but the act was noticed and he was
placed on it once more. Alone, exhausted, fearing for his life, his
work seemingly in shambles, Massignon despaired:

> Then I began to suffer from myself. Examination of conscience:
> look at how I was ending up after four and a half years of amorality,
> justly wiped out for the greediness of my science and my pleasure.
> Dying in a terrible situation; my family would be happy to forget
> me. And remembering the voices heard the night before, I decided
> to put an end to myself.[33]

Complaining that his right arm hurt from the cord, Massignon was
momentarily untied and left alone. The accounts of Hamid, Doctor
Assad, and Massignon concur that, using a blade, he wounded himself superficially near the heart, but they differ on the size of the instrument. For the captain it was, in his first report, a penknife, and
in the second a small knife. The doctor did not note the size. Massignon described it as the long straight Swedish knife which he had
concealed in a wide belt. He remembered, "Hardly had the blood
seeped out than, whether because of cowardice or physical weakness, I stopped, taken aback."[34] Those caring for him soon noticed
and bandaged him quickly. Both reports by the captain end with this
episode and the notation that Massignon was confided to the care of

Doctor Assad. The latter's written report provides the only record of Massignon's observable behavior between May 3 or 4 and May 5.

Shortly after the aborted suicide attempt and while under restraints in the captain's cabin, Massignon became more and more agitated. Dr. Assad wrote:

> But the agitation and delirium kept on increasing, so that [M. Massignon] threw off the dressings which had been applied, tore and likewise threw off his jacket as well as his sweater and shredded his shirt. His face became quite red, the congestion in his eyes and his excitement so violent that he began to throw himself at the passengers and shipmates; all this proved that a dislocation had occurred in his mental state and that he had become crazy. He kept crying out, "I want to die; leave me alone." We tried to calm him by every means and prevent him from leaving the captain's cabin so as not to give rise to other incidents.

After about three or four hours of this intense struggle, Massignon's agitation subsided and was followed by about half an hour of what appeared to be sleep:

> After a half-hour of sleep, he awakened, but I noticed first of all a state of stupor and to the question I put to him, "Do you want to eat," he limited himself to assenting by a shake of the head. I had something to eat brought to him; he ate, it's true, but by mixing together the dishes one with the other and swallowing mouthfuls without chewing them. After the meal I offered him a cigarette, but after he had taken hardly two puffs, he swallowed it.[35]

The agitation then reasserted itself, "His excitement started again, he hurled himself at me through the door and at people on board." This situation lasted until about 2:30 P.M., May 3 or 4. Massignon was then forcibly restrained by tying his hands and feet. He remained in the captain's cabin away from the other passengers.

Sometime during the peaceful intervals within that agitated period, either during the half-hour of sleep or shortly after 2:30 when he had been restrained, Massignon felt himself invaded by a mysterious presence, what he was later to call the "visitation of the Stranger." The encounter initiated an experience of spiritual transformation spanning several weeks and which culminated in his return to full participation in the Catholic Church. For the rest of his life Massignon alluded to the experience but only in telegraphic fashion. However, in 1955, responding to a questionnaire about God for a review, he was slightly more explicit. Asked about the meaning of the word *God* and its implications, he replied that "the discovery antecedes the theory, the disturbance precedes the designation." It is triggered either by "an internal rupture in our habits" or by "the realization of sin." In either case, the soul, like the Virgin Mary at the Annunciation, asks neither "the why" nor the "how" of this discovery but rather consents to the Presence. "It is not an invented idea which she [the soul] causes to evolve as it pleases her, according to nature; it is a mysterious Stranger which she adores and which orients her: she entrusts herself to it." Responding to a question about the "correspondences" of God in his own life, he used a favorite image, "it concerns a mental, Copernican decentering happening in us or, rather, experienced."[36]

These comments written toward the end of Massignon's life evoke characteristics of the 1908 experience. Certainly, events of the preceding week, coupled with Massignon's deep-seated anguish about his conflict-ridden moral life, had profoundly disrupted his mental and emotional equilibrium. His research, the escape, suicide— all had failed, and he found himself isolated and immobilized under the watchful gaze of people who thought he was either a spy or sick or both. The Stranger was perceived suddenly, a discovery which struck without warning; and Massignon was passive, helpless to resist either physically or emotionally. The change in his life was sudden, overwhelming. In the 1922 notes, he described the experience:

> Shortly after the failed knife thrust, I submitted to another stroke: interior, extraordinary, torturing, supernatural, ineffable. As if the very center of my heart were burning and my thoughts wrenched apart; my mind saw itself spinning around the wheel of its own past

judgments, struck by all the condemnation it had so liberally passed on others; "it is right and just, and yet I did not wish that." No longer alone but judged. Almost a damnation. A liberation in any case, removed from among men. And immediately the certainty that I would come back to Paris.[37]

Paul Claudel summarized in his journal the entire conversion story as recounted to him by Massignon, and his written account states that in this first dramatic phase, Massignon perceived God as simultaneously judging and liberating his life:

> He tries to commit suicide. At that moment, profound metaphysical distress, immense sorrow, irreparable privation, "damnation." All the judgments he had passed on others, he felt them turned against himself. His own measure was applied to him.[38]

In a 1910 letter to Claudel, Massignon described his psychic state at that moment of anguish: "I was in fact stripped of the pleasure of feeling my body alive and of knowing my mind in reflection, and left in this crisis with nothing more than my name to maintain the link between soul and body."[39] Massignon later summarized for Claudel the consequences of this experience for his life: his agnosticism was "cured, laid bare, cauterized, only in Mesopotamia, in May 1908, as you know."[40]

Sometime after 2:30 P.M., May 3 or 4, Massignon was removed from the relative privacy of the captain's cabin to the salon of the first-class passengers, where he remained for the last part of the trip. He remained bound and was fed during this period, which, in his own mind, formed a single block of time with his transfer to the hospital after the boat docked in Baghdad, May 5. In the salon he remembered the scent "of dry grass (alpia or hashish)" wafting in the open windows from the spring flowering along the Tigris or from the Turkish cigarettes of the other passengers: "I had dreams (a series of figures), not believing any more in my filiation or my identity. A terrible horror of myself seized me and made me keep my eyes obstinately shut for a period which I thought equal to twice

twenty-four hours."[41] Totally absorbed in the drama of his interior
life, Massignon paid no attention to his surroundings when the boat
docked, "I kept silent, my eyes closed (through horror and embar-
rassment), pretending to be mute, even accepting to be passed off as
crazy."[42]

The Austrian consul, Rosenfeld, and the French consul, Rouet,
came on board and saw Massignon still tied to a sofa; the latter refused to speak or open his eyes. They then conferred with Captain
Hamid, who gave them an oral report of events (the report was later
transcribed by Rosenfeld, the first of the captain's two reports).
When they returned to the salon, Massignon acknowledged them,
accepted a cup of tea and said his name. After consulting the wali of
Baghdad, Rouet had Massignon transported that afternoon, still
bound, to the civil hospital, a small building on the edge of the
wali's palace complex. During the transfer under the relentless Baghdad sun, first by stretcher and then in a carriage, Massignon continued to be tormented by images:

> A series of terrible mental images continued to pass before my reti-
> nas against a background of Hallajian flames (a burst of sunlight,
> transposed [Massignon's note]): faces (names) of those who had
> helped me: Foucauld, Huysmans, my mother, my aunt Thérèse
> Laurens—or tested me: A. Le Chatelier. Doubting my very person-
> ality, in a kind of forbidden initiation scene half glimpsed, I felt
> myself pursued by nothingness. I escaped finally by the willing ad-
> mission of my identity: crying out in French several times in the
> carriage taking me across the souk (native language reassumed): "I
> am Louis Massignon."[43]

In his 1922 account, Massignon added a footnote after the name of
Huysmans and stated that Léon Leclaire, Huysmans' close friend,
had told Pierre Roche in a letter how Huysmans, before his death in
May 1907, had explicitly prayed for Massignon. Another footnote,
after the name of his aunt, Thérèse Laurens, Massignon took from a
journal entry, dated July 4, 1908:

"the beloved dead," my aunt, Dulac, Huysmans especially, and Hallaj. Foucauld was only added later, in parentheses ("the living whom I have never seen"). Classification: Hallaj, Dulac, Huysmans, Foucauld.[44]

When Massignon arrived at the hospital, doctors noted his high fever, racing pulse, and inflamed face. Once again agitated and delirious, he was restrained in bed. The high fever, also mentioned by Massignon in his 1922 account, signaled an attack of malaria. Opinion was divided on what caused his other symptoms. Initially the three doctors on the case were convinced "that M. Massignon had sustained a major stroke caused by sunstroke and the fatigue of the trip." When he left the hospital, May 22, after regaining consciousness and some sense of well-being on May 8, they thought that in spite of his rapid convalescence, "this sign of suicide and the state of general and violent exaltation he had shown upon entering the hospital" suggested "mania which had manifested itself under the influence of moral and psychic fatigue . . . very probably chronic." The final report sent to the wali of Baghdad concluded that Massignon had been "afflicted with paranoia accompanied by delusions of persecution."[45] However, although Massignon suffered bouts of malaria off and on throughout his life, he never again exhibited any of the other dramatic symptoms so evident in May 1908. In 1911, when Massignon was thinking of joining Charles de Foucauld in North Africa, he recalled the diagnosis and gave his own interpretation: "I could go to Tamanrasset and come back before the heat (it is however a little risky, with my 'apoplexy' (?diagnosis of Baghdad = in reality the terrible reaction on my brain [. . .] of the *forced* conversion of my soul) three years ago."[46]

From the time he arrived at the hospital May 5, until he awakened the morning of May 8, Massignon considered himself near death and was only vaguely aware of his surroundings. He remembered hearing verses of the Qur'an prayed over him and speculated in another footnote of the 1922 account that these were "probably the sura Yasin (XXXVI), at the request of my friends, the Alussys, a wonderful alms I will never forget." A second experience of the supernatural overtook him and transformed the perception of physical death into the certitude of a spiritual death and rebirth; the "name" mentioned was undoubtedly Luis de Cuadra:

> Then, taken up for the second time into the supernatural, I felt myself warned that I was going to die: a burgeoning spiritual dawn, a serene clarity inciting me to renounce everything. I clung to a beloved name, repeating it to myself, declaring to myself "if he has betrayed me, I want to be sincere for two and carry his name with me always." The serene clarity increased in my soul: what is a name in the memory? Does not God possess this creature infinitely better than I? I abandon him to God.[47]

When Massignon awoke May 8, "the sun-speckled lapping of the flooded Tigris which had invaded the garden, played images on the plaster ceiling." And the doves called out, "haqq, haqq," from a nearby palm tree. Their gentle chant recalled the incident of two months before when he had told the young girl that her birds did not sing; the contrast suggested to him the role of Hallaj's martyrdom in his conversion. "And, in an instant, in the suspense of silence, I understood them: the Truth of my pardon came out of the broken talisman, from the veil of the torn Name."[48] In the succeeding phases of his conversion, the doves would continue to symbolize a merciful supernatural presence.

Massignon subsequently made a rapid recovery. That same day, May 8, he wrote a note to Rouet asking him to retrieve three large files about Hallaj; the next day he went with the consul for a carriage ride. On May 11, he went horseback riding and began to put in order his papers, which Rouet had remitted to him. On May 23, he was allowed to leave the hospital for his house in Hayderkhaneh, but a new attack of malaria May 28 prompted Rouet to house him at the consulate until his departure from Baghdad June 4.

At the news of Massignon's illness, Rouet had immediately alerted General de Beylié and asked him to discuss with Le Chatelier about how to communicate the news to the family. Le Chatelier did so, but Fernand Massignon initially kept the news from his wife. From May 7 onward, he maintained almost daily telegraph contact with Rouet about the details of his son's repatriation. After a flurry of memos the order was given May 14 by the French minister of education. Rouet urged a return by the Red Sea, but Massignon held out for an overland route that would take him up the Euphrates toward Aleppo (in Syria). Eventually Rouet agreed, and the Alussys' friend, Muhammad Chalabi, the head of the Baghdad merchants, found a caravan of four carriages which had come from Aleppo and wished to return. Chalabi told Massignon that he would be urged en route to change horses, but that should he do so, the caravan would never arrive at its destination. Fearing another recurrence of malaria, Rouet engaged a doctor to accompany Massignon, an Armenian, Dr. Iskenderian, a Turkish spy. In a telegram Massignon's father had asked Rouet to find a priest who would also accompany his son back to France. Rouet chose an Iraqi Carmelite whose name in religion was Père Anastase-Marie de Saint Elie; he was a scholar in Arabic and had studied in France. Given the agnosticism of his father, Massignon and his mother later wondered why the elder Massignon had requested a priest for this mission. It was "so that in case of catastrophe, there would be a hold on one of the witnesses (bound by his rule to tell his superiors the truth)."[49]

Anastase asked and was at first refused permission by the archbishop of Baghdad, Monseigneur Drure, to undertake the mission. It seemed that Massignon, in the course of a diplomatic dinner at the German consulate several months earlier, had miffed the archbishop by requesting at table that the latter cease his attacks on Clemenceau, then the French head of state. Anastase, in order to prevail and obtain a trip to France, intimated to the archbishop that the journey was not a question of accommodating Massignon but rather of saving his soul. He telegraphed Drure with the message, "conversion begun." Upon hearing of this Massignon became furious because he had told no one of the intense interior drama which had so shaken him the previous month. "I had spoken to no one of my state of mind: the slave of God without being admitted to prayer under any other form than that of obedience *hic et nunc*." Rouet demanded an explanation from Anastase, who admitted that it was a ruse. Massignon then exacted from the priest a promise, "I made him promise never to speak to me of religion during the trip."[50]

Massignon and his party left Baghdad the evening of June 4 and headed north, following the Euphrates upstream. Disquieting incidents occurred en route. At Deir ez Zor the head of the caravan camp wanted him to change horses and was furious when Massignon, remembering the counsels of Chalabi, refused. The night of the twenty-first at Maskanah, near Aleppo, the head of the escort party announced he would go no further. Massignon did not protest, "I know you are carrying out orders." When the man retorted that the caravan could not go on alone, he kept silent and the man left. The next morning before dawn, Massignon seated himself in the last carriage, as had been his custom since 1904 when his interpreter had betrayed him during the Moroccan expedition. He gave the signal to leave and the caravan pulled out. Two hours later a troop of Turkish cavalry barred the way, saying that the road was unsafe because of bandits. Fortunately, the confrontation coincided with the arrival of a messenger from Aleppo, taking a friend of Muhammad Chalabi to Baghdad. The problem was quickly resolved, and the journey to Aleppo ended June 23 without further difficulty. Massignon noted that Père Anastase was quite taken aback by the episode with the Turkish soldiers and wondered if the priest took him "for a political courier."[51]

Massignon had decided to delay for a day the trip to Beirut; he was supposed to leave Aleppo June 24. Suddenly that evening a distinct awareness of the supernatural overwhelmed him for the third time:

> A harrowing sensation, suddenly of the presence of God, no longer as a judge, but as a father inundating the prodigal child. I quietly locked the door of my room and prostrated myself on the tiles, finally weeping my prayer all night long, after five years of a dried up heart.[52]

Claudel described it as "a sudden melting of his heart, he prayed without knowing to whom or how, he prayed all night, his face to the ground."[53] In the first experience, he had been so wrenched apart by the visit of the divine "Stranger" that he could do little else but struggle to maintain some hold on his very being. The second such instance, when he had felt himself close to death, had exacted a definitive renunciation of the love he had known but had intimated spiritual rebirth. Now, in this third experience, he was able in prayer to answer a God of overwhelming mercy and compassion, a response he had abandoned five years before as a young conscript in the army.

The next morning, June 25, Massignon, Père Anastase, and the doctor boarded a train for Beirut. Shortly before Hama, as Massignon gazed through the compartment door, the same presence again took hold of him, and this time the certainty grew that the truth he had discovered was found in the Catholic faith. But the return to the Church demanded that he first confess his sins. The prospect produced instant resistance and refusal until his promise to obey in the here and now returned to Massignon with crashing force. Kneeling at the feet of the astonished Père Anastase and the amused Dr. Iskenderian, he asked to go to confession. Judging that the train was not an appropriate place, Anastase refused and the confession occurred when they arrived that evening at Baalbeck. The next day "after the Holy Sacrifice at sunrise, in the little court-yard beneath the apricot tree of the convent, I had a renewed heart and eyes as fresh as a child . . . And it was truly the dawn of a new life."[54] Massignon could not yet receive the eucharist because of sins that were reserved to a bishop.[55] Thus, the deep peace experienced at the liturgy was incomplete and alternated with obsessive images from the past which nagged at him, causing profound anguish.

This mental suffering which continued after the arrival in Beirut, prompted Massignon in desperation to visit the Church of Saint Joseph on June 28. He decided to make the way of the cross, a devotion he had totally forgotten, even to thinking that it comprised twelve stations, not fourteen. His arms in the form of a cross, his face to the ground, Massignon wrestled with his demons and became one with his struggle. "This time, my name escaped me; I had to deny myself, I was 'someone who was beginning the way of the cross.'" He glimpsed that through the crucible of his past he was called as a believer "to complete with simple and clear faith the way of the cross for those who were unable to go right to the end by their own force." Indeed, in spite of his "unworthiness, or because of it perhaps, [he had] been marked for that." The "visit of the Stranger" had laid bare and judged the fabric of Massignon's life; he had experienced rebirth and the overwhelming mercy of God. Now he rediscovered the crucified Jesus and knew that "the one in whom I believed was the One who said, 'Whoever would come after me, must deny himself and take up his cross and follow me.'" For Massignon that imperative "to carry my own cross" meant "first of all to endure myself, such as I had been made, with my habits of body and spirit: that is heavy to do alone."[56] Thus, paradoxically, the intimate suffering of his own limits and fragility became the guarantor of his call and of his identification with the One who called.

Massignon's inert figure disturbed those around him and Père Anastase was summoned. Massignon did not respond to the priest's attempt to speak with him and decided that he would stand only when explicitly asked by Anastase: this would signal that his entire confession had been received. Anastase did so; Massignon stood up and immediately the hallucinations disappeared. The papal envoy had been contacted concerning Massignon's confession; all was in order, and serenity returned.

On June 29, the Massignon party set sail from Beirut for Port Said, where Dr. Iskenderian left them. The latter noted in his report to Rouet what he termed a three-day "crisis of devotion" in Beirut but added that "it had completely ended the day of his departure."[57] On July 3, accompanied by Père Anastase, Massignon boarded the *Cordouan* for Marseille. His departure from Mesopotamia had been propitious because on July 4 the revolution of the young Turks broke out in Constantinople and began spreading rapidly throughout the crumbling empire. Shukri Alussy was sought for two days by the wali of Baghdad, who wished to imprison him; after the revolution he became the deputy of Baghdad to the new parliament.

Arriving in Marseille on July 9, Anastase and Massignon were met by the latter's father and sister. Restored to health by the long boat crossing, he was committed to deepening his rediscovered faith and fully engaged in his writing and research. After several days in Paris, Massignon spent the two weeks between July 13 and July 29 with his parents and Père Anastase at the family vacation home in Brittany. The time was devoted to preparing a paper on the discovery of the fortress of Ukhaydir, which General de Beylié presented July 31 to the Academy of Inscriptions.

Fernand Massignon was initially taken aback and disturbed by the sudden transformation of his son, and the firsthand reports of Rouet transmitted by Père Anastase did little to improve the situation. But eventually, following long conversations, the son's conversion was accepted by the father, and the two shared their many common interests as they had in the past. One bridge of understanding was found in their mutual admiration for Joan of Arc. Father and son could agree that whether her mission was divinely inspired or not, the Maid of Orleans had asserted its authenticity when challenged by Church authorities, and that she had died courageously, faithful to her belief. Fernand Massignon, the defender of Dreyfus, could accept that his son, like Joan, was attempting to remain faithful to the lived experience of his conversion.[58] Moreover, any anxiety about his son's health was quieted by Louis Massignon's complete recovery. A letter to Père Anastase in September expressed both parental solicitude and a parental judgment that the entire experience in Mesopotamia had been profitable:

> He has so completely recovered his calm that I have been able to show and discuss with him the reports of the doctors in Baghdad and the boat captain. The fever has not reappeared for a second, and I think that with a few precautions this winter, not only a complete cure but also the benefit of a hard but salutary experience will

remain with him from this dangerous sojourn in Baghdad where his simplicity and inexperience were put to such a tough test.[59]

During the next year Massignon intently pursued his professional life and his research on Hallaj. He later explained how his conversion had necessitated that he recommit himself to the project:

> Emerging from a decisive trial where the divine lesson of the present moment had struck me to my very core, I accepted the fact that at whatever cost, I would finish the scholarly work on a difficult biography begun as a whim, outside my then professional field; it was about an Arab mystic, a Muslim, al Hallaj, whom a singular accident had placed on my path. [I] considered that a significant life, a total human experience containing substantial allusions [to mystical experience] and linked to examples of heroism, all within a divinely planned scenario, could make dawn in others the desire to sublimate our common misery and the secret of how to do it, and that there was no higher lesson to pass on.[60]

Both his publications and travel mark the year as one of the most productive of Massignon's life. In August, he attended the fifteenth international congress of Orientalists in Copenhagen and presented a paper on the Muslim saints in Baghdad.[61] It earned him the encouragement of Goldziher and the beginnings of his international reputation as well. His father's technique of gypsographies had proved invaluable in Baghdad for obtaining images of inscriptions; Massignon now worked in Roche's studio to perfect the details of his etchings so that these could be included in his forthcoming volumes on the mission in Mesopotamia. He was supposed to return to Cairo and the Institut in November, but the necessity of finishing the project prompted him to request and receive a medical leave for a year so that he could stay in Paris. Under the statutes of the Institut, it was the only strategy available in order to remain salaried during that period. He finished the first volume of *Mission en Mésopotamie* in June 1909 and wrote on his work of epigraphy and archeology for numerous publications.[62]

During the same year 1908–9, he traveled extensively, not only to complete the report about the discoveries in Mesopotamia but also to research the dissertation on Hallaj. On his way to Constantinople in April, he spent four days in Berlin and questioned the German archeologists Ernst Herzfeld and Friedrich Sarre not only about epigraphy but also about why, when he had given them free rein in Samarra, they had endangered his life by denouncing him to the wali of Baghdad. No explanation was ever given. After passing through Leipzig, Massignon returned to Nancy and rejoined Fernand Massignon, whom he had persuaded to accompany him April 18 to Joan of Arc's birthplace at Domremy. It was the year of the saint's beatification, and the pilgrimage was one of thanksgiving because Joan had been the intermediary which allowed father and son to achieve mutual understanding.

The famous Orient Express eventually took Massignon to Constantinople, but only after multiple stopovers—in Vienna, Budapest, and Belgrade—for consultations with colleagues and research in libraries. The three-week stay in Constantinople (April 24–May 14) allowed him to see the definitive success of the July 1908 revolt in which members of "Union and Progress" such as Shukri and Hajj 'Ali Alussy had participated. Massignon and Shukri Alussy were reunited when the latter arrived as the deputy from Baghdad to the new parliament. The former wali of Baghdad, Hazim Bey, had been named wali of Constantinople. The sultan, Abdul Hamid II, abdicated and the minister whom Massignon had supposedly wanted to assassinate, Nazim Bey, was executed. Upon his return to Paris, Massignon wrote to Henri Maspero, "The libraries are rich and the revolution was enthralling."[63]

Massignon's intellectual life, transformed by his conversion, was certainly not diminished. Indeed, in retrospect one could say that his scholarly pursuits and religious yearnings enhanced one another. The early interest in *L'Astrée*, the steady perusal of mystical texts, and the choice of Hallaj as a dissertation topic all paved the way for the conversion. Conversely, the dramatic religious experience shaped his scholarship for the rest of his life and conferred on it the intensity and passion that was uniquely his.

The account of the conversion suggests almost paradoxically an important element both of that experience itself and the life which followed. In the final analysis the mystic in Massignon was grafted onto the artist or poet, for whom the singular person or place remains the primary way of interpreting the world. If Massignon returned to Christianity through the impact of the transcendent and inaccessible God of Islam, he did so because of the perceived influence of his own "intercessors," the most important of whom was Hallaj. If the undulating starkness of the desert signified that he must empty himself through rigorous asceticism in order to be filled by God, the very landscapes which prompted him to do so likewise impelled him to return to them throughout his life for renewal and refreshment. Beginning with the conversion, he created for himself a world of religious symbol, peopled with men and women, living or dead, legendary or historically verifiable and drawn for the most part from the three monotheistic traditions; they were included because their lives somehow touched his own. It was almost as if he transposed and made his own, not the content, but the very profusion of mythological, Christian, and patriotic figures which had inspired his father's art and graced his own childhood. Certainly the medium Massignon chose seemed almost ineffable, no longer wrought iron or Japanese paper, but rather, the texture of his own life and the words which gave it voice. That life and its telling thereby acquired a concreteness proper to art. The number of these important figures in his life would increase with the years, so that their paths intersected ever more frequently in a series of fortuitous and significant encounters labeled "intersigns." This activity occurred in an expanding world whose boundaries were determined solely by the existence of its multiple inhabitants.

He prayed to those who were saints and visited the graves of the dead: saints, family or friends. As for the living, they became part of his prayer and the recipients of numerous letters. The sheer volume of Massignon's personal correspondence is extraordinary, aside from all the letters involving his professional activity. It testifies to the fact that, perhaps in response to the solitude that he felt and that others saw in him as well, Massignon reached out to others ceaselessly to extend or request help, clarify his thinking, or assuage his own need for self-revelation. In the years immediately following his conversion it was not surprising then that, along with intense professional work, he sought counsel to guide him in his new life of faith.

THREE

The Search for Commitment

In the months that followed his return to France, the professional life of Massignon continued its steady development; but his personal life, radically altered by the conversion, underwent a profound shift as he embraced his rediscovered faith. In July he renewed contact with his boyhood spiritual director, Père Louis Poulin; and on August 8 he wrote a first letter to Paul Claudel, then stationed as a diplomat in China. Massignon had never met Claudel but around the age of twenty had begun to read his work. Their correspondence from 1908 to 1914 reflects Massignon's preoccupations during the period; a vocation struggle is closely linked to those persons and themes crucial to the conversion. The letters document how the young convert attempted to balance his longing for total dedication to God with the reality of a mind superbly prepared over the years to pursue a brilliant academic career. The themes which would preoccupy Massignon for a lifetime are already delineated, and these are clearly related to the persons (intercessors) whose presence he had felt at the moment of his conversion, among them, Huysmans, Hallaj, and Charles de Foucauld.

Chronologically, Huysmans was the first intercessor. Massignon had been so moved upon learning that the dying Huysmans had prayed for his conversion that he set out to understand the writer's spiritual legacy. The novelist's deathbed prayer and Massignon's subsequent conversion seemed to confirm the efficacy of one person's mystical substitution and atonement for the sins of another. For the rest of his life Massignon remained devoted to Huysmans' memory, and over the years he came to know and deal with various bizarre twists in the story of the writer's return to Catholicism.

Huysmans helped to popularize the doctrine of mystical substitution, but it was not original to him. It can already be found in the writings of Joseph de Maistre (1753–1821) about the reversibility of merits, which in the Catholic world of late nineteenth-century France had assumed major importance. Huysmans was introduced to the idea by the renegade priest Joseph-Antoine Boullan, who guided the novelist's unlikely journey from occultism to Catholicism.

In 1890 the then mistress of Remy de Goncourt and adept of the occult, Berthe Courrière, spoke to Huysmans about the ex-priest. The former cleric and the writer struck up a correspondence; Boullan promised to provide information for *Là-Bas*, Huysmans' forthcoming novel about the occult, published in 1891. He also promised to protect Huysmans from the evil practices of rival occult sects. The practice of occultism had convinced Huysmans that indeed the supernatural order existed, and this belief slowly paved the way for him to accept Catholic doctrine. Boullan counseled Huysmans for the next three years and in July 1891 took him to the Basilica of La Salette, near Grenoble in the French Alps. The shrine marked the spot where, in 1846, the Virgin Mary appeared, wept, and gave a secret message to two shepherd children, Maximian Giraud and Melanie Calvat. There Boullan "protected" Huysmans during religious ceremonies. The devotion to Our Lady of La Salette convinced the latter that the supernatural was not limited to the diabolical and could also exert a beneficent influence. Huysmans became a Catholic in 1892. After Boullan's death in January 1893, he visited Lyons, the longtime home of Boullan's sect, and was horrified to find papers documenting the former priest's disordered life. Included was an 1867 confession of twenty-eight pages in a pink notebook (*le cahier rose*), written for the Holy Office by Boullan while in the Vatican prison. Among other deviations the pages detailed his incarceration in Rouen (1861–1864) for having killed the newborn infant he had fathered. Huysmans kept the notebook and many papers, willing them to his longtime friend and confidant Léon Leclaire; the latter gave them over to Massignon in October 1926. With the hope that someday the documents could be studied, Massignon had them sent in 1930 to the Vatican archives, where the *cahier* either disappeared or was declared off-limits. Some claim the document never reached Rome.[1]

Although Huysmans was converted through the instrumentality of Boullan, his own writing on vicarious suffering or mystical substitution tends to avoid the priest's aberrations. Huysmans' biography of Sainte Lydwine de Schiedam, published in 1901, shortly after Massignon's sole visit with the author, influenced Catholic thinking at the turn of the century by setting forth notions that were to become the basis of Massignon's own on the subject. According to this theory, God calls certain persons in each generation throughout history; they, in turn, freely acquiesce to a vocation of suffering and thereby become substitutes for those whose evil lives wreak havoc on the world. Jesus was the first in a long line of chosen substitutes who accept personal suffering in atonement for human sin. Lydwine, who died in 1443, belongs to this lineage of substitutes, many of them women, who continued Christ's work of expiation. Huysmans and, later, Massignon were particularly struck by the case of Anna Katharina Emmerich (1774–1824), whose visions were transcribed, then edited and presented by the author Clemens Brentano.

The notion of the one suffering for the many and the succession of such consenting victims reflects certain affinities between Huysmans and Hallaj. But if Massignon had heard Huysmans speak of mystical substitution, it was only through the encounter with Hallaj that he appropriated the idea for himself. In 1907, when he first seriously confronted the life and death of Hallaj, spiritual angst and a nostalgia for heroism were the sole remnants of his Catholic upbringing. The void at the center of his life determined the overpowering force of the encounter with the Sufi martyr. Hallaj brought into focus and presented anew for Massignon the mystery of Christ, and that rediscovery permitted him to reappropriate his Christian faith.

Like Christ, Hallaj was rejected and ultimately put to death by the community he sought to save. Just as Christ became the first in the long line of substitutes within the Christian tradition, Hallaj became a substitute or *abdal* in Islam and also a witness, one of a long chain or *isnad* of persons whose lives testify to the divine presence in the world.

Here we are situated at the heart of what Hallaj meant to Louis Massignon. Hallaj brought him back to the Church but, most importantly, provided an example of mystical substitution that indicated a way for him to live out his faith. During the period of the correspondence with Claudel, he wrote his doctoral dissertation on Hallaj, so it was predictable that the latter's name should occur frequently. But the dedication of Massignon to the tenth-century mystic surpassed all traditional categories of scholarly commitment. Massignon became his disciple, and the example of the master was to determine not only a major part of his scholarly output but also the shape of his relationship to God and the world.

In the years between 1908 and 1914, the example of Hallaj helped Massignon to sort out and eventually choose a path for his life. It functioned as a bridge between his religious commitment as a Christian and his dedication to Islam. The life of Hallaj and his role in the conversion invited Massignon to become in turn a substitute, one link in the chain of those who by personal suffering break open their lives to God and in so doing intercede for others. He perceived that this role constituted a basic stance within which he could pursue a vocation embracing both the Islamic and Christian communities. Therefore, when Massignon eventually opted to marry and pursue his academic career, that choice was not a purely secular one, because it did not contradict his desire to be in turn an "intercessor" for Islam, one who would spend his life in order to achieve understanding between East and West.

The self-offering of Hallaj for the salvation of Islam flowed from his relationship with God, about which the sufi wrote extensively. The testimony of Hallaj resonated for Massignon with his own experience and provided a guide for his spiritual life. Hallaj, viewed by

many as the first mystic of Islam who wished to die for love, taught
that God initiates a relationship and human beings respond, a notion reflected in Massignon's own mystical encounter with the
Stranger. Human beings cannot somehow cajole God through formal religious practice into such a divine overture, but when it occurs, God and the respondent are experienced as one in loving
union. Therefore, union with the Divine does not contradict but
rather fulfills religious practice as such. Indeed, Massignon considered that the obedience of Hallaj to Islamic precepts guaranteed the
authenticity of his teaching; divine union constituted fulfillment
rather than escape from the discipline of the law. His own experience of belief, beginning with his dramatic conversion, seemed to
bear out the teaching of Hallaj. A practicing Catholic in the conven-
tional sense of the term, he considered that obedience to Church
law and practice was important, but he conceived of faith primarily
as a relationship initiated by God to which the believer responds in
loving surrender. As Massignon wrote toward the end of his life, in
a sentence quoted earlier, "The discovery antedates the theory, the
commotion precedes denomination."[2] The new convert expressed
the same attitude in his initial letter to Claudel (August 8, 1908)
when he recalled the Islamic practice of fixed prayers before the
empty niche, *mihrab,* which indicates the direction of Mecca. "This
illustrates many things; the effort, for example, made by the first
Sufis, ardent with remorse and filled with truth, in order to break
out of this 'enclosure of prayers.'" Massignon then cited the example of Hallaj, "the first who negated the *Hajj,*" by teaching that the
truest pilgrimage to God occurred in the heart.[3]

At one point in 1912 Massignon sent Claudel an offprint of an
article about Hallaj, to which the latter responded that Hallaj "is
hardly Christian and really gives off a kind of very dangerous spiritual sensuality. The sentiment of divine love without Christ and
without Christ crucified has inspired many heresies."[4] Undaunted,
Massignon in the next letter justified writing about Hallaj and underscored the latter's resemblance to Christ. "In the first place, it's
my thesis which I'm finishing, at the formal, repeated order of my

[spiritual] director." More fundamentally, he was repaying "a debt of gratitude," because it was Hallaj "and no one else who led me to Baghdad" and who thereby effected his return to Catholicism and hence to faith in Christ. His research had shown him that Hallaj was a Christ figure. The obedience to Islamic law which the Sufi exemplified was the touchstone of his genuineness as a mystic and an indicator of his compatability with Christianity. Like Christ "he pushed the spirit of obedience to the point of wishing to be anathema because of the law in order to save others." A host of symbols with echoes in the Christian tradition buttressed this interpretation. For example, the meaning of the word Baghdad, "in Persian the garden bestowed, the lost Eden, the Land of Captivity, [was] where Abraham came from." Moreover, according to legend, the cross on which Jesus died was at one point brought to Baghdad; the city was also the site of Hallaj's crucifixion. Finally, Massignon enumerates to Claudel certain details of Hallaj's life which resemble that of Christ in the Gospel and asserts that legends about Hallaj have not been modified by Jewish influence.[5]

During the autumn of 1908, research for material about Hallaj constituted only one element of a wider spiritual search which included both the Claudel correspondence and a series of letters to Charles de Foucauld. Massignon had had no contact with the hermit priest after the latter's 1906 note thanking him for the copy of his book on Leo Africanus. The line "I offer to God for you my poor and unworthy prayers, begging him to bless you, your work and your whole life," was ostensibly forgotten by Massignon soon after receiving the note, only to surface in the felt presence of Foucauld during the conversion. Although of different backgrounds and temperaments, the younger and older man shared a love of the desert and an experience of rediscovered faith. Moreover, the radical character of Foucauld's religious commitment struck a sympathetic note with Massignon, who thrived on risk and invested himself totally in whatever he undertook.

Eventually on November 29, 1908, the young, Sorbonne-educated intellectual wrote about his conversion to the hermit and former soldier, a product of both Saint-Cyr and seven years in a Trappist monastery. "I finished (five months of equivocation) my letter to Foucauld."[6] The letter comprised a significant step because, unlike Hallaj and Huysmans, Foucauld was a living and therefore immediately challenging example of a radically committed life. By writing, Massignon implied that he was open to such a challenge, and Christmas day found the ardent new convert at Sept Fons praying with the Trappists. Foucauld responded to Massignon's letter February 8, 1909, and announced that he would soon return to France for his first visit after eight years in Africa. Since Massignon's initial contact with him in 1906, the hermit had moved from Beni-Abbes and settled deeper in the Sahara, outside Tamanrasset, then a village in the Hoggar Mountains, near the Sudan border.

In Paris for four days, Foucauld visited Massignon at his parents' home, rue de l'Université and on February 21 took him to spend a night of prayerful vigil at the Basilica of Sacré-Coeur. He "plunged me for a whole prolonged, dismal, stark night of no consolation, in that glacial and haughty tomb of Sacré-Coeur."[7] The two continued to write after the hermit's return to Africa. All told, Massignon received seventy-nine letters from Foucauld during the period 1909–1916; those he wrote to Foucauld were destroyed by the latter.[8] Their correspondence and resulting friendship invited the new convert to choose a vocation that would encompass both his spiritual and intellectual life. The questions raised by Foucauld preoccupied him from late 1908 through the summer of 1913. In the letters to Claudel, Massignon grappled with the issue of vocation, which seems to form the leit-motif of the whole period.

Early in the friendship Foucauld thought he had found in Massignon the companion he had so long desired to share his life among the poor in the Saharan desert, and he clung to the idea even as Massignon vacillated. On May 22, 1909, Foucauld wrote, "If you are fatigued or in need of a retreat and solitary reflection, come to the hermitage of Tamanrasset."[9] By September 8 he had sketched out an entire plan of life for Massignon. The young scholar would complete the linguistic and sociological study Foucauld had begun of the Touareg people who lived in the Hoggar. While doing this, Massignon would share a common life of prayer with Foucauld and like the hermit engage in a ministry of friendship with the people; he would simultaneously prepare to be secretly ordained a priest. According to this plan, Massignon would continue to be a scholar for the world at large, but he would be nourished by a quasi-monastic life and ready one day to succeed Foucauld in the desert.[10] Those close to Massignon took a dim view of this plan; his spiritual director, Père Poulin, was skeptical because he considered Foucauld a *gyrovague*, a wandering monk. For years Madame Massignon had urged her son to marry, and the agnostic Fernand Massignon was completely closed to Foucauld's idea. Moreover, the two theses necessary to obtain the *doctorat d'état* were both unfinished.[11] On October 17 Massignon replied to Foucauld that he first must spend the year 1909–1910 in Cairo, the last year of his contract with the Institut français d'archéologie orientale; then it would be necessary to finish his thesis on Hallaj and the *thèse complémentaire* on the lexicon of Muslim mysticism.

This early response to Foucauld's project reflects well the three factors that were to pull Massignon in different directions throughout the period between 1908 and 1914: his ongoing spiritual search, the influence of his family and spiritual director, and the compelling attraction of his scholarly interests. Indeed, even as he was writing to Claudel and Foucauld concerning the life of his soul, he corresponded assiduously with eminent persons in his field about the full range of his academic interests. Letters between Massignon and Max van Berchem, a pioneer Swiss Orientalist, reveal an enthusiastic young scholar eagerly seeking advice from a celebrated elder who had created Arab epigraphy and established its paleography as a discipline.[12] One would not glean from this correspondence that Massignon was thinking of abandoning these pursuits for a life in the desert.

Indeed, his life was beset by the many influences which had brought him to this point. An interesting perception of this period is provided by a journal entry of François Mauriac, who had spent an evening with the new convert. Both men were approximately the same age and at the outset of their careers. The young writer from Bordeaux found the religious effusiveness of Massignon mystifying and somewhat doubtful:

> A curious evening at a young Orientalist's: Louis Massignon, a friend of Claudel and recently converted. He ascends to the highest levels of mysticism, and like many saints talks only about himself and offers himself endlessly as an example. He decked me out in Persian fabrics; he himself was dressed up like an Egyptian student. He talks about his disordered life when he brushed up against God in the slums of Cairo.[13]

During that same year, 1909, echoes of the past merged with voices of the present and complicated the situation still more. Massignon had maintained contact with Luis de Cuadra; he was ever mindful that the Spanish expatriate had revealed Hallaj to him in much the same way that Boullan had indicated to Huysmans the names of *compatientes*, "co-sufferers."[14] In both cases, the encounter had been life transforming. Imbued with the desire to save his Muslim friend at all costs, Massignon decided to offer himself in mystical substitution for Luis de Cuadra's conversion. On April 23, from Cairo, and May 13, from Alexandria, de Cuadra wrote and accepted the offer.[15] Massignon's gesture could be discounted as the isolated, emotional response of a recent convert wishing to share his new-found faith; but, in fact, the offering of substitution for Luis de Cuadra ran like a thread through Massignon's entire life and was manifested in different ways throughout the years.

On August 3, 1909, shortly after his twenty-sixth birthday, Massignon responded to a letter from his childhood companion Henri Maspero and compared their years of peaceful friendship with the recent, tumultuous period of the relationship with Luis de Cuadra: "My thoughts are faithful to you, do not doubt it. And I am beginning to understand that in old ties of friendship such as ours, there is a closer, more intimate brotherhood—because pure and virile—than in all the passionate embraces, desperate and empty besides, which can seduce and drag one beyond the law."[16]

Claudel, the epistolary confidante in the vocation discussion, finally met Massignon face to face on November 3, 1909. Claudel had returned from China and been recently named to the consulate in Prague. At their Paris meeting Massignon recounted his conversion; Claudel confided the account to his journal, but it was omitted at his request when his journal was published.[17]

Shortly thereafter Massignon left Europe; after conducting research on Hallaj in the libraries of Constantinople, he returned to Cairo, where in 1907, prior to his conversion, he had known such intense emotional and spiritual anguish. He was admitted to the University of Al-Azhar as a student in philosophy and at the same time began writing his dissertation. He was also supervising the publication of the first volume of *Mission en Mésopotamie*, the fruit of his 1908 expedition. The university granted him the right to wear the Arab student's toga, a privilege previously accorded only to Goldziher during the latter's stay in 1873.[18] Photographs of the period show the young Massignon staring intently at the camera, attired in flowing robes, his head swathed in a turban. The apparent degree of self-conscious awareness in this early image contrasts sharply with the worn and self-effacing figure of his later years.

The months that followed plunged Massignon once again into a crisis which lasted until the following June (1910). Although Foucauld had endorsed the return to Cairo, he foresaw that his young friend's past would weigh heavily, "Your stay in Cairo will be a trial . . ."[19] Indeed, the pull of Massignon's former life was strong, the work unending, and prayer unrewarding. He lamented in a letter to Claudel, January 1, "Where are the hours of grace I knew in Paris or those more recent, when I understood the value of a prayer that proved itself in an atmosphere of hostile ideas."[20] Moreover, Massignon felt at odds because no path for the future presented itself with clarity. Foucauld, undaunted by Massignon's hesitations, sent him, on January 13, a Touareg grammar and dictionary.[21] Claudel, for his part, answered immediately, "Why don't you park

all your books there and go throw yourself at the feet of P. de
Foucauld, who, you told me, was calling you to be with him?"[22] The
response is illuminating; it suggests not only that Massignon felt
paralyzed by the combination of work and an inability to resist the
seductions of his former life, but that, whether he knew it or not, his
scholarly work posed a stumbling block in any decision about joining Charles de Foucauld in the Sahara:

> I am overwhelmed with obligations that are late and can't get out
> of my books. Ah, certainly I don't believe in it all and would like to
> escape. But I don't have the force, and P. de Foucauld is alone in
> believing me capable of renouncing self, not just in words but in
> fact. And then, this country soaks up my will.[23]

Claudel, worried about his young friend's emotional state and seeming indecision, returned to the theme a few weeks later:

> The opinion of a saint has more weight than many empty words.
> What a unique opportunity for you to be able to live in the shadow
> of such a man! And even if you don't stay with him, a year spent at
> his side will teach you more than many books. Why not risk your-
> self in this marvelous adventure?[24]

Massignon returned to Paris from Cairo in June 1910, traveled
to London and then to the family home in Brittany, where he wrote
to Claudel in July. "I am sad but I am maintaining myself, and above
all, I am very pushed by work. It is, I believe, the only remedy."
Claudel considered that Massignon's return to the culture and place
which had supported his previous ways had contributed to the present crisis of indecision. However, Massignon missed Egypt, even
though it had been the scene of his relapse into a life he had formally rejected at his conversion. "What sadness to have left that land
of Egypt, which your [Claudel's] friendship mistreats so in your
letters."[25]

As he had done two years earlier, Massignon spent Christmas
1910 with the Trappists at Sept Fons, his vocation decision still unresolved. The next day he wrote to Claudel, "I have almost nostal-

gia for the desert, that perfect sea, serene and balanced in its very immensity by the daily passage of the sun." He remembered having been "pulled out of myself by the beauty I entered into" in the desert and hoped that its appeal would exert itself again if he returned, "I am thinking when my books are finished about going to clear up my hesitations in its great brilliance, to the Hoggar with Père de Foucauld, who's waiting for me a little, I think."[26] In the months that followed, Massignon continued to write his dissertation and published several articles. "I have my nose so close to my file cards that I can't see them any more and they are blinding me."[27] In February 1911, Foucauld returned for a second visit to France. He spent several days in Paris, and arranged for Massignon to serve his Mass on the twenty-third at the Church of Saint Augustine, where years before he had first confessed his sins to the Abbé Huvelin.

On February 28, the subject of a stay in the Sahara came up again when Massignon responded to Claudel's question about how he had come to love Arabic. In recounting his apprenticeship in the language, Massignon recalls how he first prayed in Arabic at his conversion and suggests that the language itself was encouraging him to join Foucauld:

> It is in Arabic probably that it will please [God] for me to serve Him one day. I will probably ask Him this autumn to stay with P. de Foucauld after all my books have been liquidated, down there in the heart of the Sahara, in the Hoggar, at Tamanrasset. Pray that His will be done in this and not mine.[28]

Claudel, responding March 4, encouraged the idea: "I congratulate you very much on your idea to go spend a few months this summer with P. de Foucauld. The greatest human happiness and the easiest path to perfection, the one closest to the heart of God, is certainly the company of a saint or of a man more advanced than we in perfection."[29]

In the next letter, March 23, Massignon mentioned Foucauld's visit, "Did I tell you that I just spent some very consoling moments in Paris with Père de Foucauld: a prelude, I hope, of other, longer hours in the desert."[30] Unbeknown to Massignon, the hermit had conveyed a request to Gaston Maspero that his young friend be sent to the Sahara, but the letter was ignored. After leaving France, Foucauld, ever persevering, wrote Massignon from In-Salah, an Algerian oasis, and described with an explorer's precision how to prepare for a trip to the Hoggar: civil and military authorities to contact, baggage, proper clothing, food to buy for the thirty-five day march from Touggourt to Tamanrasset, the choice of a guide and camels— nothing was left to chance. This letter of April 19 demonstrated that Foucauld really believed Massignon would one day join him, and it was quickly followed by another in the same vein.[31]

Meanwhile work on the dissertation continued, necessitating another trip to Constantinople in order to collate manuscripts needed for completing a chapter. Massignon was anxious that the entire project be finished. "And I'm eating away at myself and becoming burnt out, and I think that [the thesis] has gone on for a very long time."[32] The Sahara project was again delayed. Upon his return to Paris that spring of 1911, Massignon was asked by his father to remain in France the following winter and apply for a university post in Lyons. He seemed somewhat detached from both the idea and the process involved, and in a letter written after the fact to Max van Berchem he commented: "Since we are talking about this aborted candidacy, here is what happened. I only submitted it May 12, after coming back from Constantinople and because the contact made with literary milieux in the East seemed to me to correspond to what Lyons wanted."[33]

The possibility of being chosen for the position certainly presented Massignon with two radically different vocation alternatives. Were he to accept the position in Lyons, he would give up forever his dream of pursuing a heroic life in the desert.

> On the other hand, could he, after so many labors, give up the reward they legitimately procured for him and abandon what he could also believe to be a vocation, a university career, along with

the responsibility it would entail for bringing Europe closer to Islam?[34]

Eventually another Orientalist, Gaston Wiet, was chosen because, according to one account, the religious convictions of Massignon were an obstacle: although he never attended high-mass, he refused to promise that he would not attend.[35] Whatever the reason, the much-sought-after young scholar seemed rather bemused by his first and ultimately last experience of actively seeking a position. Undoubtedly he had assessed by this time that a prestigious academic post would be his for the taking. The comments in the letter to van Berchem reflect that sense of security:

> On the other hand I was profoundly unaware of "the art of being a candidate," and I did none of the written or verbal soliciting which it seems is expected in such a case; I never even thought of it. I wrote to the rector and the dean, considering that if they wanted more information directly, they had only to summon me. They did it only after the vote(!)—and I had quite an amusing interview with the rector, who told me his regret at having been so unaware of the fact of my candidacy—and that I should have written to the members of the Commission, had people write, given my offprints, articles and books. (My bibliography, I just noticed, already contains fifty-some entries; it's the first time I've given myself over to this work of self-contemplation . . .) In a word, I didn't know how to be a candidate according to the formula.[36]

In theory Massignon was now free to join Foucauld, "There is nothing more than the completion of my thesis and my mission which separates me from the date of my departure for the Sahara . . ."[37] However, Massignon elected to remain in France, seemingly unable to make a decisive move one way or the other. That same August of 1911 Claudel worried that Massignon remained at loose ends and that his life had no anchor. "The only thing that concerns me is your freedom: it's not good to be without a defined task, without *order*." Claudel had guessed by this time that Massignon, were he to go live with Foucauld in the Sahara, would eventually leave, "I don't think you would stay with him." However, he encouraged him again rather wistfully to consider a restricted period: "But this stopover in the middle of the desert next to a saint for several months would be such a beautiful thing."[38] In a postscript to his response (August 16), Massignon admitted that the freedom mentioned by Claudel disturbed him also, but that it was ending. He then played on the emphasis Claudel had accorded the word "order": "My order right now: to liquidate my theses and mission in Mesopotamia [the text of the 1908 mission] four months from now." All would be finished by the end of January 1912, and Massignon would be free to spend several months of the cooler season with Foucauld in Tamanrasset.[39] A letter from Foucauld, September 19, indicates that he, too, was becoming skeptical about the chances of Massignon actually joining him, "At the end of a certain time, at the hour willed by God, your director will see what Jesus asks of you, and you will find yourself equally ready for the priesthood or for a devout and scholarly life in marriage."[40]

Massignon himself remained torn. He toyed with gestures which underscored his intention to make a radical commitment. That autumn (October 13, 1911) Claudel chided him for false humility, namely for thinking about renouncing the title of "doctor" which he had labored so many years to obtain. "You would not have undertaken all those long and painful studies if God had not engaged you in them; all told, you owe your conversion to them." But along with these remarks based on "the light of natural common sense," Claudel regretted Massignon's equivocations about the Sahara: "I admit, however, that I would regret not seeing you make this trip to P. de Foucauld. It is a decisive chance in your life. Isn't there any way to reconcile it all?"[41] Massignon evoked the dilemma of the vocation crisis in the exchange of letters with Max van Berchem. After stating that he would not return to Cairo in 1911 and that both a critical bibliography and critical texts would precede the publication of the thesis, he continued:

But they are altogether secondary in my preoccupations. For three
years a secret inner ferment, more and more intense, impels me to
envisage any action from the moral perspective of charity—from
the immediate angle of charity; I feel more and more deeply the
apostolic word (Philippians 1: 23) "the desire to lift anchor, depart,
die" because I well know where the wind would lead me . . .[42]

Like the apostle, Massignon could not decide between two different
goods, in this case the call of his inner life or that, equally compelling, of his intellectual life.

In response van Berchem discreetly wrote November 7 that he
"would feel keen regret," if Massignon were to sacrifice his studies.[43] The latter wrote back two days later that he was "very touched
at the reservations you were so kind to express." There follows a
telling comment which describes Massignon's anguished state of
mind at the thought of giving up his scholarly life:

In fact for three years I've gone about liquidating my notes, with
death in my soul but resolved to go on right to the end, and then
to waste whatever months are necessary to publish successfully,
God willing, my various research notes in a really useful form.[44]

In seeming preparation for the Sahara, Massignon also destroyed
letters of friends like Luis de Cuadra, perhaps in the hope that the
gesture would somehow efface disturbing memories. However, his
director, Père Poulin, remained unenthusiastic and urged Massignon
to finish the dissertation before making a decision. With the holi-
days of 1911 approaching, Massignon decided to spend Christmas
at La Salette because he had learned of its role in Huysmans' conversion. This was the first of many pilgrimages he would make to the
celebrated and, at that time, isolated shrine in the Alps. The 1846
apparition of the weeping Virgin had drawn criticism from Massignon in 1901, when the phenomenon first came to his attention; it
had made him "judge harshly the Church that would tolerate such
stupidities" surrounding the apparitions. He remained skeptical in
the two years following his conversion but changed his mind during

the summer of 1911, thanks to "an old doctor with whom I was discussing hagiographic bibliography . . ."[45] The doctor in question was Dr. Antoine Imbert-Gourbeyre, whom Huysmans had not only consulted when composing *Sainte Lydwine* but from whose work on the saint he had extensively borrowed. Massignon had written the doctor to beg forgiveness in Huysmans' name for the plagiarism, and Imbert-Gourbeyre had responded from his home in Clermont-Ferrand that he was now ninety-four-years-old and blind but would be happy to visit with Massignon. The meeting was arranged to take place after the days at La Salette.[46]

In a portrayal reminiscent of the more hazardous moments of exploration both in North Africa and Mesopotamia, Massignon recounted to Claudel on Christmas Day how he had managed the previous evening to arrive at the hostel near the basilica. Reflected in this description is Massignon the absolutist, who had discovered the meaning of his life through confronting danger, along with Massignon the poet, ever sensitive to the beauty around him. Here, the risk of the perilous journey through the snow is heightened by passages of almost lyrical intensity which dramatize the sense of refuge produced by the sudden appearance of the moon and the church spire:

> I arrived here last evening, by Corps and the cliff path of Saint-Julien, and I thought I would perish in the thick and soft snow. Rarely have I been in such certain danger of death: in total darkness after a spectacular sunset of pale rose above the last rust-colored valleys and the last blue-black boulders, in a complete white-out and absolute isolation. I had to walk like this more than an hour and a half, stumbling, falling and catching my breath every five or six steps! I thought of sitting down and letting go . . . At that moment a pure and slender golden crescent arose between two clouds. A little later, beyond a pass, I made out the somber mass of the church and the hostel beneath the evening star. Measuring my last effort so as not to force or break anything, reciting my rosary, one syllable per step (and I said it all and more than a third more), I

crumpled against the wall of the hostel, after having seen a small light and called out in vain. The wind sprang up; I thought the frost would consume me at the door. I dragged myself along the hostel, through more than a meter of snow and, thanks be to God, I found the chain of a bell. I rang. I was saved.[47]

(The experience made such an impression on Massignon that in 1946 he described it again, in an article about the role of La Salette in the conversion of Huysmans.)[48]

Before returning to Paris, Massignon visited Dr. Imbert-Gourbeyre on December 27, and fulfilled the debt he felt Huysmans owed the old man. The doctor died soon after, but not before speaking of his visitor to a friend, Dr. Louis Pichet, who, two years later, would introduce Massignon to Jacques Maritain. The two young, fervently Catholic intellectuals were to become lifelong friends. Massignon comments: "It was with two of his friends that Jacques came to see me, December 20, 1913, in the name of an old doctor who had died happy eighteen months before, because after coming down from La Salette I had brought him a last consolation in the name of Huysmans."[49] Because their first meeting had resulted, albeit indirectly, from the pilgrimage undertaken in Huysmans' memory to Our Lady of La Salette, Massignon always considered his friendship with Maritain as a sign of the author's continuing protection.

After returning to Paris, Massignon wrote Foucauld around January 12, 1912, and asked his opinion of La Salette. The latter replied tartly: "You ask me what I think of Sister Mary of the Cross (Melanie de La Salette)—my very dear brother, I don't think anything about it, and I forbid myself to think anything. If Rome makes a decision on the subject, I will believe what Rome says."[50] This critique failed to dampen Massignon's interest in and study of La Salette throughout his life, but the topic was never reopened with Foucauld.

The vocation question remained unresolved throughout 1912, but early in January Massignon was introduced to Père Daniel Fontaine (1862–1920), who had been the last confessor of Huysmans.

Massignon saw in their meeting yet another sign of his intercessor's continuing solicitude and asked the priest to help him decide whether to marry or pursue the priesthood. Fontaine played a key role in the ultimate decision because his reluctance to push the idea of marriage gave Massignon more time to make a mature choice. "In the face of the assaults of his spiritual director [Poulin] and those of his family, Massignon found in Fontaine a refuge of peace in order to reflect."[51]

Meanwhile, work continued on the dissertation and other research. In April 1912, Massignon attended the sixteenth international congress of Orientalists in Athens and delivered a paper on the famous cry of Hallaj, *Ana'l Haqq*, which had ultimately led to the Sufi's condemnation and death. At this congress Ignaz Goldziher, who had actively encouraged Massignon since the 1908 meeting in Copenhagen, introduced his protegé to other renowned Orientalists of the time, among them Snouck Hurgronje (1875–1936) and Karl Becker (1879–1933). Goldziher and Hurgronje had been invited to Cairo by King Fuad of Egypt to teach at the university the latter had founded in 1908, the first modern university in Egypt. They proposed that Massignon be invited instead, and on their advice Fuad asked Massignon to give forty lessons in Arabic on the history of Arab philosophy at the new University of Cairo. In August, Massignon wrote Claudel about this unexpected professional opportunity which would delay yet again the long debated sojourn with Foucauld. He appeared torn:

> I would have liked to go to the Sahara this winter (a sincere wish, although intermittent). This makes me very anxious. If I refuse [Cairo], the door of the worthy ministry of I.P. is definitively closed for me: do I have the right to expose myself to that? If I accept, I can try to make the young men there *think* in Arabic about the "great problems" in a different way than Messieurs the missionaries of anarchy who have preceded me. Is my duty there? Pray for me.[52]

Claudel responded immediately: "it seems to me difficult to see in the proposition you speak of, anything except an indication of Providence to which it would be imprudent not to submit." But he reminded Massignon of the risks he would incur, "It's not that I don't understand the grave dangers of that exotic life."[53]

Indeed, the return to Egypt in November 1912 precipitated a recurrence of the moral crisis Massignon had experienced in 1907 and 1910. This manifestation of yet another state of disarray prompted Claudel to counsel that the Sahara project be deferred indefinitely: "The idea of P. de Foucauld was probably too romantic and ambitious. It is better to look for the humble ways, hidden and ordinary ones" (January 21, 1913.)[54] The months in Cairo comprised a turning point for Massignon; they brought into focus the crucial deterrents in the vocation issue: the academic credentials which assured him a distinguished career, his perceived inability to abandon all aspects of his experience prior to the conversion, and finally a series of events which, as we shall see, perhaps suggested to Massignon that his self-offering in mystical substitution for his friend Luis de Cuadra had failed.[55]

Massignon's forty conferences at the University of Cairo began November 25, 1912, and ended April 24, 1913. That experience of teaching native Arabic speakers undoubtedly played a crucial role in his final decision about joining Foucauld. Each conference was in Arabic and dealt with the technical terminology of various Arab disciplines, ranging from the physical sciences to the humanities, with a major emphasis on theology. Discussion of theological terms would later form the basis of Massignon's *thèse complémentaire*, "Essai sur les origines du lexique technique de la mystique musulmane," submitted in partial fulfillment of the requirements for the *doctorat d'état*. The sustained intellectual effort of the conferences underscored not only the expertise of Massignon in Arabic but also his ongoing commitment to the language and the civilization it expressed, a commitment that was all the more serious because of the crucial role of Arabic in his conversion, "in 1908, I had become, through the apprenticeship of Arabic, the liturgical language of Islam, an 'interiorized' *islamisant,* converted to Christianity by the witness to God implied by the Muslim faith." Massignon also knew that Arabic had interested Charles de Foucauld only marginally, "Very quickly I noted that Foucauld, self-taught in linguistics, had abandoned Arabic in order to concentrate on the Berber dialects."[56] Therefore, life in the Sahara would have meant abandoning the core of Massignon's intellectual and spiritual life at the very moment when his scholarship had begun to exert a decisive impact on Islamic studies both in Europe and the Middle East.

The work at the university occurred against a backdrop of emotional and spiritual upheaval. In the aftermath of a bout of the flu, Massignon wrote to Claudel from somewhere near the pyramids, January 28, 1913, "It is true I am poisoning myself and that I tolerate myself badly more and more [. . .]"[57] In the long passage that follows, a striking image of the desert wind propels his thought beyond the perception of beauty, beyond his ambiguous experience of human love to the imageless love of God which at that moment seemed painfully absent; similar expressions of self-deprecation linked with feelings of abandonment would recur throughout his life, although rarely with such poetry:

> Right now the low wind of the desert I know so well, which shaves the sand and sings as on the prow of a ship, this solemn wind which was there in all my perils, at Luxor, at Karbala, this strange wind shakes the threads of my life; with a rhythm so gentle and with so much grace, like a smile veiled with regrets; as if the uncertain beauty of the world were only a veil for divine grace, as if the attraction of love were only a dangling lure to draw us from ourselves and lead us into the net of the Fisherman, the great net Peter cast into the sea of Tiberias at the command of Our Lord. I can no longer love creatures totally for themselves, and I cannot invent in myself the Love God has illumined there at certain moments. And I am empty, like an empty shell and lie paralyzed, horrified by myself and the inability to love others purely. (205)

Massignon had never lost contact with Luis de Cuadra, and the two frequented the cosmopolitan society of Cairo. On December 11, 1912, the Countess Hohenwaert, the Spanish wife of the Austrian consul, introduced Massignon to a wealthy young Egyptian woman of twenty-five, Mary Kahil, descended from a Catholic family which had come to Egypt in 1775. The daughter of a Syrian father and a German mother, she reflected in her background the polyglot nature of Cairo's upper-class society at the beginning of the century. Fluent in Arabic and educated in European schools, Mary Kahil was an accomplished young woman, at home both with the Egyptian royal family and the European diplomatic corps.

Years later she remembered that at their first meeting Massignon was dressed in black and sported a monocle attached to a black ribbon. The two young people saw each other frequently in the drawing rooms of the Countess Hohenwaert, where Massignon was often accompanied by Luis de Cuadra, "a charming person, not good looking but so nice." Mary Kahil also recalled Luis's mother, the marquise of Guadalmina, "a lady of fifty-five, with white hair, but beautiful."[58] Massignon confided to Mary that he had offered himself to God in substitution for Cuadra, in order to bring about his friend's return to the Catholic faith.

Then Luis fell ill with typhus and was hospitalized in February 1913 in the Protestant hospital.[59] His condition worsened and he seemed in imminent danger of death. Massignon sent Père Alcantara, a Franciscan, to his bedside in the hope of converting him from Islam on his deathbed. Cuadra did indeed agree to confess his sins but only, as he later confided to Massignon, in order to lessen the suffering of his mother, distraught at his condition.[60] At the height of the illness, Massignon wrote an anguished letter to Claudel:

> I sought his gaze, and the lost and frightfully decomposed gaze which he returned made me remain there, inert and mute, praying. His poor mother, who had fought for five years the leprosy of his body every step of the way (he had contracted an almost uncurable illness that almost seemed to diminish the leprosy of his soul), his mother was there in the next room, suffering in timid anguish because of him, praying but so torn apart.

> And I myself, who should have been thinking of only one thing, that this was now the supreme test, where making God prevail was the issue, I, who had attempted to spur him at other times into pouring out his heart, and turning back towards God, I was inert, praying with my lips, receiving communion with my lips [. . .][61]

Luis de Cuadra did recover, and the self-offering of Massignon apparently had no further justification. However, the latter's emotional paralysis at the time, his failure to effect his friend's conversion, and Cuadra's seeming hypocrisy of going through the motions of confession, all weighed heavily on Massignon. He wondered if his offering had been rejected by God.[62]

Massignon had asked Mary Kahil, and she had agreed to join with him and offer her life too in substitution for Cuadra's conversion; but by her own account she was impelled less by the thought of the Spaniard's conversion than by hopes for his recovery, "At bottom it was rather that he might be cured."[63] Although their motivations differed, their shared offering taught Mary Kahil and Louis Massignon to pray together, and more than twenty years later that lesson would bear surprising fruit. However, at the time, early in 1913, Massignon stopped seeing her for fear, he said, that she was becoming emotionally attached to him. The Countess de Hohenwaert tried unsuccessfully to dissuade him from that decision, and the exchange between them caused Massignon to write: "I emerged troubled from this debate, beside myself to have felt weakening, beneath an unexpected feminine offensive, my sinful misogyny which has made common cause with an ascetic 'manichean' stance since my conversion. Satisfied at having backed away early enough to prevent hurt, I began to recite the Magnificat."[64]

The forty conferences at Cairo's Fuad University ended in April, and Massignon returned to Paris in June 1913 with the resolution of the vocation issue weighing ever more heavily as he approached his thirtieth birthday. The stay in Egypt, by underscoring both his professional brilliance and personal vulnerability, suggested that the Sahara project was becoming more remote than ever. The prospect of joining Foucauld had hovered in the background of Massignon's personal and professional life for five years, having been first considered soon after the conversion in 1908. That summer of 1913, while on vacation in Brittany, Massignon raised the issue again in a letter to Henri Maspero: "Here, where we were together in the old days, I continue to work—but my old desire to be a hermit still bothers me. And as soon as I can, I will try to hurry and go to the Hoggar (south Saharan)."[65] Although those words seemed to echo those of the five previous years, a final decision was close at hand, prepared by the events of the months in Egypt and precipitated by Charles de Foucauld's third and last visit to France, June 12, 1913.

Massignon prayed with Foucauld, June 22, at his mass celebrated at the parish of Saint Thomas Aquinas and several days thereafter. The two met again on September 1, when Foucauld asked Massignon to serve his mass the next day in the Crypt of the Carmelites. The occasion was the anniversary of death of Foucauld's great-uncle, Armand de Foucauld, killed on that spot in 1792, during the Terror. The hermit, usually punctual, was late that day, September 2; Massignon had been waiting forty-five minutes when a priest he did not know suddenly emerged from the sacristy and asked him to serve his mass. Massignon did so and interpreted his acquiescence as a divine sign that he and Foucauld would never be together: "a strange sign from God passed between us like a sword."[66] When he arrived, Foucauld was suprised to find Massignon occupied elsewhere but celebrated his own mass without waiting for him.

Later that day Massignon invited Foucauld to have lunch with Père Daniel Fontaine, whose counsel had been so helpful. There Foucauld explained his plan of an association of prayer open to people in all walks of life. Fontaine was interested and joined that day. He had helped a similar association, founded by Claudel, gain approval from the cardinal-archbishop of Paris. Encouraged by Massignon to also seek official approval, Foucauld several days later received a far different reception from Cardinal Amette. After the project had been laid out, the cardinal noted that Foucauld had once been a Trappist. When the latter responded that indeed he had been a monk for seven years, the cardinal suggested abruptly that he return to the monastery. The interview was over, and Foucauld was "hurriedly shown the door."[67]

The incident in the Crypt of the Carmelites helped to formulate a decision which had been in gestation for a long time: Massignon would remain in France and pursue his academic career. But he in no way distanced himself from Foucauld, and indeed his sensitivity to the solitude of the desert hermit was heightened by the reception the latter had received at the hands of Cardinal Amette. However, almost five years of indecision had ended. To reflect on his choice, Massignon went on September 6 to pray at the tomb of Anna Katharina Emmerich at Dülmen. Upon his return, he found two letters, one from Claudel and the other from Foucauld. The poet-diplomat expressed disappointment that Massignon had not opted for a life of heroic religious adventure in the Sahara:

> Marriage is a holy state. But why not admit that it is with regret that I watch you in turn enter this mediocre way where we are all floundering. Ah, I was hoping for something else from you! I saw something other for you than a life divided between a household and erudition! Your life will be a copy of mine . . . I was so happy to see you go beyond me, to know there are souls stronger and less unworthy of God than mine.[68]

Charles de Foucauld wrote in a different vein, September 16. After hoping for years that Massignon would join him, he said he warmly supported the decision:

> I too, I advise you to envisage very seriously the possibility of this marriage . . . Do what your director tells you. If need be, consult l'abbé Fontaine. For myself, I think you are made for marriage.

He returned to the same theme at the end of the month, September 30:

> If God wishes marriage for you, do not accept it as expiation, but as the state where he has reserved for you the greatest grace, the state where you are best able to glorify him, to sanctify yourself.[69]

On October 13, Massignon asked a young cousin, Marcelle Dansaert-Testelin, to become his wife. That same day, he sent Foucauld his unconditional adherance to the association of prayer founded by the latter, "I somehow knew I was alone, and I could not for all that, leave this Poor Man alone just because I was creating a family."[70] From the evidence available, it would appear that Massignon married in order to anchor his life and give it a stability which would then free him to pursue his work as teacher and scholar. Misgivings and ambivalence remained until the end of his days. A woman who knew Massignon well wrote after his death, "It seems that Massignon always bore a wound in his heart, the disappointment he caused Foucauld by not joining him."[71]

In the course of their first meeting, December 20, Massignon also spoke to Jacques Maritain of his forthcoming marriage. Their conversation about "the insertion of the eternal in the temporal," helped Massignon place his decision to marry within what he considered to be the radical and overarching commitment God had elicited from him at his conversion. Maritain's "first glance had seen the vow which no 'directorial' pressure could make me break . . ." In this context "the state of marriage, must it not be transfigured so that it tends in itself only to a life of union with God?"[72]

Massignon had earlier communicated some of his ambivalence about marriage to Père Fontaine. Unlike Massignon's family and Père Poulin, his spiritual director, Fontaine had been cautious about the idea. But once Massignon became engaged, the path seemed clear, and Fontaine responded at the end of December: "Put aside as a temptation, dear friend, any new deliberation about the choice you have made. You know that my advice was delayed the longest because it was meant to be very supernatural and reflective. The more I think about your decision, the more it seems to me that it's the Holy Spirit who has guided you." Several days later Massignon wrote the news of his forthcoming marriage to Henri Maspero, "I've reflected much, prayed, offered my life to God; and I believe it is his holy will; may he be blessed—confident in him, I am going to try and create a Christian family."[73]

January 1914 was an important month for Massignon. Five days before the wedding he deposited the completed doctoral dissertation on Hallaj at the Sorbonne. His marriage was blessed by Fontaine, January 27, 1914, in Brussels. Massignon had asked Claudel to be a witness, but the latter, then stationed in Hamburg, was unable to attend because the date conflicted with the Kaiser's birthday.[74] The young couple set out on their wedding trip for Montserrat and the Sahara. In North Africa, Massignon wanted finally to visit Charles de Foucauld so that the latter might bless his marriage. However, after the couple arrived at Touggourt, the roads were declared too unsafe to travel and their party was turned back.

Although Massignon never saw Foucauld again, their correspondence continued until the hermit's death during the First World War. After its outbreak in August 1914, Massignon was mobilized. Having decided to join the army rather than work in a government office, he then requested combat duty. In making the decision for the front lines, he sought counsel of Foucauld, "asking him if this decision seemed good (because, from the bottom of my heart, it was a meager effort to show him that I had not deserted his call, but would he understand?)."[75] Foucauld approved his young friend's course of action, "Stay on the front until the end. Assert your full claim on the common task."[76] In 1916, Foucauld himself moved from the hermitage near Tamanrasset to a small fort of his own design, whose construction he had supervised. There, although he had promised never to harbor arms, he accepted six cases of ammunition and thirty rifles from the French at nearby Fort Motylinksi. On December 1, 1916, Foucauld wrote Massignon that he had received the latter's letters of October 3 and 9:

> You have done very well to ask to move into the troops. One must never hesitate to request posts where the danger, sacrifice and devotion are greatest: honor, leave it to whoever wants it, but danger and hardship, demand them always. As Christians we must give the example of sacrifice and devotion.[77]

Several hours later that same day, December 1, Foucauld was murdered. His letter was found in the sand close to the body and received by Massignon long after. The latter received word of the hermit's death on his wedding anniversary, January 27, 1917, through a newspaper clipping sent by his wife. Massignon described his reaction: "Lifted beyond myself, overcome by a sacred joy, I climbed up on the parapet of the snow-covered trench, HE HAS FOUND THE PASSAGE, HE HAS ARRIVED." The fact that Foucauld had written that last letter the day he died profoundly affected Massignon. He considered it a striking example of mystical substitution because in the same letter Foucauld had prayed, "If God preserves your life, which I ask him with all my heart . . ." It was as if the intersection of their lives had culminated in a mysterious reversal. "By a strange exchange, he is killed and I protected."[78] The military experience had been part of their youth; the desert had brought them both to God. Now, under enemy fire on the front lines, Massignon remained alive while Foucauld, apparently secure in his desert fort, had been shot by a panicky fifteen-year-old boy guarding him while marauders pillaged the place. The latter were Senussi tribesmen from near Tripoli and allied with the Germans. Several days after news of the hermit's death, Massignon returned on furlough to Paris and began what became a lifelong task of preserving the memory and furthering the work of Charles de Foucauld.

Massignon was instrumental in obtaining approval for the association of prayer founded by Foucauld and promulgated by him while visiting Paris in 1913. René Bazin (1852–1932), a well-known novelist of the period, was contacted by Massignon in March 1917 to write Foucauld's biography. Its publication in 1921 attracted widespread notice and contributed to making the hermit known throughout the Catholic world. Foucauld had written a directory for the association of prayer and promised Massignon a copy. The latter received it in March 1917, and succeeded in having it published in 1928.

Although Massignon never fulfilled Charles de Foucauld's deepest wish for him, namely to join the hermit in the Sahara, their friendship influenced him profoundly until the end of his life. Foucauld, in Massignon's view, had been given him "as an older brother," whose experience of rediscovering Christian faith through Islam was paralleled in the life of the younger man. These similarities helped Massignon to validate his own experience. As he explained, "Foucauld made me abandon the classic problem of the connections between science and faith, of pure theory" and demonstrated instead that belief in God could arise when one observed the clash between "the monotheistic, monolithic faith of the Muslims" and "the perforating technique of colonial penetration by Western culture."[79]

The point of departure in the spiritual odyssey of both men had been a love of the Maghreb, and that provided yet another enduring legacy of Foucauld. The topographical and linguistic studies of the former soldier-explorer exemplified an approach to Islam that influenced the research of Massignon, the scholar-teacher:

> I owe a debt to Charles de Foucauld, for having laid out methods of sociological research on Islam, through many "explorations" and experiences of everyday life in Muslim countries. They have guided me throughout more than thirty years of teaching at the Collège de France: beginning with the internal structure of the corporate links between the groups of craftsmen in Fez and the rest of Morocco, and culminating in the discovery of the permanent social value of the only Semitic language of international, technical development: Arabic, the liturgical language of the Qur'an, whose adaptation to modern life I have studied since 1933.[80]

The Islamic code of hospitality had enabled both Foucauld and Massignon in their explorations to penetrate the Muslim world. It had not only saved their lives but proved to be the touchstone of rediscovered faith. After their respective conversions, hospitality prefigured for them the stance of God himself toward human beings. The sacredness of the guest and his right of asylum guided Foucauld's activity among the poor of the Hoggar. By exercising the same hospitality and compassion he had once been shown, Foucauld wished to suggest divine compassion. From that example Massignon, the Christian whose faith had been restored through contact with Islam, discovered "in all other human beings, beginning with the most abandoned, [his] brothers." Foucauld's lesson was not theoretical but rather what Massignon termed an "experiential knowledge of the sacred":

> I needed him to communicate to me, by spiritual contact and in very simple words, conversations and letters, his experiential initiation into true understanding of the human condition and his experiential science of compassion which led him to bind himself to the most abandoned of people.[81]

Foucauld's stance became the basis of what Massignon would term *l'hospitalité sacrée*, or "the acceptance, the transfer to ourselves of the sufferings of others." Fidelity to such an experience calls people "to go out from themselves towards the other, to love fraternally beyond their milieu and their relationships in time and space here below, within a community directed towards the universal."[82] It was a concept that evolved for Massignon throughout his life even as it nurtured him. He wrote in 1961, a year before his death:

> This notion of sacred hospitality that I have deepened over many years, since 1908, when Foucauld supported me like an older brother, seems to me essential in the search for Truth among men, in our journeying and work here below, up until the very threshold of the beyond.[83]

In Foucauld's eyes the life of the priest embodied the gift of self to others through mystical substitution and compassion. He himself was a priest and had suggested that Massignon be secretly ordained. In abandoning the Sahara project, Massignon also renounced the possibility of ordination, but the seed had been planted. In his mind the priesthood remained inseparable from "the experiential science of compassion" he had seen realized in Foucauld's life. As the years passed and Massignon became ever more deeply committed to "sacred hospitality," his desire for the priesthood never left him. Foucauld's dream for his would-be successor would surprisingly be realized in 1950.

That same year, Massignon ultimately fulfilled another aborted dream when he and his wife completed the visit to Tamanrasset that had been interrupted during their January 1914 wedding trip. The night of October 19, from 11:00 P.M. until 4 A.M., Massignon spent in prayer at the fort where Foucauld was killed. He described it as "a dark night, darker than our first night of adoration together at Sacré Coeur in 1909; poorer yet and reduced to ashes."[84]

As Massignon neared the end of his own life amid the apparent failure of his opposition to the Algerian war, then raging, he recalled his night of prayer at Tamanrasset. There he had understood the lesson of Foucauld's death—how ultimately prayer is sustained only by the desire for God; faith subsists solely on divine resources; and only God can determine the significance of one's existence. In the case of Foucauld, death seemingly confirmed the evidence of his life. He had realized none of his missionary projects, from converting the Touareg to Christianity, to founding a religious community; he had never succeeded in attracting companions. His death, caused by an adolescent's panic, could hardly be considered martyrdom. The arms cache in his possession suggested that he was allied with the French, and this fact certainly mitigated the guilt of the tribesman supporting Germany who killed him. As a "substitute," Foucauld had, in Massignon's view, willfully chosen the random and meaningless death suffered by many of the poor he served. From the evidence of Massignon's own life, the lesson seemed clear—to let God determine the significance of his death, "not to make of it a kind of proof," but a last act of loving surrender to His purposes.[85]

FOUR

Military and Diplomatic Service

The years of the First World War constituted a crucial period of transition for Massignon because during this time he in effect rounded out his education. An intellectual apprenticeship had formed the scholar, and his conversion had produced the committed believer. These two fundamental aspects of Massignon's identity were completed by a third: military and diplomatic service paved the way for him to become an active and outspoken participant in the world of his time. His knowledge of the Middle East and commitment to the Muslim ideal of religious hospitality would shape how he interpreted the events he witnessed from 1914 to 1920. Massignon's thinking was never static, but it followed a consistent path. The injustices he saw perpetrated by the European allies on Muslims during those years provided the basis for his later interventions, first on behalf of the Palestinian refugees and then in the Maghreb. The early military and diplomatic experience laid the groundwork for positions he later held and fueled his determination not only to speak out but to risk his very person in doing so. The scholar and mystic would also become an activist involved in critical social and political issues affecting the Muslim world.

During this period Massignon's personal life was transformed as well. With marriage came an address of his own and the responsibility of children. In the year following his marriage, Massignon and his wife settled in what became their lifelong home, 21, rue Monsieur in the seventh arrondissement of Paris, not far from where he had grown up. The apartment was spacious and the neighborhood, affluent. However, the location was chosen because the apartment was situated across the street from the Benedictine convent where Huysmans had resided in 1901. (After leaving his home in Ligugé, the author had occupied a large flat in the convent annex.)[1] Massignon's young family grew: Yves, the first of three children, was born March 1, 1915; Daniel, born in 1919, was named after Père Daniel Fontaine, and a daughter, Genevieve, was born after the war, in April 1921.

These years also saw the loss of mentors and of childhood friends in the First World War. Ernest Psichari, a companion at the Sorbonne, who, like Massignon, had rediscovered Christianity through Islam, was killed in combat during the first month of hostilities, August 1914. Besides the death of Foucauld in 1916, the war claimed Henri Maspero's brother, Jean, killed in February 1915. Gaston Maspero died of a heart attack the following year. The war also delayed publication of Massignon's two doctoral theses. The *thèse complémentaire* on the technical lexicon of Sufi mysticism was being typeset in Louvain, Belgium, when the fighting began. The first half of the dissertation was destroyed by fire following a German bombing raid and later had to be reconstituted.

Massignon's military service was varied. After the war's outbreak in August 1914, he was mobilized. Because of his linguistic ability and knowledge of the Arab world, he was first assigned to the ministry of foreign affairs. As part of the press service his task was to summarize print news from the Arab world. However, Massignon held out for active duty and in accord with his wishes was allowed to join the army, October 29, 1914.

Almost two years passed before his desire to serve in combat was realized. In March 1915, as a second lieutenant of the Zouaves and stationed at Saint-Denis, he became an English interpreter. Such a position could not satisfy his deep-seated need to risk everything, and he requested frontline duty. In April he received word of his transfer to the Dardanelles and the eastern front and toward the end of the month left Paris for the East. On April 28, however, during a stopover in Lyons, Massignon was recalled to Paris by the ministry of foreign affairs, thanks to the intervention of his family and Paul Claudel.[2] Finally, at the end of July, his request was honored and on August 8 he wrote to Foucauld from Marseille on his way to the Dardanelles. There he again served as an interpreter, this time at the front, first for an air unit, then for the headquarters of the Seventeenth Colonial Infantry Division in Macedonia. Only on October 4, 1916, at his request, did Massignon join the ground troops; five days later, October 9, he went to the trenches, where he spent the next four months. Enemy contact occurred during seventy-five days of that tour. On November 21, Massignon participated in an attack during which his commander was killed but enemy territory was regained.[3] His combat stint on the Macedonian front earned him a *croix de guerre* with several citations.

If the war experience undoubtedly influenced his later commitment to nonviolence, it provoked in him no antipathy towards the military as such, nor any critique of his choice of combat duty. Besides providing a way to demonstrate patriotism, the army taught discipline and exemplified human solidarity in the service of a common cause. Military vocabulary recurs in his self-descriptions throughout his life. Indeed, because of Massignon's affection for the army he was doubly outraged at reports of its use of torture to extract information during the Algerian War. Early photos show a young Massignon, resplendent in his uniform and proudly conscious of the dignity it conferred.

Yet, in terms of his dedication to the Muslim world, the diplomatic assignments from 1917 until 1920 were ultimately more formative because as a firsthand observer, he watched French and British diplomats create the postwar world of the Middle East. Both his intellectual development and personal experience led him to sympathize with the Muslim perspective promoting religious unity for Islam and political autonomy for Arab countries. The perception that his country was betraying those who had saved his life came only a few years after he had been transformed through living in Muslim countries, and with this realization began a lifelong tension between his belief that France had a mission in the world and his

disavowal of any colonial ambitions on its part.[4] His memories of
Faisal and Lawrence, recorded in 1946 and 1960 respectively, describe the origins of that tension which years of contact with the
Muslim world only served to heighten and which in some sense was
never resolved.

After returning on leave to Paris early in 1917, Massignon was
detached March 17 to the ministry of foreign affairs, which in turn
named him to the high commissioner for Syria, Palestine, and Cilicia.
This assignment allowed him to follow the twists and turns of French
and British diplomacy in the Middle East at the end of the war. In
May 1916 a commission headed by Sir Mark Sykes on behalf of the
English and François Georges-Picot for the French had drawn up
what came to be known as the Sykes-Picot agreement. Under its
terms the former Ottoman provinces of Baghdad and Basra were
placed under direct British rule and the coastal regions of Syria,
under direct French rule. An area west of Baghdad and north of
Arabia would be declared independent but under British influence;
an independent state in western Syria and northern Iraq would be
guided by the French. Palestine would be under international control. Through his work as as adjunct for the Sykes-Picot mission
Massignon witnessed how the promise of an independent Arab state
was modified by Britain and France both during and after the war.

Picot and his staff, including Massignon, arrived in Port-Saïd in
April 1917, en route to Cairo; their mission, according to one his-
torian, was "to further the cause of French interests in Syria by means
of political action among the Arab leaders in Egypt."[5] Years later
Massignon remembered his first glimpse of "the slender and proud
silhouette" of Faisal (1883–1933), Husayn of Mecca's son.[6] On
May 17, 1917, Faisal boarded the British vessel *Northbrook* on the
northern coast of the Hejaz to join his father's discussions with the
Sykes-Picot mission at Jidda. A year before, Husayn, supported by
British promises of Arab independence, had launched the armed
Arab revolt against the Ottoman Turks, and at the time of the May
1917 meeting he did not know that Sykes and Picot had been simultaneously negotiating about how to partition the Middle East after

the war. Nevertheless, Picot's arrival in Cairo had aroused Husayn's anxieties about allied intentions. The Arab leader had asked the British for assurances, and Sykes had been dispatched in order to allay Husayn's fears. Assigned by Sykes to write up the four days of discussion with Husayn, Massignon had ample opportunity to observe Faisal. He remarked that the "revolutionary leader's youthful ardor was quickly calmed before the calm and patient serenity of his father." In 1946 Massignon did not mention the substance of the May 17–20 meetings or that the Sykes-Picot agreement was never revealed to Husayn, but he alludes sympathetically to the obstacles Faisal encountered on the road to Arab independence, "He realized, little by little, that the national Arab movement of which he was soon to become the guide was to thread its way through much foreign opposition."[7]

Several months later the Sykes-Picot mission put Massignon in contact with a key person in the Arab revolt, the legendary T. E. Lawrence, whose published work never mentions his French counterpart. However, in 1960, when Massignon recorded their 1917 encounters, his recollections, filtered and perhaps modified by time, remained vivid. Their first meeting occurred August 8, at the Arab Bureau in Cairo, where the two conversed alone for two hours in English, French, and finally Arabic:

> For me he already possessed his legend; I saw with surprise an Englishman who was still very young, quite free from all convention, almost an outlaw, but so discreet, at once gentle and bitter, with the timidity of a young girl, and then with the harsh intonations in a low voice, of a prisoner.[8]

Massignon perceived Lawrence as someone who, despite his role among the Arabs, remained very much alone, and Lawrence, speaking in the staccato Arab dialect which reflected his months with the Bedouin fighters, seemed to put his French counterpart in the same category. He tried "to make me rediscover the mentality of a masked nomadic archeologist, but nine years had passed since Ukhaydir," the fortified palace Massignon had discovered in the Mesopotamian desert. The sentence reveals how much Massignon judged he had changed between 1908 and 1917. A month before his conversion, unaware of how deeply he was being transformed by prolonged contact with his Arab hosts, he had styled himself a European researcher whose sole tie to the region was his thirst for exploration, "the secular rage to understand." By 1917 he had become a different man. From this conversation with Lawrence, Massignon concluded that the latter's solitude was irrevocable. "And from that day on, I felt Lawrence would slip away from any attempt at sharing life; 'you love the Arabs more than I do,' he concluded."[9] That impression was reinforced at their next meeting, in a tent on the edge of the Gaza desert. During two separate conversations of October 12 Massignon remembered the seemingly timeless detachment of Lawrence:

> He was the one who spoke, not about a future to construct together, but from within a kind of aloneness *à deux*, in a strange detachment from the world; he made me think of a sort of essential liberty, created from an asceticism so drastic that all my own stripped-down faith collided with it. In a no man's land.[10]

In October 1917, General Allenby, head of the British forces in Egypt, summoned Massignon from Cairo to his Gaza headquarters and asked him to become the adjunct French officer to Faisal's army in the north. He had perhaps been chosen because, unlike some French members of the Picot mission, he was well regarded by the British.[11] Both the Foreign Office and the Quai d'Orsay endorsed the assignment, but it subsequently "encountered the formal veto of Colonel Lawrence."[12] According to Massignon, Lawrence did not want a French Orientalist to dissuade Faisal from relying exclusively on the British in his pursuit of Arab independence.

In the intervening two years before Massignon and Faisal met again, events moved rapidly. After the Bolshevik revolution removed the Russians from the war, the new regime nullified arrangements made under the czar and in November 1917 revealed the existence of the Sykes-Picot agreement to the unsuspecting Husayn. However, shifting Allied interests had already indicated the need for revisions because around this time the Balfour Declaration was published. By endorsing the idea of a "Jewish homeland" in Palestine, Balfour withdrew that area from either Arab or international control and reserved its fate to the British. Thus, in Husayn's eyes, the betrayal was twofold, first through the Sykes-Picot agreement and then through the Balfour Declaration.

Meanwhile, the Arab revolt made rapid progress throughout 1917, thanks in large measure to British gold. Its distribution involved many people, and in his 1960 reminiscences about Lawrence, Massignon ruefully described his experience of autumn 1917, while awaiting assignment to Faisal's army:

> On the edge of the desert in this forbidden Arabia, which I had longed for and surrendered to as an outlaw nine years before in such a primitive and naked rush, I awaited my destiny, which depended on Lawrence. I had no illusions: my leaders wanted to give me a large budget in order to "corrupt the Syrian bedouins"; I was to take gold with me; I would surely get myself killed: More surely yet, I felt my damnation for buying friends, I who had known the sacred hospitality of the Arabs. I had just escorted to Suez . . . 950,000 francs in gold for King Husayn, and Sharif Nasser was to recount to me later with what terrifying disdain Lawrence threw guineas at their open palms in return for armed attacks.[13]

Massignon and Lawrence met for the last time December 11, 1917, when the victorious British under General Allenby officially entered Jerusalem, an act which concretized British rather than international control of Palestine and prepared the creation of a Jewish state. It was a painful moment for the French contingent because both they and the Arabs had been outmaneuvered. In order to save face for the Sykes-Picot mission, Allenby and Picot rode together in the first car of the official party; Massignon and Lawrence were in the fourth car:

> I spent the entire morning with Lawrence. The proclamation of martial law by Allenby in front of the tower of David removed the

Sykes-Picot mission from any diplomatic involvement in the Holy City (coveted by London alone); Allenby harshly threatened to have Picot arrested if he infringed on this. Lawrence stayed next to me. His defeat equaled mine and was even worse, and his innate nobility opened his heart to me; assigned to make King Husayn believe they would turn over the Holy City to him, Lawrence had just learned about the dealings of Lord Balfour with Lord Rothschild over the Jewish homeland.[14]

Massignon concluded that "our entry into the Holy City was made under the sign of desecration," and recounted an incident which occurred later that day when the two arrived late for an official lunch organized by Allenby. As they crossed a large courtyard under the eyes of watchful officers, Massignon noticed that Lawrence's left epaulette needed reattaching. Lawrence was disdainful:

"Do you think I have any consideration for these people?" he said; and at that moment he made the gesture of opening his pants to urinate in front of headquarters; it was in a minor mode, the gesture of Sir Thomas More at the Tower of London, but without his gaiety.[15]

Massignon noted elsewhere that Charles de Foucauld and Lawrence were often compared with one another by those who thought they "had both abused Arab and Muslim hospitality," a judgment which aroused his ire. Both men were involved with the political interests of their respective countries. However, as Massignon explained it, Foucauld had founded his entire ministry in North Africa on hospitality or care for the population. Lawrence fought for Arab independence, but his relationship to that concept was at best indirect; ultimately he had rejected British military honors for his work among the Arabs because he considered that his country had betrayed them: "If he rejected his stripes, if he willingly died in abjection, a simple airman of the ground personnel, it was out of disgust for having been assigned to the rebelling Turkish Arabs, whom we allied with us in order to use and then abandon them, as if it were permitted for a man of honor to hand over his guests."[16]

If Lawrence felt acutely that his country had betrayed the Arabs by promoting Zionist aspirations in Palestine at the expense of the indigenous population, Massignon shared his distress. Moreover, as a Frenchman he experienced similar feelings when he observed what happened to Faisal at the hands of the French in Syria. The king's fate resulted from the contradictory agreements of the war years. On one hand, the Sykes-Picot agreement had mandated portions of Syria to French control. On the other hand, British forces had liberated Syria from the Turks and occupied the region at the war's end. The British, faced with French resentment, were fearful that their military presence in Syria would jeopardize future Anglo-French relations. Under the terms of the Anglo-French agreement of September 15, 1919, the military command and provision of garrisons in western Syria and Cilicia were handed over to the French under the command of General Gouraud. When Faisal protested because the move seemed to indicate French plans to dominate all of Syria, the British advised him to negotiate his own agreement with the French.

In November 1919 Faisal returned to Paris, where, from the end of the month through January 6, 1920, he and Massignon had daily contact as various aspects of the agreement with Clemenceau were negotiated. From this vantage point, Massignon "was able truly to know, appreciate and admire through firsthand knowledge the character of the emir."[17] Their conversations were often in Arabic, and the two became friends:

> During the informal conversations I held with Prince Faisal (the future king) in 1919–1920, the Arabic we spoke together was in terms deliberately "chosen": but I systematically avoided our obscure abstract words. Neither did I try to to compete with the dialectical Arabic which Lawrence . . . had forged, . . . that of a gang leader discussing a heist. That wasn't what I was looking for with Faisal, but rather to gain access to the meaning of his own tradi-

tion, to the formation of ideas I wished later to exchange for my own. I then attempted to make him understand that his system of ideas was not exactly mine, but that nevertheless, there could be shared elements of hope.[18]

The provisional agreement signed by Faisal was never implemented; it assured Arab independence for inland Syria but stipulated that the Arab state be defended, advised, and represented abroad by France. Lebanon would be recognized as a mandated region, separated from Syria by the neutral Bekáa Valley. Within Syria, the Druze remained autonomous. In Massignon's eyes, the agreement, however restrictive, signified that Damascus would become "the capital of the Arab renaissance, halfway between Baghdad, Cairo, and Medina." Believing in France's traditional role as educator, Massignon considered that "France was destined to help the emir in his task as sovereign, as a founder of a new state." He recalled Faisal's hope that the two of them would work together in Damascus to implement the agreement; but Massignon, recently named to the Collège de France, was by then unavailable. No mention is made whether the misgivings he conveyed to Faisal touched on the agreement itself or the emir's response to it. But when placed in the light of what followed, as Massignon recounts the incident, Faisal's misgivings seemed to revolve around differing French and Syrian interpretations of the agreement: "The emir in a quick glance, as discreet as it was noble, made me understand that he had guessed certain fears I had not dared admit to him except through silences. I understood at that moment that the emir had committed his loyalty without reserve to the provisional agreement he had signed."[19]

What followed disturbed Massignon all the more, since he believed that France in the person of Clemenceau had negotiated honorably with Faisal and that assurances of an independent Arab state were genuine. However, the Clemenceau government fell and was succeeded in early 1920 by one which was increasingly concerned about growing nationalist fervor throughout the region. For their part Faisal's supporters thought he had compromised Syria's chances for independence and unity. Since the agreement he had signed was provisional, Faisal felt he needed a national mandate in order to go to San Remo for the final peace negotiations of the war. To that end he reconvened the Syrian National Congress, whose aspirations were far more radical than his own. On March 7 that body proclaimed the existence of an independent Syria which included Palestine and Lebanon within its boundaries. Faisal was named the constitutional monarch of the new state.

London and Paris opposed the declarations of the Congress and its enthronement of Faisal. In May the San Remo peace conference mandated Syria and Lebanon to France; and Palestine, Transjordan, and Iraq to Britain. Although these decisions in and of themselves did not preclude the existence of an independent Arab state in inland Syria, they were met in Damascus with violent opposition. On May 8, the Assembly voted to reject all mandatory tutelage and reasserted its demand for an independent Syria that included Palestine. Positions hardened on both sides, and on July 14, General Gouraud, commander of French forces in the region, demanded in an ultimatum to Faisal that he accept the mandate. The violent response this move provoked both in the street and the Congress resulted in the latter's dissolution by Faisal. Realizing that non-acceptance of the ultimatum would inevitably precipitate the fall of his government, Faisal sent a personal telegram to Gouraud on July 19 in which he accepted the conditions of the mandate. The Syrian government telegraphed its official agreement on July 20, and orders to demobilize were issued in Damascus, but because of downed lines, the telegram failed to arrive in time, and French troops began advancing July 21. On July 24, French forces defeated the Syrians at the Maysalun Pass, marched on Damascus, and forced Faisal into exile. Later, thanks to the British, Faisal was installed as king of Iraq (1921–33).

In 1946, when the Hachemites celebrated their silver anniversery as Iraq's monarchs, Massignon recalled the abortive reign of Faisal in Syria. He contrasted French betrayal with the nobility of the king's response; but he also reasserted his belief in a unique

French honor, sullied by this episode but historically grounded and thus redeemable:

> And the tragic episode of Maysalun, several months later, showed all informed Frenchmen (but there are still very few) with what determination this Arab emir had kept his pledged word until the end. My respectful friendship for him bled then; that day we did not know how to show the Arabs in Damascus and in Syria the true face of our country, the face which the emir had seen in Paris with Monsieur Clemenceau, the pure face of our true historic vocation, which we must someday make clear to all Arab nations. But that day, he showed us, in all its nobility, the Arab sense of honor intact and the silent claim of misunderstood justice which ultimately triumphs.[20]

Massignon returned to Damascus in November 1920, on an official diplomatic mission designed to safeguard the cultural institutions created by the former king; and he "saw with such sadness that years would be necessary for the normalization of French-Arab relations to occur."[21]

The reminiscences about Faisal and Lawrence, recorded years later, show that British and French dealings with the Arabs during and after the First World War created strong ambivalences in Massignon. It could be argued that such comments, written long after the fact, inaccurately reflect his opinion when the events occurred. But the pull he felt between Anglo-French policy and Arab aspirations is already evident in 1919. Seen within the context of his later positions, these earlier writings show that he walked a fine line between faith in his country's good intentions and solidarity with Arab aspirations for independence. When Sir Mark Sykes died in 1919, Massignon eulogized the ex-officer turned diplomat and unambiguously praised his efforts on behalf of the Arabs: "Sir Mark Sykes constructed, from his studies and experiences, a wholly new British Arab policy, neither of Anglo-Indian, nor Anglo-Egyptian origin: no longer founded on what Arabs can mean for England, but on what Arabs can become for themselves."[22] This new Arab policy, while it promoted autonomy, did not exclude "the urgency of temporary help, of a guardianship by a European power, "provided for by the Sykes-Picot agreement. Massignon believed that in spite of the evidence the former allies could assist the Arab world in its quest for autonomy, if not independence. However, in 1920 as the mandates were implemented, he cautioned that unless France, England, and Italy "followed an interallied policy embracing the whole Muslim world and eliminated all discord among themselves" they would be incapable of handling regional conflict. Massignon saw that it was essential to resolve the local clashes which had multiplied after 1914, because these "resulted from an internal and generalized transformation of Islam, a transformation which went far beyond the artificial compartmentalizing and the so-called airtight partitions of the present borders" established by the postwar treaties.[23] Even as he spoke of the need for European guidance of the emerging Arab states, Massignon felt that their evolution transcended the limits of isolated efforts to create or maintain structures for them. The drama of these countries belonged to a wider upheaval, that of the Muslim world seeking its own identity.

By the time Massignon spoke to the Société de sociologie de Paris in November 1921 about "L'Arabie et le problème arabe," he could assert without question that his competence to examine the issue came from years of observation and experience:

> The documentation I am going to assess here, both theoretical and practical, was gathered on the scene, privately at first, for seventeen years, not only in Arab-speaking countries, but in Arabia itself, by visiting Jidda, Aden, Muscat, Basra, Jericho, Damascus, Aleppo, almost all the gateways of the desert, and by asking those who could best explain the bases of the problem. Then, in a totally unexpected fashion, through practical experience, in the course of the Anglo-Arab bargaining which took place from 1917 until last year and even now, by dealings which have been followed up in the home area, in Jidda, Aden, Cairo, Jerusalem, Damascus, and Paris itself.[24]

Such claims of expertise were well-founded, and these years of experience proved invaluable to Massignon in the decades to come. Not only had he been exposed firsthand to the process of postwar diplomacy in the Middle East, but government service had given him an entree to the halls of state, which he would use effectively and fearlessly later in life. Moreover, it had provided him with a political apprenticeship that would save him from naiveté, however unrealistic his positions often sounded to opponents.

This talk to sociologists in Paris reveals a nuanced position because Massignon was addressing Frenchmen, and the French were very uneasy about Arab autonomy, especially since British moves in this regard had encroached on what had long been considered French spheres of interest in the Middle East. Massignon carefully threaded his way, neither strongly endorsing French policy nor unreservedly upholding Arab nationalism. By stating at the outset that he would examine the Arab question objectively, he seemed to imply no objection to French policy in Syria:

> I will try to detach myself from all the passions [undoubtedly British] which I viewed as inflammatory and that were limited not simply to sneaking off with what was ours or to taking shots at us and multiplying all sorts of hasty procedures in order to be rid of legitimate French objections that could not be dismissed any other way.[25]

Yet if Massignon asserts the legitimacy of French claims in Syria, he also suggests that their preservation rested on the uncertain ground of secret British diplomacy. "We had a series of diplomatic agreements which spilled a lot of ink . . . because they were secret." Massignon outlines these agreements, first the McMahon-Husayn exchange of letters, promising an independent Arab state:

> There were, however, two slightly reserved questions: the question of the Syrian coast and the question of Palestine; but these were two questions the king [Husayn] did not dare press and about which England did not insist on informing him.[26]

The implicit irony of that sentence continues in the following paragraph. Massignon underscores the secrecy of both the Sykes-Picot agreement and the Balfour Declaration and heightens the resulting duplicity toward the Arabs by personifying it in a victim— not the Arab leader, Husayn, but the British agent, Lawrence. Such embodiment, in someone who could be considered a peer of Massignon, renders more striking the impact of a broken promise. Although mentioned here only in passing, the pledged word of hospitality which became increasingly central to Massignon's thought, already underlies this 1921 critique of allied treatment of the Arabs:

> Meanwhile, there intervened the agreements which the Bolsheviks have since published and which I think have been officially published. These are the Sykes-Picot agreements of 1916 between the French government and the British government about the question of delimiting the Anglo-French spheres of influence on the northern slope of the Arab territory, treaties which, as Pan-Arab English officers like Colonel Lawrence have remarked, contradicted the word pledged to King Husayn. I still remember the discontent shown by Colonel Lawrence at Allenby's headquarters; he was faced with this series of contradictory, secret agreements published successively as the troops pushed forward, and these alongside the one he had negotiated. In November it was the Balfour Declaration (Zionism) that wiped out the promises he had made to the Arab nationalists about Palestine, and then when we arrived in Syria, the gradual implementation of the Sykes-Picot agreement, which until the last moment he had hoped would be rejected.[27]

Subsequent French activity in Syria is sketched out in the same ironic and implicitly critical tone. In Massignon's account, it was decided that Damascus could become the center of the Arab people:

> but Damascus, naturally, was delicate, since Damascus had been promised by another secret [Sykes-Picot] treaty to France. France was asked to arbitrate, a very tactful move, seeing that what was promised her had likewise been promised to her adversaries. We

tried to arbitrate; we negotiated with Faisal and let him move into Damascus. For multiple reasons that could not last, and the event is still too present for me to insist on it.[28]

Since discussion of the French role in Faisal's downfall is reduced to "multiple reasons," potentially embarrassing specifics are avoided. However, that failure had also been hastened by "blunders on the part of the Arab nationalists," who "decided to go too fast."[29]

As an Arab state Syria also belonged to the emerging Arab world, and Massignon had approved the choice of Damascus as its center: "For myself I regret our failed experiment of 1920."[30] He regretted it all the more since whatever sympathy he had for Arab nationalism was rooted in his wider concern for Arab civilization. And when he thought of the *mission civilisatrice* of France in Arab lands, that role meant, first and foremost, French support for Arabic language and culture.

The issue held special urgency for Massignon even in this early period because of the French colonies in the Maghreb, which from childhood he had come to know and love deeply. The cultural heritage of Syria was shared by Morocco, Tunisia, and most importantly, Algeria, a key French colony since 1830 and France's most important possession in North Africa. Thus, French policy in Syria would have important consequences for the entire Maghreb as the cultural origins of four-fifths of its people lay in the Arabian peninsula. Massignon felt that the Algerians carefully observed French moves in the Middle East: "On this bank, this western slope of Arabia, we have placed our feet; but our Arabs of Africa have their eyes open and are watching us attentively."[31] When he cautions that French civilization must not be fostered in Syria at the expense of Arabic language and culture, he is also thinking of North Africa. There the issue concerned not only the promotion of the indigenous culture but the choice of which one to favor. In Massignon's eyes, the clear choice over a language such as Berber must be classical Arabic:

> One must not forget that this is not a rudimentary language; that it
> is important not only for our local mandate in Syria, whether tem-
> porary or not; our local mandate is a relatively secondary question,
> but what is more serious, what is important, is our permanent fu-
> ture in North Africa, where in questions concerning the Arabic
> alphabet and education it would be silly to continue playing off di-
> alectical autonomy against classical Arabic, an instrument of inter-
> national exchange.[32]

However, since classical Arab culture had originated in the Middle
East, Massignon also underlined that "we cannot constitute a serious Arabic culture in our North Africans without taking into account
our actions in the East vis-à-vis their brothers in the language."[33]

The following year, in 1922, he again outlined the role of
France in Syria and foresaw repercussions a generation later in the
Maghreb. The discussion was placed within the context of the over-
all evolution of the Middle East:

> For twenty years the astonishingly disparate populations of the
> Middle East have been gradually coming together, by taking as the
> basis for political grouping the idea of linguistic and cultural na-
> tionality—no longer the idea of a religious confession, which has
> receded in the political arena, nor the idea of social class, which
> insufficient industrial development has not yet allowed them to
> envisage.[34]

When Massignon considered the French role in Syria, national interest was not discounted, but the mission of France as educator was
the primary justification for her presence in the Middle East: "the
importance of our material interests in the Orient has consistently
followed the course of our ethical influence."[35] Indeed, the success
of the former is predicated on the latter: "French culture has fertil-
ized Syrian social milieux in the past through this '*francisation*' . . .
only because it was not an instrument of political domination but of
intellectual reform and moral liberation. To use her language, peda-
gogy and literature in such a role would be to betray the very soul of

France." On the other hand by being faithful to its mission, France would further her own interests and enhance her standing in the region, for Massignon estimated that Franco-Arab conflict had diminished since the events of 1920 in Syria:

> it is certain that if we show ourselves worthy of the mission confided to us, Arabian Syria will count for much in the overseas expansion and influence of France tomorrow. Through Syria, France is positioned at the very heart of the Middle East. . . . If France so wishes, the gradual emancipation of the Arab nationality—which she can guide and help, from Damascus to the center [of the Middle East]—will make her, more than ever before, the uncontested educator of the East, the inspirer in whom all the neighboring nationalities, from Egypt to Persia, will have confidence.[36]

Texts such as this one, when read in isolation could seemingly imply that Massignon was promoting nineteenth-century French imperialism. Certainly such was not the case at the end of his life. But even early on his position was more nuanced. When he used the term *francisation*, he had in mind, not a relationship of colonizer to colonized, but rather one which placed French and Arabic culture on an equal footing. Through this partnership of equals, Arab values such as hospitality and fidelity to the pledged word would be restored in French society, where they had, in his eyes, long since disappeared. Conversely, through French efforts Arab independence in Syria would be assured. Thus, because Massignon himself had been so radically transformed by exposure to Islam, his own profound respect for Arab culture and language dictated what he proposed as French policy in both the Middle East and North Africa. One might argue that such a position provided no practical framework within which to construct policy, but that does not imply that the position itself secretly promoted French imperialism.

To buttress his country's role of arbitrator and educator in Syria, Massignon counseled that troops be maintained there, although not in great number. He evinced the hope, futile as it turned out, that France could thereby resolve regional conflict and "cement little by little the national unity of Syria, in conformity with the very wishes of the inhabitants."[37] Success in this endeavor was crucial because the outcome of French policy in Syria was inextricably linked, he believed, to the future of France in North Africa. Within this perspective his closing remarks are curious because he suggests, perhaps unconsciously, that in the case of North Africa the dream of mutual understanding might ultimately prove untenable:

> France must remain present on all the fronts where history has engaged her; she cannot retreat with impunity between the Pyrenees and the Rhine. It is in Syria that she will discover this Muslim policy which is needed so that North Africa might become truly French; a question of life or death for the generation to come.[38]

Since the legitimacy of French extraterritorial claims depended on French success in promoting *francisation* as Massignon understood it, he implies that failure in that effort will jeopardize any French presence beyond its borders. As one commentator of that passage observed: "Does one not read here, along with the generous will to help growth, justice, and peace, the observation that '*francisation*' has not happened and a prophetic premonition, in the form of a threat, that success is impossible."[39] While we cannot know if Massignon himself thought of his words as a "prophetic premonition," in fact they were. As successive French governments ignored or mismanaged critical situations in the Maghreb, the tension he felt between his love of France and his dismay at its colonial policies deepened with the years. He saw that the word pledged to the Arabs, already betrayed in the Middle East by the European allies in their dealings with Husayn, was likewise betrayed by France in the Maghreb. Years later his sense of longstanding injustices perpetrated against Muslim peoples would impel him to intervene publicly as events unfolded, first in Palestine and then North Africa.

FIVE

Hallaj, Abraham, and
the Scholar of Islam

During the 1920s Massignon became the foremost Orientalist in France and achieved international renown. His academic career at the Collège de France began soon after the war's end and would span a thirty-five-year period. The chair of Sociologie et Sociographic musulmanes was then held by its creator, Massignon's former professor, Alfred le Chatelier. On June 15, 1919, the assembly of professors at the Collège met to consider Chatelier's request that Massignon be engaged to replace him provisionally as a *suppléant*; and on July 5, shortly before Massignon's thirty-sixth birthday, the ministry of education formally named him to the position. He brought to this teaching post a unique depth and range of experience. The diplomatic experience and sojourns in the Middle East complemented his formal education by providing ongoing information and experience about contemporary Islam. He could situate his insights about the present within a broad historical context because, although not an archeologist, he had been trained in that field and contributed significantly to it by discovering the palace of Ukhaydir in the Mesopotamian desert. He thought of himself as a religious historian, but his research was enhanced by his expertise as a philologist, born of the commitment to Arabic and evidenced in Cairo by the series of classes he had given on technical Arabic for Egyptian students.

As his professional life became established, Massignon seemingly settled into a predictable and secure rhythm marked by steady professional advancement. The family lived in Paris most of the year and vacationed each summer in Brittany. Every winter he spent several weeks in Muslim countries; the travel expenses were minimized thanks to the diplomatic privileges granted him during his wartime service at the ministry of foreign affairs. In January 1926, Alfred Le Chatelier retired, vacating the chair of Muslim sociology. Silvain Lévi presented the candidacy of his former student in Sanskrit to the assembly of professors at the Collège de France, "M. Massignon is not only a scholar of the first order; he is an elite personality, an exquisite spirit."[1] Among those who voted him unanimously to the post was his childhood friend Henri Maspero, who occupied the chair of Chinese literature and language.

The professional success Massignon achieved during this period stood in marked contrast to the sudden and disquieting losses he sustained at the same time. Only two months after the birth of his daughter Geneviève in April 1921, Massignon learned of the suicide, June 30, of Pierre Sainte, the sculptor who had accompanied him on his 1904 expedition to Morocco. He had offered himself in mystical substitution for Pierre Sainte and repeatedly for Luis de Cuadra. Moreover, after his May 1908 conversion, Massignon had written the Spaniard every week. The correspondence ended when news came of Luis de Cuadra's suicide, August 12, 1921, in a prison of Valencia. The reasons for his incarceration have always remained unclear. The following January Massignon wrote to Luis's father requesting details, but he received no response. Finally, he learned from Asin Palacios that Cuadra's father had likewise committed suicide. The memory of Luis, like that of other close friends who died, remained with Massignon for the rest of his life, but in this instance it provoked special anguish because of the unique significance of their relationship and because he felt uncertain about the fate of Luis before God.[2]

Similar feelings recurred when Fernand Massignon suddenly died less than six months later, January 18, 1922, without receiving the last sacraments. Only the day before, Massignon had received Asin Palacios's letter about de Cuadra's father, and that very morning, two hours before discovering Fernand Massignon's body, he had offered his communion for the father of his friend. This uncanny convergence of significant events was no mere coincidence for Massignon. Rather, as with General de Beylié's project of sending him to Baghdad, the home of Hallaj, it functioned as an "intersign" or marker, pointing up events as relevatory and giving direction for the future. And if the coincidence concerning Luis de Cuadra's father were not enough, the lives of J. K. Huysmans and Louis Massignon intersected once again. Death found the elder Massignon working on a bust of Huysmans, to be placed in the inner court of Saint-Severin, the church where his old friend had habitually worshipped. Massignon recalled that his father had begun carving out the hunk of plaster from which the bust was to emerge:

> and it was in front of this unfinished memorial that he was going to work on again (he had just thrown aside his gloves), that he fell, head forward, struck down by an attack of hypertension. His daughter [Henriette, Massignon's sister] and I found him there, having had to push open the door of that studio, 25, rue Vaneau, where Huysmans had long ago come, since Pierre Roche is the author of the sole remaining bust of this great writer.[3]

A sentence Massignon expurgated from the final version of *Parole donnée* described his father's death as "the strangest and most cruel intersign" of his life.[4] Fernand Massignon had introduced Huysmans to his son and told him that the writer on his deathbed had prayed for him. The doctrine of mystical substitution, central to Massignon's rediscovery of faith and the dissertation on Hallaj, had been learned from Huysmans. That Pierre Roche should die while sculpting Huysmans's memorial, Massignon could never forget. It was a clear summons that he should offer himself for his father's salvation as Huysmans had done so long ago for him and as he had already done for Luis de Cuadra.

Massignon's ardent faith and the doctrine of mystical substitution influenced how he interpreted events in his personal life and altered his professional life as well; in point of fact, the two tended to become one intensely focused existence. The transforming experience of Muslim hospitality and religious conversion also radically changed the approach to Islamic studies Massignon had learned as a student under Le Chatelier. His wide-ranging expertise now concentrated primarily on the religious history of Islam and those contemporary issues which reflected his deep personal commitment to the Muslim world. In contrast, the formation of his former professor, like that of the young Charles de Foucauld, belonged to the tradition of the "specialized officer of the Arab bureaus" and involved the scientific gathering of data in order to promote direct French control of North Africa. Such work had served a colonial policy Massignon opposed, because it used information to subjugate the population rather than to understand social structures within the context of the culture. Le Chatelier had assigned his student to produce similar work, "from which I distanced myself progressively and systematically after my conversion, as a 'violation of the virginal point' of Muslims."[5] However, rather than completely abandoning the approach, Massignon used it to encourage understanding of contemporary Muslim society. In Cairo, during the war, Mark Sykes had set him to studying the British diplomatic *Handbooks*, which Massignon characterized as "admirable" and observed, "It is to this study that I owe the conception of the *Annuaire du monde musulman*."[6]

The first edition of the *Annuaire,* a study of contemporary Muslim society based on surveys and data collection, appeared in 1923 and was dedicated to Charles de Foucauld in memory of the latter's exhaustive exploration of Morocco. Religious, cultural, social, and economic questions were treated. That same year Massignon was contacted by General Hubert Lyautey, who years before had transmitted Massignon's book on Leo Africanus to his friend Charles de Foucauld. Lyautey, the *résident général* and founder of the protectorate of Morocco, was a strong proponent of self-rule if not independence in the French colonies of North Africa. He asked Massignon to survey the Moroccan craft guilds so that their structures could be renewed, especially in Fez, thereby promoting economic growth. Le Chatelier, who espoused a North African policy of direct French control emanating from Paris, strongly opposed

Lyautey's ideas and forbade his *suppléant* Massignon to contact the general. Predictably, Massignon did so anyway and undertook the survey because he had little sympathy with the school of thought represented by his former professor. In his words, Le Chatelier was "in rivalry with the school of Lyautey which triumphed, and whose style, charm, and noble sympathy towards Islam, I, along with Castries, much preferred."[7]

Three more editions of the *Annuaire musulman* were published, in 1926, 1929, and finally, in 1954, the year Massignon retired. "It was this work, so meticulous and so original, which earned for its author, his election, in 1924 [sic], to the chair which he occupied for thirty years at the Collège de France."[8] In 1919 Massignon also became editor of the *Revue du monde musulman,* where his writing had already appeared for over a decade. He later became the journal's director and remained in that position when, in 1927, it evolved into the *Revue des études islamiques.*

Research and publication about the changing face of the Muslim world remained a constant for Massignon, but the particular flavor of this work derived from its connection to other aspects of his scholarly life. In the course of his career the religious history of Islam, Sufi mysticism, and most centrally, Hallaj provided the fulcrum which gave that life coherence and continuity. After eight years of interruptions, the printed versions of Massignon's two dissertations were finally deposited at the Sorbonne, March 26, 1922, exactly one thousand years after the martyrdom of Hallaj. They were defended May 24 and published that same year. Both works were specially dedicated: the *Essai* to "the comrades of the fifty-sixth regiment of the colonial infantry, who died on the Eastern Front (1916–1917)"; the two-volume *Passion d'al-Hallaj* is inscribed, among others, to Huysmans, Foucauld, and the Alussys, key figures in the conversion. Publication brought international acclaim and election in 1924 to the Royal Asiatic Society of London and the Academy of Sciences in the Soviet Union.

However, for Massignon, academic recognition for these works was secondary to the profound motivation which had produced them. They culminated only one phase of his life-long veneration of Hallaj. Research on the Sufi martyr continued until the end, and death found him in the midst of preparations for the much expanded second edition of the *Passion,* ultimately published in 1975. In the preface he wrote for that second edition, Massignon testified that his deepest self had been plumbed by Hallaj, one of the "'royal' souls" whose sacrificial life transforms human history, "Not that the study of his life, which was full and strong, upright and whole, rising and given, has yielded to me the secret of his heart. It is rather he who has fathomed mine and who probes it still."[9] The eminent scholar and the faithful disciple were one.

In the eyes of contemporaries, a whole new approach to Muslim mysticism was created by the biography of Hallaj and the *Essai* on the lexicon of Muslim mysticism. Their publication sparked an interest in the topic which has never ceased to grow. Important research in the area already existed but had focused on external influences rather than on what Muslim mysticism constituted in itself:

> Massignon was the first in the West to provoke a kind of "Copernican revolution" and, according to an expression dear to him, a "decentering," and even a "mental stripping," which led researchers following his example in regard to Sufism, to proceed through attempts at internal reconstitution and no longer by examinations "from outside" to which "their patient erudition" was limited.[10]

The basis of this novel approach was ultimately linguistic. The Arabic language, so integrally a part of his own conversion, undergirded all of Massignon's research on mysticism. Language existed to convey ideas, and the latter were molded by the language used to communicate them. "It is useless to scrutinize the works of the Muslim mystics if one does not study very closely the mechanism of Arab grammar, lexicography, morphology, syntax."[11]

Mysticism was for Massignon at once universal in nature and concrete in expression. Using a definition of Ghazali, he defined it as the believer's "methodical introspection" about the experience and results of religious practice. Accordingly, "in any religious milieu where there exist really sincere and reflective souls, cases of mysticism can be found." As a "human phenomenon," it knows no limits of "race, language, or nation," although the expression of that phenomenon necessarily occurs through the language of a given culture. Evidence of borrowing, especially of vocabulary, does not prove that the entire tradition has been derived. Massignon reacted with particular vigor to racial theories propogated by Gobineau and Renan among others, which contended that, as "Semites," Muslims could not possess an indigenous mystical tradition. Proponents of such theories "decreed the absolute inaptitude of Semites for the arts and sciences in general and asserted the 'Aryan' origin of mysticism in religions said to be semitic."[12]

Massignon used linguistic evidence to refute Gobineau's claims and build his own argument. He pointed out that when so-called Semitic and Aryan cultures were compared, immense differences in language structure were readily apparent. However, those who maintained that Indo-European languages were superior because their periphrastic structure allowed the gradual unfolding and nuancing of ideas did not understand the "powerful and explosive concision of Semitic languages." The latter were characterized by a staccato word order and punctuated with formulas or pithy maxims; words were formed from fixed roots and admitted little modulation. Variation occurred from inside the word, and verb tenses related only to the action, not to its subject. Far from considering that these qualities prevented languages such as Arabic from being suitable vehicles for mysticism, Massignon contended that their structure was much more adequate than that of Indo-European languages for articulating the ineffable experience of an encounter with God. The condensed and disjunctive structure of Arabic corresponded to the disruption caused by such an encounter, when a transcendent God enters human finiteness.

Basing his assertions on a philological analysis of their writings, Massignon asserted that Sufi mysticism could be traced to the Qur'an. "It is from the Qur'an, constantly recited, meditated, and practiced, that Muslim mysticism proceeds, in its origins and its development."[13] As a result, Sufism was integral both to the growth of Islam and the development of the Arabic language. The early mystics interiorized the vocabulary of the Qur'an by making it part of their daily cultic practice. This was "the oldest effort of appropriation of the Arab idiom" and resulted in "a method of psychological introspection, in a moral theology, the first version of a critical lexicon of philosophical questions."[14] Moreover, Islam owed its international character to the Sufis. Mystics such as Hallaj had traveled far beyond Arabian borders, learned other languages, and converted more people to Islam by their example than did their compatriots by the sword.[15]

The preface of the *Essai* outlines how Massignon had proceeded: "the only way to arrive at the formation process of their vocabulary is to confront the succession of their works with the stages of their career."[16] For each author studied, a researcher must make "a direct and exhaustive examination of homogeneous lexicons, one per author."[17] Such a lexicon allowed one, first to distinguish between borrowings and an author's own unique use of Arabic vocabulary and, second, to see parallels between that original development and the author's growth as a mystic. In the case of Hallaj, Massignon culled a lexicon from the recurring, favored terms of the martyr's work, noting how their meanings evolved at progressive stages and determining where they might have been discovered. Hallaj, like Arab mystics before him, had appropriated vocabulary from primarily Arabic sources: the Qur'an, early Arab disciplines such as grammar, early Arab schools of theology, and scientific teaching diffused first in Aramaic and then in Arabic. Having analyzed the vocabulary of Hallaj, Massignon realized "how much the doctrinal presentation of the works of Hallaj depends on the terminology fixed little by little by his predecessors. Almost all his vocabulary, his principal allegories, his very rule of life, are found in previous Muslim mystics."[18]

The originality of Hallaj lay not in his vocabulary but rather in the single-mindedness which led him to affirm publicly "at the cost of his life, a doctrine his masters had not dared render accessible to everyone."[19] The life of Hallaj is seen to crown that of his predecessors because he alone explicated the central issue of mystical union, "the intermittent identification of the subject [man] and the Object [God]."[20] Mentioned only briefly in the *Essai*, the originality of Hallaj is exhaustively treated in the *Passion*, the monumental biography which recreates the social, political, and economic ambiance surrounding the tenth-century martyr and analyzes his doctrine in the light of Muslim dogma. In both editions, the first section contains (in the words of the preface of 1914) "the stages in the life of Hallaj and their social repercussions, from his first efforts of personal asceticism until the unofficial accounts of his trial and the 'acta sincera' of his martyrdom." In the second section one finds "the systematic account, in the framework of the actual theology of his time, of his teaching, reconstructed from his own works."[21]

Massignon's manner of proceeding followed from careful choice. He later described the method and explained how essential it was for verifying the authenticity of all mystical experience. As Massignon had done for Hallaj, the historian "establishes two chronological series of personal facts constituting a serious biography: a series of acts effectively accomplished, a series of ideas publicly communicated." He then examines "how the ideas and actions of the person were greeted by his entourage." For Massignon the reception accorded Hallaj by his contemporaries constituted a template of veritable mysticism because the true mystic is "raised up 'as a sign of contradiction' for many; just as a torch, lighting up, suddenly reveals while casting shadow, the passions and crimes which make their way in the night." The theologian confronts the two series of documents, the actions and the teachings of the mystic which have been prepared by the historian. "The rules of moral theology concerning the discernment of spirits" are set against the actions of the mystic and the ideas of the latter, within the framework of dogma, "the indispensable minimum of dogmatic elements properly expected from their author."[22]

Massignon concluded that Hallaj not only understood and experienced mystical union more deeply than his predecessors, but that his life and death constituted the fulfillment of Islam. Since the cornerstone of Muslim law rests on the notion of divine transcendence in contrast to human contingency, worship consists in affirming that transcendence, and the fact that God is inaccessible. Hallaj was ultimately killed because he publicly asserted, in opposition to Islamic law, that he had achieved mystical union with God. Whereas his predecessors had hidden their mystical experience in order to shield themselves, Hallaj accepted the consequences of his open preaching and acquiesced to the law which decreed his death. In so doing he transformed his ordeal into a sacrifice of reparation, offered in love for the community of Islam.

This view of the importance of Hallaj has, of course, been criticized because it seemingly equates the role of Hallaj in Islam with that of Jesus in Christianity, and thereby elevates a marginal figure in the history of Islam to a position denied him within the culture. Sir Hamilton Gibb and other Western colleagues thought that Massignon ascribed too much importance to the role of mysticism in the development of Islam. Some Muslim scholars also shared these reserves, recalling "the ancient separation between the mystical way and the way of religious Law" and added: "The greatest portion of what Orientalists call Muslim mysticism has nothing to do with Islam."[23] One of the most trenchant reproaches is found in Edward Said's *Orientalism*, where his comments echo in part those mentioned above. However, they are also based on debatable assumptions about Massignon's personal motivations for studying Muslim doctrine and Hallaj in the first place:

> The disproportionate importance accorded al-Hallaj by Massignon signifies, first, the scholar's decision to promote one figure above his sustaining culture, and second, the fact that al-Hallaj had come to represent a constant challenge, even an irritant, to the Western Christian for whom belief was not (and perhaps could not be) the extreme self-sacrifice it was for the Sufi. In either case, Massignon's al-Hallaj was intended literally to embody, to incarnate, values essentially outlawed by the main doctrinal system of Islam, a system

that Massignon himself described mainly in order to circumvent it with al-Hallaj.[24]

If certain Muslims thought that Massignon interpeted Hallaj and Muslim mysticism in the light of his own Catholic faith, his interpretation of the links between that faith and Islam also drew criticism from Catholics. Over the years both Christians and Muslims inevitably held reservations about the significance he assigned to religious figures whose stories seemingly bridged the gap between Islam and Christianity. His religious intuition, born in the intimacy of his own experience of faith, outstripped any ability to reconcile differences in dogmatic formulation.

Abraham was the first and pivotal figure in the long line which Massignon singled out after Hallaj, and the patriarch came to exemplify for him not only the earliest link between Christianity and Islam but also the notions of mystical substitution, hospitality, and compassion. The three monotheistic religious traditions trace their beginnings to the story of God's revelation to Abraham in the Bible and the Qur'an. Muhammad taught that just as the Jewish people traced their lineage through Isaac to Abraham, now the Arabs could claim divine favor through Ismael, Abraham's son by Hagar, the slave-girl. Before sending mother and child off to the desert at his wife Sarah's request, Abraham had blessed the child. For Muslims, the revelation to Muhammad and subsequent rise of Islam fulfilled a more ancient divine promise than the one made to Isaac because, although Judaism was blessed through Isaac, Ismael, as Abraham's first-born, was blessed first.

Since Abraham was central to divine revelation in all three faiths, he constituted a bridge between them. Moreover, since the patriarch is portrayed in the Bible as having a direct experience of God, Massignon felt a kinship with him because of his own mystical experience of conversion. Finally, the Genesis account of Abraham's relation with God illustrated Massignon's concept of hospitality and ntercession on behalf of others. Even before the dissertation was completed he began reflecting on the prayers of Abraham for Sodom, at Beersheba and finally Moria, as well as about the prophetic role of Ismael. Composition of the "Prière sur Sodome" dates from 1920, but the essay was published in a limited edition only in 1929. The introductory note to the "Hégire d'Ismael," begun as early as 1912, was completed in 1925–27 and published along with the "Prière sur Sodome" only in 1935, under the title "Les Trois Prières d'Abraham." The third prayer, for Isaac, was never published as such but incorporated into an abridged version which appeared in 1949 in *Dieu vivant*, the review Massignon co-edited for a time after the Second World War.[25] Shortly before his death, he chose the abridged version for the collection of his articles in *Parole donnée*. The publication history of these essays undoubtedly reflects that Massignon knew well how problematic his ideas about Abraham would appear to the Catholic hierarchy, intent upon preserving doctrinal orthodoxy.

It was one thing to assert that Hallaj had received special favors from God because these could be considered as an exception to the norm, limited to a few individuals. But Massignon's views, by extending the notion of divine revelation to include the entire Islamic community, implicitly questioned traditional Catholic teaching about salvation history, which restricts divine revelation to Judaism and Christianity and specifies that such revelation, contained in the Bible, ended with the death of the last apostle. In Massignon's interpretation Islam signified—six hundred years later—the "mysterious resurgence of the patriarchal cult prior to the Mosaic decalogue and the beatitudes" or again, "a mysterious response of grace to the prayer of Abraham for Ismael and the Arabs."[26] Within this context, the Qur'an is related to the Bible in a way analogous to the relationship between Ismael and Isaac. Abraham blessed both his sons. The existence of the Qur'an testifies that his blessing of Ismael was realized through Muhammad just as Christ fulfills the blessing of Isaac.

On the one hand, during the Second Vatican Council, Massignon's writings on Islam, of which these reflections formed a part, were crucial in reshaping the Catholic vision of the Muslim faith.

On the other hand, the question of Abraham and Ismael provoked reservations among Catholic theologians, which remain to this day:

> The most acute problem was using the specifically Muslim schema from among the three monotheisms descended from Abraham. One touches there at the very heart of the Christian faith, which, aside from dogma properly speaking, establishes through the 'Christian event,' its meaning within the history of salvation and the irreducible originality of the furrow thus traced in human history.[27]

The dilemma for the theologian then becomes the task of finding a middle ground which at one and the same time upholds Catholic dogma as divinely revealed and still affirms that God provides in multiple ways for the salvation of all people. Whatever the doctrinal implications of Massignon's theories about Abraham and Ismael, his ideas deepened Catholic reflection about the Muslim faith, and the story of the patriarch in Genesis remained for him a rich source of inspiration throughout his life. By integrating the key themes of sacred hospitality and sacrificial intercession for others, the story of Abraham exemplified the heroism which modifies the course of human history, a heroism which Massignon sought to emulate.

In "Les Trois Prières" Massignon portrayed Abraham as a biblical example of hospitality: he had been both guest and host. Because he had left his own country at God's demand and settled in the land of Canaan, Abraham had "come into this land as a stranger, *gèr*: a guest."[28] In gratitude for Sodomite hospitality he had saved their town a first time, through a military victory over an alliance of kings ranged against it. When later near Mamre he received three young men as guests, unaware that they were angels, "his perfect hospitality towards his three mysterious visitors" was rewarded by their promise of the birth of Isaac. The fidelity of Abraham to the Sodomites was demonstrated after the heavenly visitors headed toward Sodom, where his nephew Lot had settled. The inhabitants surrounded Lot's home, demanding that the visitors come out so that they could be seduced. "Sodom is the city which loves itself, which refuses the visitation of angels or wants to abuse them." It was also the city where the male affiliations of soldiers, priests, and merchants necessary for maintaining a society had led to homosexual activity. Abraham, faithful to his pledged word of hospitality, begged God to spare the city if ten just men could be found among its inhabitants. In Massignon's meditation, the plea was heard, even though Abraham could not find ten just men, and even though four of the five towns in the area were ultimately destroyed when he could only find three.

The unsuccessful outcome of Abraham's efforts to save Sodom was secondary to the faithfulness which prompted it. Singled out as the key element of hospitality and the central lesson to be learned from the Genesis account, faithfulness is linked to the necessity for compassion. Because Abraham practiced it to a heroic degree, Massignon was led to consider him as an early example of mystical substitution and the related Muslim notion of the *abdal* or ongoing chain of substitutes throughout time. In this perspective the patriarch prefigures both Jesus and Hallaj, and his hospitality toward the stranger resonates far beyond his own story. It stands in contrast to much human behavior and like a beacon illuminates the goal of human history, which is union with God. Heroic lives, like that of Abraham, reveal "in the perishable world, the incorruptible presence of a sacred Truth." They involve great suffering and thereby serve to uncover the redemptive meaning of the "crises of collective suffering—famines, epidemics, wars, persecutions—suffered by the masses of unfortunate people." Such are the lives of the "substitute" saints, who through their suffering intercede "for an immense number of souls who have remained behind somewhere along the way." Massignon concludes that "the religious life of believer groups is protected against rotting from hypocrisy by an intermittent treatment, in infinitesimal homeopathic doses, of 'substitute' sanctity." In sacred history this occurred for the first time through "the prayer of intercession of the first of the *abdal*, Abraham, on behalf of Sodom."[29]

Such reflections were not mere theorizing from a sacred text;

Massignon was outlining the direction of his own life. The profound conviction of having been chosen like Abraham for a special vocation of hospitality and intercession remained ever with him, but became refocused with new urgency early in 1927. He had given a paper at the University of London on "The Present Condition of the Muhammadan World," and while in the city, he suffered a cardiac episode. Massignon assessed his reaction in a letter written sometime after 1935:

> From 1922 to 1927, the time spent in consolidating my official position—Collège de France, journals, *Annuaire du monde musulman*, [ministry of] Foreign Affairs—might make one think from the outside that my life as an Islamist and Arabist was going to become that of a scholar in his study, swathing his arthritis in worldly honors, but some doubted it . . . And when, January 26, 1927, after praying to God the night before to reclaim me for Himself, I had the cardiac episode in London, which almost carried me off, I understood clearly that I had to fulfill my vocation to the very end, the way God had presented it to me in 1908 from May third to June 28. Not simply to find shelter in my family life and my scientific and social activity, more or less useful and so perishable, but to remain available, remain at the front until the end, as I had sworn to Foucauld; that is to say, to give more to Muslim souls, make the subject of my courses converge with my prayer for them, go every year at any price to their country, offer more and more of my life for them. The rectification has taken time, but I am trying to keep all my promises and those of my predecessors . . .[30]

Toward the end of 1927, while on one of his periodic diplomatic missions to the Middle East, Massignon encountered yet another spiritual figure with whom he felt akin. The trip to Palestine, Syria, and Iraq allowed him to pursue his interests in contemporary Islam; he was assigned to observe the social evolution of those countries, the development of Arab higher education, and the professional organizations of artisans and workers groups in Syria. Days in Iraq included visits to the tomb of Hallaj in Baghdad and the ruins of Ctesiphon, a palace on the eastern bank of the Tigris below Baghdad. Massignon already knew the place because, immediately before his conversion in May 1908, he had attempted to flee the steamer after it had run aground near Ctesiphon. However, at that time he knew nothing of Salman Pak who was buried there, an Iranian Christian who became a Muslim and one of the first companions of Muhammad. The discovery of Salman's tomb in 1927 led Massignon to believe that he had found yet another "intercessor" in his conversion near this spot so many years before.

He began to research the legend of Salman Pak because he was intrigued by the "historical contrast" between "the single vault remaining upright from the palace of Ctesiphon" and the "hidden tomb" of the foreigner who became part of Muhammad's inner circle. Accounts of early Muslim heresies and tribal alliances contained elements similar to details found in his legend and thus provided a basis for asserting the historicity of Salman Pak. Although venerated by the minority Shi'ites, he did not possess the importance for the majority Sunni Muslims that Abraham did in both Judaism and Christianity. However, purely scholarly pursuits did not exist for Massignon; they were all subsumed within the passionate pursuit of his life's meaning. As in the case of Hallaj, he studied the story of Salman Pak because of its affinity with his own and continued to reflect on it for the rest of his life. In so doing, he would discover ever closer links with other figures in his spiritual universe.

The Frenchman and the Iranian, were both foreigners to the geographic origins of Islam; their religious roots lay in Christianity, and both engaged in a spiritual search involving Islam, which led the one to rediscover Christianity and the other to embrace Islam. By his pronounced asceticism Salman Pak could be considered the first Sufi and thus the first of a long line of mystics leading to Hallaj. He was a wisdom figure whose Christian background had, according to legend, helped Muhammad understand the meaning of the Hebrew scriptures and the Gospel. Although a foreigner, he became one of Muhammad's intimates, councilor and companion, first to the prophet and later to Fatima, his daughter, and 'Ali, his son-in-law.

In this position Salman Pak witnessed many key moments in the development of Islam, including one which became central to the ever widening circle of Massignon's personal symbol system, the *mubahala*. In the Shi'ite tradition this event marked the spiritual adoption of non-Arabs converted to Islam. In 10/631 A.D., a Christian delegation from Najran (Yemen) came to negotiate with Muhammad. After considerable discussion during which the prophet criticized the group for believing in the divinity of Christ and invited them to become Muslims, an ordeal of mutual malediction was proposed to establish which side possessed religious truth. The next morning Muhammad appeared before the Christians using his family—'Ali, Fatima, and his two grandsons—as guarantors of the truth of Islam. The five, cloaked in the prophet's coat, were surrounded by thunder and light, in what Massignon described as a revelation of divine presence. At this sight the Christians capitulated and signed a treaty with the Muslims. A witness to this scene, Salman was charged to explain its significance to the other observers, so that they might see in it "a new manifestation of this same Divine Spirit which anointed the Messiah [Christ] as royalty."[31]

Massignon was attracted to the tradition of Salman as bridge builder between Christianity and Islam; it was a role he had espoused for himself. His assertion that heroic individuals shape history reflected another of Salman's roles according to Shi'ite tradition. After Muhammad's death, the Iranians recognized 'Ali as the prophet's successor and thus became one of the divine instruments who intuitively discover those whose lives change the course of history. He became identified with a kind of divine intuition which "identifies within each generation, those who personify the immutable protagonists in the human drama of obedience to God . . ."[32] Salman's link with 'Ali also introduced Massignon to various themes related to the thirst for justice, the reparative value of suffering, and the vindication of the oppressed at the last judgment. When Ali was displaced by an elected caliph, Salman defended his legitimacy as Muhammad's successor and came to be regarded as the prototype of those who demand justice. Because of his role with both Muhammad and 'Ali, he constitutes for the Shi'ites the essential link guaranteeing the latter's legitimacy; in their eyes he became one of the first Muslims in a chain of witnesses or *isnad,* whose existence guaranteed the truth of Islam. Because of his own asceticism and link to 'Ali, he was also related to the notion of the *abdal* or substitute, whose suffering ultimately saves humanity. The Iranian's identification with justice divinely wrought at the end of time became an increasing source of inspiration to Massignon. This was particularly true toward the end of his life as he became ever more absorbed by the suffering of Muslim populations in the Near East, the Maghreb, and France.

Within the Christian tradition a parallel example of mystical substitution and convergence between Christianity and Islam was provided by Francis of Assisi. Massignon was especially drawn to an incident in the saint's life which recalled the encounter witnessed by Salman Pak between Muhammad and the Christians from Najran. In 1219, after the defeat of the crusaders at Damietta in the Nile delta, Francis of Assisi left the Christian encampment to seek out the Sultan al-Malik al-Kamil. Whereas Muhammad had challenged the Christians to establish the truth of their faith by seeing whose curses were strongest, Francis offered to undergo an ordeal by fire to prove the truth of Christ and thereby convert the sultan. The latter rejected the offer, and Francis, having refused the sultan's gifts, was sent back to the Christian lines. Years before, during Massignon's religious crisis, Paul Claudel had suggested that his friend become a lay member of the Franciscans by joining the Third Order. But it was only in November 1931, having long meditated on the link between Francis and Islam, that Massignon became a Franciscan tertiary; he took the name of "Ibrahim" or Abraham in recognition of the biblical patriarch's central role in the sacred history of both Christianity and Islam. The following year, 1932, he took vows.

Massignon was in his late forties as the 1920s ended and the 1930s began, securely established in the top ranks of European scholars. His work and his life continued to reflect both his intellectual and spiritual preoccupations. His 1928–29 classes at the Collège de France drew on the findings of his mission to the Middle East the previous year and focused on the "artisanal and agricultural organizations in Muslim Syria." The foundation of the Institut d'études islamiques by Massignon dates from 1929. That same year his commitment to the disenfranchised took a decisive first step towards the "activism" which so characterized his later years. He realized "from 1929 on, that it was only by private social action, allying him with the life of Muslim workers that he would arrive at serious results."[33] Therefore he organized and began teaching night classes for illiterate North African workers living in Paris. The following year, the work, under the name Equipes sociales nord africaines was located permanently in Gennevilliers, a northern, working-class suburb of Paris; Massignon continued teaching with this group until his death.

In 1929 also, the issue of justice in Algeria began to elicit a response from Massignon. At a time when the independence movement was beginning to take shape in Algeria, he belonged to an interministerial commission which was preparing a survey on the status of Algeria for the approaching centenary of 1930. Years later he reported what happened:

> I investigated on site without going through the administration and returned convinced that, in justice, reforms were urgent; President Tardieu had the Commission reject them en masse by means of a classic ruse, by having read to it a police report truncated of its second section proving me right. He could not restrain himself from bragging about it later . . . insinuating that I had changed my mind. Always the same procedure: disqualify the witness whom one does not succeed in winning over.[34]

During the century of French control, the European settlers and the indigenous Muslim majority of Algeria had become increasingly separated from each other. The former automatically became naturalized French citizens, whereas that possibility was closed to the latter, ostensibly in order to preserve their distinctive cultural character. The very success of the colonization effort had impoverished the Muslim population, and for years the French government had failed either to improve their economic condition or arbitrate between them and the Europeans. Members of the educated Muslim elite had attempted several times unsuccessfully to negotiate the progressive integration of the Muslims into the French electorate. Both the indifference of the French government and the hostility of the Europeans effectively destroyed any possibility of collaboration between the indigenous population and the settlers, and thus, any hope of eventually creating a Franco-Muslim society.

The idea of collaboration received support from a few liberals, who invoked basic principles of the Republic, and also from Louis Massignon. In a 1930 essay outlining his opinion of French Algerian policy, he did not mention his experience with the commission but advocated a policy based on mutual respect, much as he had in 1921–22 concerning *francisation* and the French mandate in Syria. His ideas about Algeria remained founded on the notion of equality among all elements of the population and the shared destiny of France and Algeria. Independence was not then and never became an issue for him because in his eyes Algeria formed part of France: "one must continue to repeat without flagging, that the Algerian problem is not a colonial but a mainland problem, that Algeria is composed of three departments, that it depends on the Ministry of the Interior and not on the Ministry of the Colonies."[35]

Therefore, while an indirect administration should eventually lead to Syrian autonomy, in Algeria, "a loyal *francisation* of the Muslim element" was required. For Massignon this signified both finding a way for Muslims and Europeans to work together and allowing Muslims to enjoy those benefits French citizens took for granted. Citing "years of personal experience," as his basis of observation, he described two categories of "administrative tendencies" which he deplored in Algeria. The weary colonial bureaucrat operates by "administrative cynicism" that tolerates and even encourages corruption because it is seen as the only available means of governing. The notion of "benevolent association" promotes limited material and educational well-being for native Algerians but discourages them from attaining elite positions. Massignon would substitute a tendency deriving "from a more immediate and simpler loyalty, that of being 'shoulder to shoulder' which imposes itself when one journeys together: not to refuse a priori to others what one has found good for oneself."[36] He believed that Algeria, juridically a part of France, shared with her a common destiny and that the country's two disparate communities could learn to live in harmony with each other. Although this essay did not say so, Massignon's hopes for Algeria were rooted in his belief that relationships among peoples were grounded in the spiritual order, in the sacred hospitality he had first experienced as a young man in the Middle East and found exemplified in the story of Abraham.

In the early 1930s the Algerian independence movement began to take hold for multiple reasons. Not only was the French government's Algerian policy stagnant, but a new Arab consciousness in the Middle East had strengthened the Islamic community's awareness of itself. The French Communist Party, which was opposed to colonialism, was growing in influence. Finally, the French protectorates of the Maghreb, particularly Morocco under Lyautey, enjoyed more liberal policies than did Algeria. More than a generation would pass and another war would occur before frustration in both Morocco and Algeria erupted into conflicts which led to their independence. Massignon would be deeply involved in this painful decolonization, brought about in part by the new geopolitical realities produced by the war. However, in 1931, a year after the French celebrated the centenary of the Algerian conquest, he briefly encountered someone whose life and work were dedicated to freeing his people from foreign domination. Years later the example of Mahatma Gandhi would concretely direct Massignon's reponse to the upheavals which shook the Arab world after World War II.

If Charles de Foucauld had exemplified how to live out the radical faith which had first attracted Massignon to Hallaj, the life of Mahatma Gandhi demonstrated how to integrate such a faith with the struggle for political and social justice. When the Hindu first came to his attention a decade earlier, in 1921, he was immediately struck by the power of his thought but could not foresee that

Gandhi's influence would prove so decisive and far-reaching for his own life. Through the Collège de France, Massignon was visited in 1921 by two Muslims heading the commission which attempted to preserve the Muslim caliphate (the historic institution of Muslim governance, abolished in 1924). They cited Gandhi's example to Massignon:

> It was through Muslims that I knew Gandhi and I understood the ideals of Gandhi, the ideal of *satyagraha*, the pursuit of truth by steadfastness in will, by *vrata*, by oath. I also learned . . . that *satyagraha* was a sacred thing for the Muslims also. I realized immediately there was something in Gandhi that was valuable. For perhaps the first time in the world, there was a man influencing people of other religions and with great social results.[37]

The two visitors gave a copy of the *satyagraha* pledge to Massignon, who published it in the April 1921 issue of the *Revue du monde musulman*. Part of Gandhi's appeal for Massignon stemmed from the fact that Hindu understanding and respect for the minority Muslim population were fundamental to Gandhi's program. In the struggle for Indian independence, Gandhi considered that the crucial issue of national unity depended on mutual understanding between Hindus and Muslims. Thus, his support for retaining the caliphate was based on his respect for Muslim religious values. This attitude paralleled Massignon's own views about the appropriate stance of France vis-à-vis Muslims in the Middle East and North Africa. But most importantly, the *satyagraha* of Gandhi placed political action within an overall commitment to the truth, which began with the truth of one's own life. Such a view corresponded to Massignon's own demand that government policy be founded on sacred hospitality. Throughout the 1920s, Massignon worked informally with others "trying to see how the *satyagraha* pledge of truth could be made to capture the French mind."[38]

The single meeting with Gandhi occurred December 5, 1931. The latter had arrived from London that day; there, as the delegate of the Indian Congress, he had attended the Round Table Conference convened to discuss the Indian question. The Paris stopover was brief; he was traveling to Switzerland for a visit with Romain Rolland, the writer who spearheaded French interest in Gandhi and his movement. The meeting with Massignon occurred at the apartment of Mme Louise Guieysse, who in 1932 founded the group Amis de Gandhi and who along with Rolland sponsored a newsletter, *Nouvelles de l'Inde*. That same evening Massignon went to hear the Hindu speak at an open meeting. He recalled that during his visit, Gandhi was asked, "How and in what way could religion help in advocating the suppression of war?" and that "Gandhi very simply replied: 'Official religions are very weak in stopping war.'" The response certainly agreed with Massignon's own life-long suspicion, which co-existed with his religious commitment, that official religious leaders and their churches were more aligned with wealth than worship. He joined the Amis de Gandhi and supported the newsletter which, he explained, "was not much of a success. We could not get the support of bankers."[39] Nevertheless, thanks to the interest of the small group of French intellectuals who had gathered to meet Gandhi, the latter's ongoing efforts to gain independence for India were well-known in Paris during the thirties. Massignon followed those events and pondered Gandhi's message. Years later it would nurture and direct his own response when he confronted the dramas in the Middle East and the Maghreb created by the Israeli-Arab conflict, the removal of the sultan of Morocco, and the Algerian War.

SIX

The Vocation Renewed and Tested

The interest in Gandhi, long before the latter became a personal model, reflected both Massignon's capacity to nurture his thought from diverse cultures and his consistent desire to live in such a manner that his entire life bore witness to his committed faith. During the 1930s, the academic honors continued, as did the ever deepening search to express his unique devotion to Islam. Topics such as Shi'ite Islam, which had begun to interest Massignon in the 1920s, were pursued in greater depth. The study of new themes came to enrich the kaleidoscope of persons, places, and things that constituted his personal universe of intersigns.

Professional recognition of Massignon during these years confirmed his rank at the forefront of Orientalists worldwide. In 1933 he was named director of studies in the section *sciences religieuses* at the Ecole Pratique des Hautes Etudes, a post he held until his retirement in 1954. In 1933 also, King Fuad of Egypt named him to the Royal Academy of the Arabic language, which the monarch had created in 1932 in order to address the problems of Arabic in the twentieth century and to produce an Arabic dictionary. Along with Sir Hamilton Gibb, Massignon was among the five European Orientalists so honored by the king. Their task was to suggest methods for creating the dictionary and ways of carrying out the academy's programs. Except for the war years and until 1960 he met with scholars in Cairo each winter to work on his assigned area of the dictionary, the social sciences and literature. Over time it was he who demonstrated the greatest interest in the academy's work.[1]

On January 23, 1934, Massignon arrived in Cairo for the first meeting of the academy, but the sojourn proved memorable for other reasons as well. He had not seen Mary Kahil in twenty-one years, since 1913 when the two had become acquainted in the salon of the Countess Hohenwaert and later had offered their lives in mystical substitution for the recovery of Luis de Cuadra. Their reunion January 29, 1934, when Massignon was fifty-one and Mary Kahil, forty-six, led to a deep and lasting relationship that ended only with Massignon's death. Vivacious and socially well-connected, Kahil had never married. She participated in the Egyptian feminist movement and devoted her considerable resources to charitable work among the Muslims.

Years after rediscovering Massignon she reminisced about the incident in the easy conversational style that was hers. While having tea at the home of friends, she heard he had come to Cairo and was staying at the Institut francais d'archéologie orientale. "I said nothing, then I left, and without anyone seeing me I went to the Institut . . . " to inquire if Massignon was indeed there. And when told that he could be found in the library, she went looking for him upstairs:

> Then I saw coming towards me a strange silhouette, a man bent over, with his head tilted, while I myself had known him as very tall. He said to me, 'Ah, is it you? You haven't changed.' 'Nor you!' This wasn't true. Both of us were remnants . . . So we went downstairs. On the mezzanine there was a divan covered with a rug. He began talking then about his life. And he talked, and he talked. It was like a river.[2]

Indeed, Massignon's appearance had changed considerably since they had known each other in 1913 or in the photos taken soon afterward that show him proudly erect in his army uniform. A black suit and tie had constituted his invariable attire since his father's death in 1922;[3] for bad weather he put on a beret and a worn raincoat tied at the waist. With the years, his physical stature had seemingly diminished, as if all his life energy were increasingly concentrated in the realm of the spirit and revealed in the penetrating gaze of his eyes.

The following morning Kahil drove Massignon to mass, and in the course of the next few weeks they became reacquainted. His volubility amazed her as did his capacity to ignore his surroundings while talking:

> One day we went to Damietta. The chauffeur accompanied us in the little Mercedes. All along the way Massignon talked to me about his life and the vices of his past. And as for me, I understood nothing and was bored. My little dog spent the time licking his hands. And as for him, he talked and talked and seemed to find it normal that my dog should be licking his hands.[4]

Massignon discovered in Mary Kahil not only an important link with his personal history but also someone whose life, like his, had been shaped by contact with the Islamic world. When he in turn asked Kahil about her own life, she recalled explaining, "I'm not involved with Christian organizations. I'm involved with Muslim good works. I joined the Muhammad Ali group and the Union féministe égyptienne. And thus I try to make contact with Muslim women." Massignon immediately responded that her choice had not been a random one, that indeed she was called to consecrate her life to the Muslims. Reflecting on that exchange, Kahil stated that this observation determined the rest of her life: "It seemed to me then that Massignon had confirmed me in my path when he said that I had a vocation to live among the Muslims, and I devoted myself totally to them."[5]

His affirmation of her work prompted her to become deeply devoted to her rediscovered friend, primarily but not exclusively as a spiritual mentor, "I attached myself to Massignon as a spiritual master and not as a man. It was a silent call, unhoped for, from the depths of myself."[6] Since he was married and both were deeply committed Catholics, the relationship was always articulated at the level of their mutual interest in Islam and search for God. However, evidence suggests a bond far transcending that of spiritual director and directee; they occupied a unique place in each other's lives, based on their shared experience in 1913 and a Christian faith lived out within a deep commitment to Islam. Their devotion to each other was reciprocal, expressed in regular and voluminous correspondence between them; it extended from 1934 to 1962 and was interrupted only by the war and during a period in the 1950s, when his asceticism prompted Massignon to interrupt contact for a time. Kahil saved his letters and eventually had them deposited in the Vatican. The total comprised 1,488 manuscript pages, only extracts of which have been published. Her letters to him were evidently destroyed.[7]

Because various critical aspects of his past suddenly converged in this unexpected meeting, Massignon interpreted it as yet another "intersign," very different from the death of his father or the discovery of Salman Pak, but structured in much the same way and with an identical mandate. The unforeseen coming together of important elements of his life in the person of Mary Kahil was a sign from God that must be heeded. Portions of the available correspondence detail how their renewed contact rekindled the religious fervor of his 1908 conversion, which he had shared with her in 1913. Several weeks after their 1934 meeting he wrote Kahil about his profound emotion at seeing her again:

> This meeting, after what will soon be twenty-one years, pierced my heart right through to the burning wound of my conversion during the nights of May 1–3 and revived within me in a wrenching manner my promises to belong to God alone, in all holiness, forever.[8]

Through the experience of their reunion Massignon reexamined the commitment of those early years and knew again its fervor. In the same letter he also recalled the offering they had shared in 1913 for "the soul of my friend, Luis, who . . . must be out of the fire now, or quite close to being saved." In 1934, twenty-one years later, the memory of that offering seemed to embody the trajectory of Massignon's life, namely the single-minded search for God expressed in his self-offering for Islam. In Mary Kahil he discovered someone who, having been present as that vocation was formulated, could both understand its significance and share its demands. If other intersigns had and would occur in Massignon's life, no parallel existed for the depth of understanding he found in her—as he himself recognized early on:

> When I speak, in the inflections of my voice; when I grow silent, within the recesses of my mind, in my heart's desires, from time to time I find something that astonishes me, that expands and unfetters me, and I think it is our Angels who are communicating. How silent it is, the wonderful perfume of incense, the mute prayer of my Arab sister, of Maryam which rises toward God and reaches me here by a supernatural delicacy of grace . . .
>
> This grace I had never known in such a direct way, constituted by the spiritual presence of a soul-friend who understands and who shares. It is such a direct sign to my heart of my membership in the community of the Church that I praise God for it with all my soul and beg him on my knees to bless us.[9]

Massignon and Kahil wished to ritualize their shared sense of commitment to Islam, renewed by their surprising rediscovery of each other after so many years. They did so in a place that epitomized how places and events converged for Massignon in an intricate pattern of symbol. On February 9, 1934, they returned to the abandoned Franciscan church at Damietta made famous by the crusaders and by Francis of Assisi, who had offered to be tested by fire in order to prove the truth of Christianity to the sultan. For Massignon that episode was linked to the encounter of Muhammad with the Christians of Najran or the *mubahala* witnessed by Salman Pak. In turn, Salman was linked both to the long line of Muslim witnesses, the *isnad* who testify to the truth of an event and preserve its memory across generations, and the *abdal,* or substitutes, whose act of self-donation is salvific because their holy lives make reparation for others.[10] At Damietta, Massignon and Kahil vowed together to offer their lives for the Muslims, "not so they would be converted, but so that the will of God might be accomplished in them and through them."[11] This offering was termed *badaliya*, after the Arab word signifying "to be in the place of" or a substitute. It gave expression to Massignon's convictions about mystical substitution encountered first in Huysmans and echoed in the Muslim notion of the *abdal.* Later that year, on July 18, Massignon wrote Kahil that Pius XI in a private audience had approved their action, "he blessed by name our offering of Damietta."[12]

These were the small beginnings of what would eventually become the association of the Badaliya, a "sodality of prayer" whose members, like the founders, offered themselves in mystical substitution for the salvation of the Muslim community. However, Massignon explained in the statutes he wrote for the group in 1943 that "salvation did not necessarily mean exterior conversion. It is already a great deal to obtain that a larger number belong to the soul of the Church, and live and die in the state of grace."[13] The association was formally approved in 1947, and the annual letters Massignon wrote to the membership until his death reveal that he wrestled with the seeming contradiction of his desire to bring Muslims to faith in Christ even as he asserted that Islam was an authentic vehicle of grace.

Kahil also encouraged Massignon not to abandon his lifelong dream of the priesthood, a dream ended apparently forever in 1914 when he married and thereby renounced the possibility of joining Charles de Foucauld in the Sahara. However, the feelings of ambivalence which accompanied that choice remained over the years. Massignon resolutely asserted that his commitment to God, as lived out through his dedication to the Muslims, superseded all others. Yet his work on their behalf failed to allay that ambivalence. He felt constantly torn between his desire to live more radically and the obligations necessarily imposed by family life. One day in early 1934, Kahil questioned him on the topic of priesthood:

> One day I asked him why he hadn't become a priest. He told me that it was in order to obey his confessor, who had asked him to marry. I showed my astonishment at seeing a man his age obey his

confessor. He confided to me then that he still wanted to be a priest and that he would then be closer to the Lord Jesus. And I, I told him: "It's still possible!" He responded, "I will mull on it."[14]

Before the unexpected reunion with Mary Kahil, Massignon had considered Baghdad his spiritual home in the Middle East, because it had been the scene of his conversion and that of the death of Hallaj. Indeed, during his 1934 sojourn he wrote to her from Iraq where, on March 7, he visited the tombs of Hallaj in Baghdad, Salman Pak in Ctesiphon, and also of his friend King Faisal, who had died in 1933. Several days later he returned to Karbala, Najaf, and Kufah, cities crucial both to the history of Shi'ism and the saga of Massignon's conversion. (This excursion was accomplished thanks to an automobile and guide supplied by Shi'ite friends, a far cry from the caravan of horses needed in 1908 for the same itinerary.)[15] However, after the winter of 1934 Cairo replaced Baghdad as the center of his activities in the Middle East; he returned yearly to work on the dictionary, visit Mary Kahil, and renew with her at Damietta the vow of *badaliya*.

The months in Cairo marked yet another critical turning point for Massignon, because seeing Kahil resurrected the latent tension between his life as constituted and the kind of heroism to which he aspired. Therefore, when at the beginning of April, Massignon returned to the full range of his activities in Paris, he experienced more acutely than ever the familiar tension between his daily existence and the longing for a life crowned with martyrdom, as exemplified by Hallaj and Foucauld. He wrote to Kahil on Easter Monday:

> Suffering has begun for me in this "classic and normal" framework of my life in Paris, which I have never believed in—but which, for two years, I had consented to in lukewarm and cowardly abandon. Your spiritual presence, so direct and so fraternal, is a piercing reminder to me, like some suddenly felt anxiety: it has made me realize that God did not raise me up, praying in Arabic in 1908, so I could doze in France, surrounded by general regard—scorning the example of the mystics who guided me and whose study has

earned me my name and my position. What shamefulness! They themselves chose exile, the desert, deprivation, persecution, and torture—and I, the friend of Hallaj and Foucauld, I was thinking about staying alive by comfortably exploiting their works until my death. May you be blessed for having called me back to the desire for martyrdom. My heart is once more enkindled, and I have promised God to tear myself away from everything gradually, gently, but implacably—so as to be judged worthy of martyrdom in a Muslim land if God permits.[16]

In point of fact, Massignon continued his normal round in Paris, and inevitably the tension persisted. Commenting several days later that mystical poetry celebrated the dead of night as a propitious moment for prayer, Massignon noted to Kahil that he could not follow such an example, "For I must not prevent my family from sleeping, and all the doors of the apartment creak."[17] In yet another letter to Kahil on June 27, the day after returning from a pilgrimage to La Salette, Massignon returns to the theme of family obligations versus commitment to Islam and suggests that resolution of the problem rests in the hands of God:

> Pray that I succeed in giving my family all the good God wants me to give them. Evidently, my offering to Islam is prior and it governs everything. But the God I have sought to love extravagantly in this same world that ignores him (and in this bourgeois "moderation" that does not want to understand the passion of the Cross) will be able to find an exquisite (and probably atrocious) means of arranging everything. Because I cannot bring harm to my family.[18]

At the end of the year Massignon expresses the tension in slightly different terms; the implacable givens of his daily life are seemingly balanced and ultimately surmounted by an equally imperious reality within him, namely the thirst for God:

> There is nothing good in me, nothing but a certain wound, a thirst for God such that the most bitter premonitions, even while twisting me around as if beneath the lashes of a whip, no longer succeed

in uprooting hope from my heart, a hope, moreover, as childlike as it is crazy because at the age of 51, I see my lacks, my handicaps, and above all, this empty labor which absorbs the best of my energy. But in spite of everything, this thirst for God tears me away from all that and, in the midst of pain, pulls me along towards the sunlit high seas, serene and trembling under a great wind.[19]

In 1934, then, Massignon's life seemed to offer little room for substantial change. The possibility of priesthood seemed remote since, aside from the Roman Catholic objection to married clergy, he was committed to professional and family responsibilities. Whatever his regrets, they did not affect his professional life. His days were crowded with classes at the Collège de France and the Ecole Pratique des Hautes Etudes, conferences in Europe and the Middle East, and numerous articles for scholarly revues. He continued to study and lecture on religious themes linked to Shi'ism. Many of these, such as the legend of Salman Pak, resonated with his own ever-deepening belief that justice and mutual understanding among peoples could be achieved only through suffering, compassion, and mystical substitution. One article, "Salman Pak and the Beginnings of Iranian Islam" was initially presented in 1933 to a meeting of the Society of Iranian Studies. A course at the Collège de France in 1936 was devoted to the role of Ali, the prophet's son-in-law counseled by Salman Pak.[20]

Soon after returning from the Middle East in April 1934, Massignon had visited with Paul Claudel and later wrote to his one-time spiritual mentor about the restlessness intensified by the winter months in Cairo.[21] They had seen each other only intermittently after the war, but remained friends because of the bond created by Massignon's conversion and their links with Père Daniel Fontaine; in May 1925, Massignon and Claudel placed flowers on the tomb of Daniel Fontaine.[22] The poet was also the godfather of Massignon's daughter, Genevieve. However, the two men were of quite different temperaments. Claudel took a dim view of Massignon's ability to talk endlessly and of what he considered his excessive asceticism. Moreover, because he was more conservative than his friend, their religious and political views diverged more and more with the years. In 1925, upon returning from Japan, Claudel noted in his journal: "Holy Saturday. Massignon, still ascetic but a more joyous air. He's suffering from a knee inflammation, the 'malady of monks,' the result of too protracted prayers. He talks incessantly."[23] Claudel could also muster but little enthusiasm for the Muslim mysticism that nurtured his friend's spiritual life. He commented in November, "Saw L. Massignon, who reminded me what I had written him about the Arab Sufis. Not love but desire, a kind of desire without charity, an 'ontological' desire."[24]

Yet the friendship endured, perhaps because Claudel remained indissolubly linked in the younger man's mind with the years of spiritual crisis following the conversion. Massignon's attentiveness was not reserved solely for his one-time spiritual mentor. It was as if all those who touched his life, be they living or dead, formed a kind of spiritual constellation with which Massignon stayed in contact. He visited the graves of the dead. The living received letters to mark occasions important either to them or him. Thus, in August 1934, six months after the reunion with Kahil, he wrote Claudel and recalled the latter's response to the letter which had launched their correspondence:

> Tomorrow is the feast of Saint Augustine, and within me is imprinted the old and gentle custom of thinking and praying especially with you that day, to thank you and thank God for the elder who responded so fraternally in 1908, and who helped me so much.
>
> So many passages in your work resonate intimately within me, so many sentences from your letters and our conversations, where our common experience and our greatest supernatural hope call out to God.
>
> This year has brought me wrenchingly back to my first solemn promises of 1908, to love God alone, and recalls that first letter I dared write you in Tien-Tsin; it was August 8, 1908.[25]

The following year, Massignon contributed to a special issue of *La Vie intellectuelle* honoring Claudel (July 10, 1935). Contributors

included G. K. Chesterton and the best-known French Catholic intellectuals: Jacques Maritain, Francis Jammes, Georges Cattaui, Henri
Ghéon, Gabriel Marcel, Charles Du Bos, and François Mauriac.
Massignon's tribute, even as it acknowledged Claudel's literary
achievements, focused on the importance of their correspondence
during the years of the vocation crisis. In evoking the period 1908–
1914 Massignon alludes to his preoccupations of 1935, namely the
renewed sense of urgency about how to integrate his professional
and spiritual aspirations. He remembers that Claudel's letters arrived
"always at the right moment, bringing me with patient attention the
counsel of a wise, older brother who was willing to stay with me 'in
that hard struggle over vocation, as severe as that of death' (Oct. 12,
1909)." He goes on to say that this same struggle "will last until
death" without weakening either the link between them or Massignon's "fraternal gratitude."[26]

Curiously and perhaps significantly, Massignon altered the text
of Claudel's 1909 letter, which compared the severity of the vocation crisis not immediately to death but to the struggle involved in
religious conversion, "My thought is with you in this hard struggle
over vocation, as severe as that of conversion. But there, it is a battle
one wages all alone like that of death."[27] Massignon had always
characterized his conversion as a kind of death, because in seemingly
an instant it had so radically transformed the whole of his life. It is
not surprising, then, that he telescoped the two images Claudel had
used to describe vocation into the single word, *death*. Moreover,
given the context of the 1934 experience in Cairo, one might also
conclude that the transposition came from an insight that was certainly evident in Massignon's life, namely that as events unfolded his
religious commitment exacted ever new responses. The tension involved in choosing such responses would prove unrelenting until
the end.

The short article for Claudel ends with a quote from another
Claudel letter, where the poet wrote that his vocation as a Christian
winning souls for God outweighed his achievements as a literary figure delighting audiences and readers through his art: "When we

have written a few articles and, as I have, composed a few plays filled with artificial emotions, *quid hoc ad aeternitatem?*"[28] In citing his friend, Massignon was also echoing his own preoccupations and weighing the relative importance of his professional life against that of eternity. A different but analogous note was struck a year later when, under the same title, "Sortes claudelianae," he composed a short article paying explicit homage to Claudel as author. In this instance, Massignon wrote that the encounter with Claudel, the writer, "facilitates the mental decentering of the reader," a notion Massignon often used to describe his discovery of Islamic culture in the secular order and of God in mystical prayer. Indeed, Massignon suggests that the power of such writing and his own response to it are based on the fact that both he and Claudel, however disparate their views, had undergone profound religious experience. Therefore Claudel's texts or a given sentence succeed in producing "the gently persuasive intervention of another personality, triggering a relationship. Personal, spontaneous, and incisive, such a sentence burrows its way in, secretly reminding us of the original upheaval that marked us both with a single and identical sign."[29]

However deeply and irrevocably conversion had changed him, Massignon never attempted to proselytize. Indeed, such an effort ran counter to his cherished notion of sacred hospitality and acceptance of the other on his own terms. Unable to attend a July 1936 meeting in London of the World Congress of Faith, where he had been invited to speak, Massignon sent instead a summary of the proposed talk. In his sometimes uncertain English, it outlined his deeply held notion that a fellowship of believers could be achieved only through a mutual respect which celebrates and transcends dogmatic differences. Those he mentions are subsumed under the mantle of a common Abrahamic origin:

> If we take . . . the three "Abrahamic" religions, Israel, Christianity, Islam, we realize that between Israel's jealous segregation and Islam's open easiness (and readiness to evolve universalism, [*sic*] simple and clear worship), room remains for Christians to elaborate

the gradual incorporation of all men, through good will and good works, into the "Church's soul." Meanwhile Islam exists as a supreme divine summons, on behalf of all unprivileged believers faced with Israel's and Christendom's special privileges, recalling to them both that the "legacies" they boast of may condemn them on the Day of Doom.[30]

In 1935 and 1937 Massignon lectured at the Ecole Pratique des Hautes Etudes on sura 18, "the Cave," of the Qur'an. In this tale which he called "the apocalypse of Islam," he discovered yet another link between Islam and Christianity, one that grew up spontaneously as a popular devotion in both traditions. Recited during the Friday noon worship in the mosque, the sura evokes the end of time and the legend of the Seven Sleepers. The theme itself was of Christian origin, and like other references to Christian themes in the Qur'an, went back to "ancient, apocryphal traditions, developed at the beginning of the second century A.D., and which oral renderings by unlettered believers kept alive in the desert."[31]

In both traditions, the legend concerns seven young men fleeing religious persecution who took refuge with their dog in a cave, walled themselves in, and fell into a mysterious sleep. At the end of some three hundred years they awoke, testified to those around them that their hope of resurrection was real, and then died several hours later. In 1926 ruins of a basilica dedicated to the Seven Sleepers were discovered near Ephesus, the first site in Christianity where they were venerated. The foundations of the basilica dated from 448 and the reign of Theodosius II. Ephesus was also the city where, according to Christian tradition, Mary, the mother of Jesus, had lived with the apostle John until her death and "assumption," body and soul, into heaven. The primitive tomb of Mary Magdalen, the first witness of Jesus' resurrection, was supposedly situated at the edge of the cave where the young men hid.

Because the tale of the Seven Sleepers combined major themes and personnages of both traditions, Massignon considered it powerful evidence of the basis of understanding between Christians and

Muslims, all children of Abraham. Just as Abraham had abandoned Isaac to God, so too, the young men in the cave had confidently given themselves over to seeming death. In both cases their faith in a resurrection beyond death was realized. Massignon presented a paper on the Seven Sleepers in November 1938, at the twentieth congress of Orientalists in Brussels; it was entitled "The Seven Sleepers: Research on the Eschatological Value of the Legend in Islam." However, as a devotion the Seven Sleepers assumed major importance for him only later, after the war, when he promoted it as a symbol of reconciliation between Christians and Muslims during the Algerian crisis.

As the 1930s advanced, the conflicts of decolonization were still remote, but catastrophe at home was becoming imminent. Family events and repercussions from the gathering storm of European fascism left Massignon little time to seek solutions to the interior struggles evident in his writings to and about Claudel or in letters to Mary Kahil. The middle 1930s was a period of profound personal loss for him, set against the background of a country increasingly menaced by its neighbors.

Because of his close-knit family, Massignon had felt keenly the loss of his parents; he had discovered his father struck dead by a heart attack in 1922 and was present when his mother died in 1931. Their memories, along with all his beloved dead, he honored for the rest of his life, but his grief was necessarily tempered by the knowledge that his parents had lived full lives. However, the death at age twenty of his first-born son, Yves, opened a whole new dimension of sorrow. On October 29, 1935 the young man succumbed after an eleven-year struggle with tuberculosis. Massignon telegraphed and wrote the news to his friends, his sorrow eloquent in its simplicity, "Yves died yesterday morning, at two-thirty, his hands clasped in mine."[32] He was deeply affected by the loss and in an explicit reference to Abraham, often spoke "of the son God did not give back."

Using the notes Yves had gathered for a study of the French Canadians in the Saint Jean Valley of Maine and Eastern Canada, he summarized his son's research in an article and thereby wrote his eulogy, "the sustained study [of the Acadians and Canadians] had thoroughly educated him in how to surmount the long trial of his own suffering." Massignon recounted that the August before his death, Yves had confided to his father how he identified with the patience of this people, a cultural minority in a foreign land: "betrayed, forgotten, oppressed, they did not blaspheme, or despair; they did not revolt but remained patient; they maintained their confidence, and they could not be deformed; I identified myself with them; they became my own; my life is for them."[33] Massignon selected his article about his son's research for inclusion in *Parole donnée* under the rubric "Non-Violent Resistance." To the original piece he added a footnote stating that Yves's sister, Geneviève, had followed in her brother's footsteps and chosen as topics for her two doctoral theses "the French dialect of Acadia" and "popular tales of Acadia." Massignon himself, during his 1952 trip to the United States, visited as a kind of pilgrimage the area in northern Maine studied by his son and also Louisiana. In these regions settled by the French, "he became recollected and meditated on the example of this oldest son, 'who had gone before him' in death."[34]

Less than a year later, Massignon's sister, Henriette Girard, died April 26, 1936, at the age of forty-eight. Nevertheless, personal loss interrupted neither the steady pace of Massignon's professional life nor his preoccupation with situations in the Islamic world. The Maghreb remained an ongoing preoccupation even at the height of Yves's illness. A short article in the October 1935 issue of the journal *Esprit* posed the dilemma of the Christian conscience faced with the consequences of French colonialism in Algeria. Massignon sketched two scenarios. One concerned a young man about to assume his first post as a civil servant in Algeria who wondered "how will I be able to reconcile the colonialist directives of my supervisors with my obligations as a Catholic." The other concerned a young Algerian who, after spending some time in France, wrote Massignon: "I cannot . . . forgive you this one thing, that I loved you, you who were humane to me, because in so doing you were my worst enemy, causing me to risk losing my hatred for a race and culture different from my own and one capable of giving my people only ruin and despair."[35]

The response to the first case was not cause for "despairing," since it involved well-known, if not always practiced, Christian principles of "humble works of mercy," and Massignon felt that such action extended well beyond the Christian community properly speaking. However the second case, that of the young North African, evoked an anguished observation, and it reveals how simultaneously implicated and powerless Massignon felt about the ongoing situation in Algeria:

> The best among us are not only hostages but also accomplices in the abuses and illegal profits our colonists have endured because of our country. In spite of ourselves, we are an integral part of an implacable machinery, of an inert mass that is becoming heavier and heavier. Those who have come to France, whether to blow up all this machinery or to try and make it backfire against us, must understand that the true secret of our momentary force depends on the survival of the effects of a superior spiritual discipline. It is reserved not for Europe alone, today less than half Christianized, but for all those colonized, upright people whose suffering caused by our crimes predisposes [them] to practice [it] better than we can.[36]

The pattern of winter travel to the Middle East remained sacred. Massignon returned to Cairo in the winter of 1936 to work on the Arab dictionary and, of course, to see Mary Kahil. Together the two renewed their vow of *badaliya* at Damietta. That same year Massignon met the future Paul VI, then Monsignor Montini. The meeting was auspicious in its consequences: Montini became a friend, a member of the Badaliya when it was officially constituted, and later the pope who, at the Second Vatican Council, promoted understanding between Christians and Muslims.

No doubt because of his commitment to the Muslim world and in contrast to his passionate involvement after World War II in the political upheavals of the Middle East and North Africa, Massignon remained seemingly distant from the political turmoil that began to swirl across the European continent in the mid-thirties. As the communist regime in the Soviet Union and fascist governments in Germany and Italy increasingly darkened European politics, other Catholic intellectuals such as Mauriac and Maritain initiated public responses to the worsening political situation. However, Massignon's name rarely appears with those of his compatriots. One exception involved the Spanish civil war, a subject of considerable debate and division in Massignon's circle.

The victory of the Spanish Frente Popular in February 1936 raised fears that the Church would be eradicated in Spain and that international communism would triumph. Such fears were intensifed in the first days of the popular uprisings in July when thousands of priests and religious were murdered. The Catholics in Massignon's circle protested the atrocities with almost a single voice. However, their censure extended also to Franco when the latter's forces retaliated with atrocities such as the massacre of republicans in the bullring of Badajoz on August 15, the feast of the Assumption, and the saturation bombing of Spanish cities. Maritain and others publicly denounced the bombings of Madrid in March 1937; the bombing of Guernica, April 26, prompted Maritain to draw up a manifesto "For the Basque People" and circulate it for signatures.

Nevertheless, like other groups French Catholics were divided, and Franco's forces had their sympathizers, among them Paul Claudel. That same spring Claudel wrote a poem "To the Spanish Martyrs"; he had been inspired by a papal declaration that the priests and religious killed during the early days of the popular uprising would henceforth be included in the official list of Church martyrs. Besides celebrating the new martyrs, the poem also expressed allegiance to Franco, although the latter remained unnamed. In his journal Claudel noted with satisfaction that his poem had generated "enormous publicity and that it was the thing which had touched off the letter from the bishops and the whole movement that followed. . . . I am rewriting my project of a letter from French intellectuals to Spanish intellectuals."[37] However, when he approached Massignon for his signature, the latter refused to sign.[38] The episode provides another instance of the increasing distance between their political outlooks.

The views of Massignon, for his part, were much more closely aligned with those of Catholics and others who opposed the war. He recalled how both he and Jean-Richard Bloch, once companions as army draftees, had stood "side by side to protest against Guernica."[39] Many of those with whom he aligned himself in this struggle joined him sixteen years later when successive crises in Morocco and Algeria again divided French public opinion. Early in the summer of 1937 Maritain helped found the Committee for Civil and Religious Peace in Spain in an attempt to move beyond hardened positions on both sides and end the killing. The committee, with French, British, and Spanish branches, hoped to alleviate the consequences of the war for the general population and influence public opinion in such a way that other governments might be encouraged to mediate the dispute. Along with notables such as Georges Duhamel, Gabriel Marcel, Jacques Maritain, François Mauriac, and Emmanuel Mounier, Massignon sat on the board of directors of the French committee.[40] Maritain outlined its purpose in the introduction to a pamphlet he wrote explaining to Americans his position on the war: "It seems to these diverse personalities that if Spain is to be saved both from the risk of communist hegemony inspired by Moscow and the risk of totalitarian hegemony inspired by Italian fascism and German national socialism, this can only in fact be realized thanks to a peace based on reconciliation."[41] The primary focus on peaceful resolution echoed what Massignon had already learned from Gandhi's example and prefigured his later positions in regard to Algeria, Morocco, and the plight of the Palestinians.

That same year the Vatican ordered *Sept,* a modest weekly newspaper published by the Dominicans, to cease publication because it opposed the war. François Mauriac spearheaded a move to resurrect the paper under lay leadership and a new name, *Le Temps Présent.* In the first issue, November 5, 1937, he wrote an editorial and presented a list of collaborators which read like the "who's who" of Christian intellectuals. It included Karl Barth, Georges

Bernanos, Charles Du Bos, Henri Ghéon, Pierre-Henri Simon, Jacques Madaule, Gabriel Marcel, Maritain, Massignon, Mauriac, and Emmanuel Mounier, founder and editor of *Esprit.* Only Claudel had refused.[42] If the alliance between Church authorities and Franco was the primary target of the paper, this same group also criticized colonial abuses in the Maghreb, as they would again many years and another war later.

During this period, Massignon wrote articles and took positions that prefigured his later activism, but any political involvement remained secondary to his work as scholar and teacher. In 1937 he signed a contract with the Gallimard publishing house for a second edition of the *Hallaj,* which ultimately appeared only in 1975, thirteen years after his death. By a strange coincidence the English version of that second edition indirectly owes its existence to a conference Massignon began attending that same year. He first lectured at the Eranos Conference in Ascona, Switzerland in 1937, where he participated regularly for years, along with Carl Jung and others. There he met Paul and Mary Mellon, who became interested in his work and decided to help underwrite the English edition of the *Hallaj* through the Bollingen series of Princeton Press.

As 1938 began, Massignon was again able to return to Cairo and renew the vow of *badaliya* at Damietta. Once back in Paris near the end of February, he voiced to Kahil the familiar lament about his overcrowded life, "The atmosphere of my life in Paris is so overcrowded with parasite cares that I often need to turn eastward in prayer in order to take heart."[43] Yet his multiple involvements reveal that he thrived on activity and drove himself relentlessly. Besides his professional commitments, he received a steady stream of visitors at home. Monteil provides a portrait of Massignon during this period, recounting how, like so many others, he himself "took the path of the rue Monsieur, for the first time." Like them, he entered the study overlooking the street and across from the then Benedictine monastery and Huysmans' one-time home: "In a little office flooded with papers and books was seated a slender figure clothed in black and enveloped that day in a kind of brown shawl . . . On his emaciated and weatherbeaten face, spirituality alternated with humor and intelligence."[44]

October found Massignon in Rome where, in the midst of a congress, he found time "to see at [his] convenience several intelligent and upright prelates." (The adjectives are significant because Massignon did not automatically associate these qualities with clerics.) He pressed Cardinal Tisserant to complete an Eastern canon law code and found that Monsignor Montini, then the deputy of the future Pius XII, Cardinal Pacelli, "understood well the case of Hallaj."[45]

In November of that year he wrote Kahil in response to her suggestion that he, together with his family, spend six months of 1939 in Cairo, presumably as part of his annual winter trip. His comments reveal once more that, whatever ambivalence he felt about his life in Paris, Massignon never seriously considered walking away from professional and family considerations in order to alleviate the strain:

> About your suggestion of coming to Cairo for six months with my family, that would destroy the future of my children and force me to hand over a part of my teaching in Paris to my colleagues, who would hang on to it. And the life of Cairo would be impossible for my wife and children, who would be bored at the end of two weeks, or else attach themselves to whom? [46]

At the same time, awareness of family obligations did not prevent Massignon from a certain distaste for the whole question of money, a discomfort he could hardly resolve to his satisfaction, given those same family obligations. Because of his pronounced asceticism, he spent next to nothing on himself. By this time his eternal black suit, faded trench coat, and beret had become his trademark, while by all accounts food was simply a necessity for remaining alive. Yet, since he had inherited property from his parents and, as an eminent professor, received a comfortable salary, his relative affluence made him uncomfortable. In that same letter to Kahil there is question of Massignon giving ten conferences on the history of Muslim philosophy during the forthcoming two-month stay in Cairo. Aside from the time involved in such a commitment, he was worried about being paid by both the university and the academy:

> Yesterday I saw Taha; I explained to him that it was impossible for me, what with cashing in already from the Academy during these two months, to take the 360 pounds he was offering me for these conferences at the University. That would have perverted my life and our friendship. I don't want, either up close or from afar, to imitate the chase after the dollar of so many Europeans and Frenchmen . . . Taha understood—he will give me a sum for each conference—and I will only do five or six, as I wish. My friend, I would like to be naked. I vomit over these money questions (alas . . .).

Even as the threat of war loomed ever more menacingly at the beginning of 1939, Massignon made his annual trip to Egypt and the Middle East. André Gide makes interesting mention of a visit with him in his *Souvenirs d'Egypte*. Massignon showed Gide the city from the heights of a neighboring monastery, took him on a tour of the mosques, and walked with him through the old city. More significantly, because it suggests Massignon's ability to welcome and dialogue with people very different from himself, Gide noted that "upon returning to the hotel, we talked for almost an hour, much more intimately than I would have believed possible. But already in Paris, and from a very first meeting, we broached the most serious subjects."[47] Ever the faithful pilgrim, Massignon also visited the tomb of Hallaj in Baghdad during his second-to-last extended stay in the Middle East before the outbreak of war.

Massignon frequently performed diplomatic functions for France in the Middle East. In October 1939 he returned to Cairo along with Maxime Weygand, the ill-fated general who less than a year later would see the French army defeated by the Nazis. That eventuality seemed remote as the two represented France at the marriage of the shah of Iran to King Farouk's sister. A story told by a scholar friend about Massignon at this event illustrates how single-minded he could be. Over the years he had acquired an uncanny ability to utter statements which his listeners found at best disconcerting. Based on profound conviction and drawn from somewhere deep within, such declarations either had no bearing on the situation at hand, involved intimate self-revelation, or inflamed opposition because of their severity. In this instance the effect was highly amusing. After the wedding ceremony, the guests formed two lines for the final procession headed by the young couple; then followed the reigning shah and his wife; the mother of the bride, the queen of Egypt; and other dignitaries from around the world:

> Before the procession, I found myself behind General Weygand and the French minister and next to Louis Massignon. As the procession was slow in starting, Massignon was talking to me about the Gospel, the love of God and the Samaritan woman in such passionate terms that he ended by shouting, "Don't forget; the prostitutes are the ones who will enter first into the kingdom of heaven." General Weygand and M. Bodard turned around abruptly.[48]

Massignon would make only one more winter journey to the Middle East before the Second World War cut him off from that beloved world for five years. By early 1940, with Eastern Europe already overrun, France nervously awaited the seemingly inevitable invasion of its territory. The so-called "phoney war" had begun, and Massignon, now almost fifty-seven years old, was mobilized along with his son Daniel.[49] On March 20, 1940, shortly after Massignon returned from that last trip to Cairo, Vincent Monteil visited him and recounted that his friend was "in anguish over the destiny of his homeland."[50] Writing years later about that same visit, Monteil stated, "We talked about Morocco and the war. Accompanying me to the door of his apartment, my friend said, "My homeland is the Arab world.'" Evidently Monteil felt the comment needed explanation because he added, "Of course, he was talking about his 'spiritual' country, and this was not restrictive, because no one was more attached than he to 'a certain idea of France' . . ."[51]

Indeed, on the basis of his military service alone, Massignon amply demonstrated his devotion to France. Once again in the army, he was assigned to his rank as head of a colonial battalion within the overseas section of headquarters; there he served as an adjutant to the writer Jean Giraudoux in the ministry of information. However one senses from what is known about Massignon during this period, that in contrast to his passionate involvement in later events in the Middle East, the prospect of another devastating conflict within his lifetime evoked a certain fatalistic resignation. Beyond his awareness born of experience about the destruction and suffering to come, his outlook can be attributed to several causes. Massignon's emotional, religious, and intellectual life was nourished primarily through his contact with the Arab world, and hostilities would sever that lifeline. To this prospect must be added his deepening attraction to nonviolence as a response to oppression of all sorts. In a segment ultimately omitted from the introduction to *Parole donnée*, Massignon explained that his experience during the debacle of the French defeat by the Germans confirmed him in the stance of nonviolence which Gandhi's example made so compelling.[52]

The culmination of the drama that began with the German invasion of France came for Massignon in June 1940, when his unit was forced back to Courtine, a military base and town northwest of Bordeaux. There he escaped, ultimately reaching Bordeaux and the remnants of the French army under General Weygand. The latter, considering that further resistance was hopeless, refused to have him leave for Algiers. Petain signed the armistice with the Germans on June 22, and on June 28, Massignon was designated to hand over the keys of Dax, a town near Bordeaux. He refused, a gesture he considered "his sole act of national 'resistance.'" That same day the occupying army consigned him to the barracks at Mont-de-Marsan, a nearby military town, and confiscated his revolver, the last weapon he ever carried. Massignon eventually succeeded in making his way east to the free zone. According to the account omitted from the introduction to *Parole donnée*, his will to escape had been motivated by the desire "to save his notes on Hallaj, the single precious deposit which pushed him to survive the disaster." Then, heading north in civilian dress, he reached the occupied zone via Clermont-Ferrand,

July 27, the feast of the Seven Sleepers and "decided to wall himself up in silence, mourning in Paris."[53]

Indeed, silence in the public forum seemingly constituted Massignon's response during the war, even as he pursued his regular rhythm of teaching and research. Daily life continued, although the prevailing atmosphere among his peers can be sensed from Claudel's brief mention of seeing them in October 1942, "three ravaged and tragic faces: Duhamel, Massignon, Dullin."[54] Unlike Claudel, Massignon gave no sign of supporting Petain and the Vichy government. If he aided the Resistance, that fact is not known, but it appears doubtful since he had espoused nonviolence. Moreover, as he recalled years later to Monteil, "Gandhi condemned all clandestine activity . . ."[55]

During the war years, Massignon's scholarship and classes reflected his deepening interest in eschatology: Shi'ite themes and the legend of the Seven Sleepers were recurring topics. In 1943 he succeeded in having the statues of the Badaliya union of prayer provisionally approved by Church authorities. However, contact with Mary Kahil was interrupted and travel to the Middle East, impossible. The health of his two surviving children preoccupied him because both became ill as living conditions in Paris gradually worsened under the Occupation. Above all, Massignon was lonely, cut off from his Muslim colleagues and friends such as Jacques Maritain, who spent the war years in the United States. The horror reached him personally: his childhood friend, the eminent Sinologist Henri Maspero, was deported and died in Buchenwald March 17, 1945. An excerpt of a letter written to Mary Kahil several months after the Liberation of Paris in August 1944 gives some idea of Massignon's suffering during the years of Occupation and war:

> it is certainly into death that this terrible divine trial has made me enter little by little, along with my unhappy country, and I have suffered in all those who have been killed, raped, sullied, wounded, and mutilated through the fathomless bestiality of beings who for the most part received Christian baptism—supreme horror! I suffer

in so many friends who are still deported, more or less desperate prisoners, and because of so many compatriots whom the enemy occupation has intoxicated to the point of making them into horrible torturers, who now apply the pagan law of talion. However, through the depths of my separation from the Arab and Muslim countries where I wish to die, through a separation whose end I don't yet foresee, by inflicting this on me, God has discovered such an atrocious way of making me suffer that I can't conceive how any consolation could put my heart at peace. And this in addition to the illness which is raging, caused by deprivations of all sorts.[56]

As Massignon kept his long and silent vigil, the world was inexorably remade. After the war, emerging conflicts involving both the Arab world and France challenged his lifelong commitment to the Muslim world and his love of country. New political configurations would elicit from him a new and intense involvement in political issues. In writing and speaking to a postwar world whose conflicts touched him deeply and personally, he would utilize the intricate web of his thought and symbol system, carefully fashioned by religious faith, personal experience, and years of scholarship. In retrospect, it would seem that the first sixty years of his life were an apprenticeship for the last nineteen years.

SEVEN

Conflict in the Middle East

After the Liberation Massignon began to travel again, and the familiar prewar rhythm of teaching, writing, and winter sojourns in the Arab world resumed. Friendships and correspondence interrupted by the war were renewed. He returned to the Middle East in the winter of 1945 when the interim French government sent him on a marathon, six-month mission with a mandate to renew France's historic cultural ties with various countries in the region. The itinerary included Egypt, Palestine, Syria, Lebanon, Turkey, Iraq, Iran, and Afghanistan. He was also invited to India where he had hoped to see Mahatma Gandhi, but the latter was not in New Delhi during the June 1945 visit.

In Cairo, Massignon saw Mary Kahil and soon became involved in projects she had pursued during the war. On December 5, 1941, she had bought an abandoned Anglican Church in the middle of Cairo, then had it refurbished and consecrated in the Melkite rite of the Greek Catholic Church under the name, Sainte Marie de la Paix. In an adjacent building she and Massignon together founded the Dar-el-Salam Center, whose purpose was to facilitate encounters and exchange between Christians and Muslims. An annual cycle of conferences was begun, certain of which were published under the title *Mardis de dar-el-Salam*. The work, funded by Kahil, continued until 1976.[1]

Another project concerned the Badaliya, created when Massignon and Kahil rediscovered each other in 1934. Together they had drawn up statutes for this prayer group which formalized their mutual self-offering at Damietta, and in 1943 these had been circulated to a limited group of friends in Cairo. Finally, in January 1947, the statutes were officially approved by the Church, in the person of Archbishop Kamel Medawar, then the auxiliary to the Greek Catholic patriarch. The annual Christmas letter to the Badaliya, which Massignon wrote until his death, reflected both his ongoing commitment to the Muslims and the evolving expression of that commitment as crises unfolded in the Middle East and the Maghreb. For if Massignon's life did in some ways revert to long-established patterns, both the aftermath of the war and renewed conflict in the Arab-speaking world changed it forever.

In his own surroundings Massignon was faced with a society needing to be rebuilt in the wake of the Nazi occupation. Predictably, his response was expressed initially through the written word. During the war Marcel Moré, a Catholic layman, had met regularly with Massignon and a group of intellectuals of different faith traditions; many of these same people had worked on *Esprit,* which was suppressed during the Occupation. Together this group laid plans for a new journal of religious thought to be directed by laymen.

The first *cahier* of *Dieu vivant* appeared after the Liberation, in April 1945, with Maurice de Gandillac, Massignon, and Moré as its first codirectors. Gandillac would withdraw as codirector in 1946 because he "often felt ill at ease," seeing "Moré's strong personality sometimes at odds with Massignon's." After his replacement, Brice Parain, left, Moré and Massignon remained codirectors until the latter quit in 1950, undoubtedly because their differences had become too great. When the journal ended in 1955, Jules Monchanin, a frequent contributor and friend of Massignon, mused: "*Dieu vivant* where I published four articles has ceased publication. Moré has an irascible temperament and broke off with several of his collaborators. . . . Is that why?"[2] However, in 1945, the project was in its beginnings, and Moré's introduction to the first issue outlined the circumstances of its creation: "The *cahiers* of *Dieu vivant* were born in a period that recalls the darkest pages of the Apocalypse because of the violence and extent of the catyclysm unleashed, and likewise because of the atmosphere of spiritual death that is suffocating the world."[3]

Massignon had been increasingly attracted by eschatalogical themes throughout the 1930s, as evidenced not only in his reflections on the meaning of history but also by his growing interest in Shi'ite formulations of Islam. The enormity of the recent conflict had certainly reinforced the attraction such themes held for him. Since the carnage of the war surpassed any kind of human measure, only descriptions linked to and ultimately resolved by a transcendent order seemed an appropriate response to what he had lived. It was not surprising, then, that he contributed to a journal which asserted that divine intervention in human history constituted the world's only hope. Such a position is theologically conservative, because it tends to reduce human responsibility for resolving human problems and to place them primarily in the hands of an immutable God. In light of Massignon's fiercely independent thought, unhindered by confessional, philosophical, or political categories, his collaboration with such a journal might seem surprising. Yet certain affinities beyond the sympathy for eschatological themes drew him; he shared *Dieu vivant*'s mistrust of science, long a trait of conservative Catholics and articulated by Moré:

> The world of human servitude and destruction cannot be combatted by more refined and subtle techniques, but broken open only through the irruption in the visible world of an invisible world rooted in Transcendence: the one belonging to the Poor One and the Eternal Beggar of eschatological holiness.[4]

The war arsenal of the belligerents demonstrated how Western technology had so refined the art of destruction that the capability now existed to destroy the planet. However, the reservations Massignon held about the ability of technology to improve the human condition antedated the war. He had seen firsthand how the inroads of Western, industrial economies had disrupted and impoverished the traditional societies of the Middle East and how the policies of the former towards the region were increasingly dictated by their ever-growing dependence on oil.

Massignon published five articles in *Dieu vivant* during the five years he was associated with the journal.[5] His first two contributions reflect the theology which undergirded the writings chosen for publication. The material of "Hallaj, Mystic and Martyr of Islam," came from Massignon's dissertation. The parallelism he had seen between the life of the Sufi and that of Jesus was based on a theology compatible with that of *Dieu Vivant*. In a world torn apart by the inveterate human capacity for destruction, the cross of Christ stands at the center of history as humanity's single hope. The Christian, like Jesus, must be prepared to die for his beliefs, and holiness is intimately related to suffering and asceticism. Human effort of itself cannot effect positive change in the world, which comes only from direct intervention by God.

Massignon's second contribution, "Our Lady of La Salette," can be understood within the context of this same attitude. Its underlying view of history opposes human sinfulness to Divine transcendence and to those intermittent revelations of God's presence that modify the course of world events. In a February 1949 letter to Claudel, Massignon takes this same position and asserts that the evils of the modern world are overcome supernaturally, in this instance through the witness of Melanie, the seer of the apparitions at La Salette. The comments occur after Massignon mentions how sick he was while making the way of the cross in Jerusalem the previous November. He implicitly links his physical weakness to the cross of Jesus and juxtaposes both to what he perceives as the failures of both Jews and Christians to deal with the Palestinian refugee problem caused by the first Arab-Israeli war. The next paragraph suggests that any solution could only come from the supernatural valorization of suffering:

> I was in Jerusalem for the thirteenth time, on November 28. The base of both lungs already blocked by pneumonia, I did the "Via Dolorosa," all the while gasping under the sympathetic gaze of two

policemen—my heart wrenched by the ignominy of the Jews and the Christians of the West.

In this terrible time of planetary suicide—when the modernists dance with evolutionary joy to the flute of P. Teilhard and Emmanuel Mounier—I send you this photo of the face of a skeleton marked by the terrible joy of the Divine Test, Melanie at her 1918 exhumation by the bishop of Altamura, fourteen years after her saintly death. This extraordinary photo [. . .] is sustaining me at this moment, like a sound of the Church triumphant over and above the radios paid for by Truman or by Stalin: "*Solve vincla reis!*"[6]

An eschatalogical focus that discounts the impact of human effort necessarily distances one from the ever-shifting issues and crises of the world. When seen against the backdrop of final divine intervention, any human response to such crises, other than that of prayer and suffering, ultimately becomes meaningless. Massignon's affiliation with *Dieu vivant* might seem to foreshadow how he would respond to religious and political issues in the postwar era. Harpigny notes that he could have become "a man outside his own time," someone who, as he advanced into his sixties, would continue to write and teach but who would not examine his ideas within the context of a rapidly changing world.[7] His involvement would be limited to prayer, suffering, and occasional commentary on the evils of a world gone awry. However, such would not be the case, and several factors could explain why Massignon did not become disengaged from the crises that almost immediately began to swirl around him after the war.

Both the underlying premises of his thought and his own personal history of devotion to Islam committed Massignon to being intensely involved in the world of his time. Although he thought of history as tending towards a finality known only to God and therefore possessing an eschatological dimension, the "transhistorical continuity" by which the end point was reached was populated by heroic persons whose suffering in mystical substitution for others

redeemed their era. Formulated in this manner, such a notion precluded abstractions, because it involved concrete persons and a
lived history. If the doctrine could be considered abstractly within
a certain nineteenth-century Catholic theology of atonement, for
Massignon it became a concrete reality from the moment of his conversion, when, beginning with Huysmans, he had perceived intercessors in his life.

Moreover, mystical substitution was seen by Massignon as the
ultimate expression of the hospitality he had found in Islam before
his conversion and which became a paradigm for his own Christian
life. He understood from his own experience that the practice of
hospitality implied putting oneself in the other's place and necessarily led to compassion for others' suffering. Most radically, such a
stance could lead to substitution for another. Thus, his self-offering
for Islam expressed a personal religious commitment founded on
experience. After discovering Hallaj and returning to Christianity
Massignon had uncovered other figures in both Islam and Christianity whose self-offering imaged his own. Salman Pak, Francis of
Assisi at Damietta, and the Seven Sleepers all belonged to this network which expressed his vow of mystical substitution for Muslims
and the hoped-for outcome of that vow, the rapprochement of
Christianity and Islam.

However, almost immediately after the war, events in both the
Middle East and the Maghreb seemed to belie such hopes in either
the religious or political spheres. In Algeria the right to vote had
been extended to all Muslim men in 1944. This step towards political parity by assimilation would have been welcomed by the Muslim
elite in the 1930s, but after the war it was received with indifference.
In Syria although the French Mandate was finally about to end, independence had been achieved at the cost of blood. Syrian and
Lebanese nationalists had demonstrated when the French were un-
willing to grant independence prior to negotiating a treaty. When
protest demonstrations erupted in May 1946, French forces retaliated May 29 and 30 with an air attack on Damascus. Commenting
on these situations to Monteil in June, during their first conversa-

tion after the war, Massignon expressed solidarity with the emerging Muslim consciousness in Algeria, Syria, and Morocco and criticized the obtuseness and foot dragging of French colonial policy:

> When will we stop exporting "impossible" notions? Our own Joan of Arc and our Revolution formed nationalists here for independence. Instead of repression, as pernicious in Sétif [a department of Algeria and scene of anti-French demonstrations in 1945] as in Damascus, we needed to be sincere. We should not have waited until 1944 to give the right to vote to the Algerians and to understand in Morocco that the circumcized Berbers have at least a kind of "baptism of desire" which draws them to solidarity with Muslims. In Morocco as elsewhere, the protectorate is outdated: why didn't we make a treaty with Syria in time![8]

Formulated initially as compassion and mystical substitution, the response of Massignon to the increasing turmoil in the postwar Arab world expressed itself in various ways. The Badaliya provided a union of prayer on behalf of issues involving Muslims in the Middle East, France, and the Maghreb. Another strategy consisted in founding or participating in groups which defended the political and religious rights of Muslims in France and the emerging countries of the Maghreb. In this context his keen intellect and forceful presence as a public speaker allowed him to articulate his passionately held convictions. Some would discount Massignon; others would be angered by him; however, the sheer force of his mind and personality meant, to the frustration of some, that he could never be ignored. He became a public figure in ways he had not been before and thereby exposed himself to all the criticism and even danger inherent in such a position.

In 1947 Massignon, along with his friends, Jean Scelles and André de Peretti, created the Comité chrétien d'Entente France-Islam. For a generation now, Massignon had vehemently defended the rights of colonized peoples who, in his view, had initially accepted Western colonizers as guests in the name of sacred hospitality. The *comité* gave him a more focused way of speaking out at a time when the full force of independence movements was beginning to be felt. The move further distanced him politically from Paul Claudel and the Catholic right but placed him in contact with a wide range of people concerned about the deteriorating situation in the French colonies of the Maghreb. The June 17, 1947, manifesto of the group reflected Massignon's concern that Muslim demands for social justice be honored and also his conviction that possibilities for mutual understanding still existed:

> We know the superhuman confidence in God's judgment that inspires the Muslim world right now, what with its social demands misunderstood and scoffed at everywhere. It will not be said that Christendom remains deaf to this appeal for sovereign justice because it has ceased believing in it. As Christians in France we want to be the first to bear witness: to commit ourselves to work for loyal civic and social understanding with the Muslims: for our common destiny.[9]

Massignon considered that witnessing to the truth through groups like France-Islam constituted the most potent arm of all in the fight for justice. Over the next fifteen years he would participate in several such groups, and the example of Mahatma Gandhi would influence him profoundly. Since 1921 he had been familiar with the teaching of *satyagraha* or nonviolent proclamation of the truth in the face of adversaries, a stance founded on personal self-discipline and respect for that adversary. Now the example of Gandhi's own practice of *satyagraha* in the struggle for the independence of India seemed to indicate the path he himself should follow.

"A very curious incident" in 1948 was reported by Massignon in order to illustrate Gandhi's decisive impact on him in the postwar period of decolonization. A new statute concerning Algeria had been passed in 1947, and Massignon had participated in its redaction. Although not radically different from the 1944 law, the new statute did provide for the election of an Algerian assembly with certain powers. Most importantly, the bill implicitly recognized the uniqueness of Algeria and its Muslim population, a position in marked contrast to the colonial policy of assimilation. Massignon recounted how, prior to the final vote on the bill, the minister of the interior, Edouard Dépreux, had cited Massignon's name to the two French assemblies "to back up his [Dépreux's] promise: justice would be done, our word kept both to the Arabic language and Islam."[10] However, a new governor general opposed to Algerian nationalism delayed the election of the assembly mandated by the new law. Massignon found himself in a difficult position "The guaranty was ridiculed, and I did not feel the least courage to come forth and protest as a *satyagrahi*." However, in Egypt pilgrims on their way to Mecca had heard Algerian complaints about the French breach of promise, "It was said that perhaps I would not turn a deaf ear indefinitely to the pleas of the oppressed." In February 1947, during his annual visit to Cairo, Massignon went to see the sheik of Al Azhar, Shannawi. During their conversation the Algerian question was never raised:

> Notwithstanding, Shannawi planned to circulate an interview the next day, in which he had me responding about the brutalities of the state of siege endured by the Muslims in Algeria and saying that I would work to make them stop (sic). Immediately, there were cries of alarm from the French Information Service in Cairo, cabling Paris against me and a call from the ambassador who asked me to retract. Literally I should have done so, having said nothing of the sort. Morally that option was closed to me. Shannawi had read in my heart my silent shame at having tolerated for so long this behavior of my own people in the land of Joan of Arc. I limited myself to having the press services of the embassy circulate a "parallel communique" to Shannawi's, stating only what I had said, and silent about what I had not said. Shannawi accused me of cowardice. But the truth of his point had sunk in: henceforth, I would act publicly, even if I were accused of the deed of Ham [treason against one's country].[11]

Massignon was true to his word and spoke out passionately and tirelessly for the rest of his life. Gandhi's teaching provided guidance as he became personally and deeply involved in successive conflicts, first, between the Palestinians and the Israelis over the creation of Israel, then between the French government and the sultan of Morocco, and finally between France and Algeria over that country's independence. The power of the teaching was heightened by the parallels he discovered between the situation faced by Gandhi during the struggle for India's independence and the political situations in Palestine and Algeria. In all three instances Massignon saw that colonial interests were at stake, and that hostility between diverse ethnic groups was a key factor. The most overt examples of Gandhi's influence occurred after 1954, as the Algerian conflict erupted into violence. However, Massignon's increasing activism and references to Gandhi were already evident in 1948, the year of the latter's assassination and the first Israeli-Arab war, thus two years before Massignon ended his association with *Dieu vivant*.

It was a critical and violence-filled time. In February 1947 the Palestinian question had been referred by Britain to the fledgling United Nations. At the end of November 1947 the U.N. voted to end the British mandate and partition Palestine into two states, one Jewish and one Arab; British troops were to be evacuated before August 1 of the following year. Britain refused to be associated with this plan and announced in January 1948 that it was ending the British mandate in Palestine on May 15 at midnight. The armed confrontations between Arabs and Jews, which had gone on for some time, escalated into war while Palestinians by the thousands either fled the region or were relocated. On April 2, after returning from the Middle East, Massignon worried aloud to Vincent Monteil about the deteriorating situation and the widespread arms trafficking.[12] Civilian casualties were mounting, whole villages destroyed, their inhabitants either killed or displaced. The day before the British mandate was to end, on May 14, 1948, the National Jewish Council proclaimed the independence of the state of Israel; the next day the armies of the Arab League invaded Israel. The war, the terrorist attacks on both sides, and the plight of the refugees, most of them Palestinians, elicited impassioned and anguished pleas from

Massignon to end the violence and work for mutual understanding and cooperation. He called on Jews and Arabs, as Semitic peoples descended from Abraham, to understand that because the future of both groups lay in Asia, they should together resist Anglo-American influence, share the Holy Land as their joint home, and protect its integrity as the religious space sacred to Jews, Christians, and Muslims.

Massignon was often accused during his lifetime of being anti-Semitic because of his unwavering support for the Palestinians and opposition to Zionism. Anti-Semitic he was not, but he came to equate Zionism with French practices in North Africa: the movement excluded Palestinians in the same way that French colonialism denied benefits to Muslims. For this reason he adamantly opposed the notion of a separate Jewish state which disenfranchised Palestinians. In 1949 as the refugee problem was becoming more and more acute, he wrote that he had favored Israel's desire to return to the land of its origins: "Israel wanted to return to the land, and from 1918 onward I supported that aspiration, but it was not in order to make other Displaced Persons! Because ultimately one can't say that 700,000 Arabs are not Palestinians."[13]

From around 1924 Massignon had distanced himself from Zionism when he saw that some of its leaders like Vladimir Jabotinsky (1880–1940) advocated massive Jewish immigration and competition rather than cooperation with the existing Arab population in Palestine. His objections were many. He felt that secular Zionist goals for a Jewish state were divorced from Jewish religious history and ignored the validity of Muslim claims to the same territory, claims based on their own religious heritage and centuries of life on the land. Moreover, the newcomers had European roots and were far removed from the culture of the Middle East, shared by both Sephardic Jews and Arabs, a factor which aggravated tensions from the outset and diminished possibilities for mutual understanding. Beginning in the late nineteenth century many of these immigrants had come to Palestine in order to escape persecution. While sympathizing with their plight, Massignon noted that their tortured history caused them to be understandably suspicious in their new land of those whom they found already settled there for centuries. In a move of instinctive self-protection the newcomers then inevitably duplicated the self-contained life of their former homes and sealed themselves off from any exchange with the Arab population. Massignon had observed this phenomenon over the years, and a 1946 article summarized his dismay: "One might have hoped, and I have been among those who did, that the remaking of the new Hebrew reality in Palestine would be done by taking into account the shared Judeo-Arab elements of acculturation (familiar to the great Jewish authors of the Middle Ages, who wrote in Arabic), but it has been done within a Germano-American direction which is disquieting."[14]

Some critics felt that Massignon distanced himself from the struggle of his Jewish contemporaries and that, in his dedication to the Muslims and their interests, he failed to grasp the reality of a Jewish community decimated by war and genocide. Thus, in evaluating the uncertain beginnings of the new state, he was considered too harsh. In the context of an imaginary letter of tribute to Massignon after his death, his old friend Gabriel Marcel summarized well these reservations:

> I would not be completely sincere if I did not admit to you that the severity of your judgments sometimes troubled me. I am thinking very specifically of the severity you demonstrated towards the State of Israel after the Judeo-Arab war of 1947. Generally speaking you estimated that the act of taking over (in part) Palestine by the Jews, made possible by American gold, had occurred in radically impure conditions and constituted a flagrant injustice towards the Arabs, who thus found themselves expelled from a land they had occupied for centuries. From my own reflections, it was impossible to subscribe to this condemnation. What alone mattered in my eyes was that, after the extermination of six million Jews, the survivors could finally find permanent refuge, which doesn't mean, however, that I am insensitive to the misery of refugees camped in Jordan

and elsewhere. Everyone will agree that an injustice exists there which must be remedied; but one must admit that with the Arabs one does not find the minimum good will necessary to begin negotiations with Israel on this point.[15]

According to such criticism, the position of Massignon concerning the Jewish people ignored their actual plight and focused instead either on the origins of Israel in the story of Abraham or else on the future of Israel in the Parousia at the end of time.[16] This kind of atemporal and religious perspective was understandably dismissed as irrelevant by some, especially those involved in mutually exclusive claims to the same land. However, his prophecy that the cultural disparity between Israel and its Arab neighbors portended nothing but conflict has certainly been validated by half a century of unabated terror and hostility in the region.

In the summer of 1948 Massignon wrote numerous articles about the war and the Palestinian plight. His own rhetoric became more impassioned as the situation in the fledgling state deteriorated. One of these articles, "Palestine and Peace with Justice," was composed shortly after the July 17 capture of Nazareth by Israeli forces and published by *Dieu vivant* in December. It reflects both Gandhi's profound influence on Massignon and the extent to which the latter felt that the hostility between Arabs and Jews in Palestine was echoed by the growing impasse in North Africa between French colonists and Algerians. The life of Gandhi and his assassination the previous January had validated Massignon's theory that the intractable conflicts of human history are resolved only through the lives and deaths of holy persons. Only peaceful witness to the truth in the face of opposition—and, most strikingly, death incurred in serving that truth—could break the repeated cycles of human violence. In an effort to promote the teaching of nonviolence, Massignon had reactivated the group Amis de Gandhi the month of the assassination.[17]

The *Dieu vivant* article begins by recalling how years before, in 1921, Massignon had published the "Satyagraha" of Gandhi in the *Revue du monde musulman*. He had been struck then by similarities between Gandhi's notion of civic duty and the Muslim notion of treating the stranger as guest. In both instances one is asked to look beyond differences and find a common basis for solidarity. Behavior then is governed by a law of love which posits the common good as its goal and the family as the archetypal model of how differences are mediated within a community. Rather than seeking vengeance, the wronged family member bears the injustice without rancor, loving the offender and knowing that this response provides the most effective means of ultimately resolving the issue. Within a larger society groups must find ways to implement a like attitude if peace is to be achieved with their neighbors.

Massignon agreed with Gandhi that groups who had long shared the same territory could not ultimately resolve their differences by separating themselves geographically. In August 1947 the latter had opposed the creation of Pakistan as a separate state and for the same reasons had objected to the partition of Palestine. According to Massignon, Gandhi "would have wanted the Jews to reach an understanding, directly and freely, on an equal footing with the Arabs."[18] Killed by a Hindu extremist as he attempted to promote Muslim/Hindu unity, Gandhi exemplified by his own death the ultimate price for peacefully upholding truth even in the face of violent opposition.

Referring to Gandhi within the context of his own notion of sacred hospitality, Massignon adamantly denounced the idea that segregating warring parties (in this case, Jews and Arabs) would resolve the conflict: "It is not permissible to partition, that is, to effect segregation between two momentarily adverse elements, under the pretext that the method of territorial "relocations" would finally lead to an umbrella confederation of the nationalities concentrated each one within its own borders."[19] Only dialogue and an honest effort to understand differences—in a word the hospitality accorded the guest—could replace suspicion and hostility with respect and trust. In this regard he cited and then explained an Arab proverb, "First the neighbor, then the house." Building a house was useless if the location worried the neighbors or the builder ignored them. If the

Jews arriving in Palestine and the Arabs already there were to live together in peace, it was essential that they come to understand their shared history as children of Abraham and respect each other's cultures.

Although the Algerian conflict was at this point six years away, Massignon saw a parallel between the drama unfolding in Palestine and the worsening situation in North Africa: "I well know, alas, that French colonists of Algeria have little desire to apply this proverb vis-à-vis Arabs in North Africa."[20] Muslims and Europeans existed as two separate and increasingly hostile societies, the one poor and the other relatively affluent by comparison. Significantly, the French Algerians had publicly supported the Zionist effort in Palestine and opposed the newly formed Arab League.

If Massignon strongly opposed juridical divisions as a means of resolving conflicts between all groups, his conviction rang out most clearly in regard to the Holy Land: "which should not be an object for the privileged to carve up, but the seamless garment of world-wide reconciliation, a place of intimate sharing among all, and to begin with, among those who have, just the same, more reasons to join with than to hate each other: Semites, Jews and Arabs, sons of Abraham; and Christians, spiritual Semites, who should all of them have renouced the cult of idols."[21] However, his conviction was accompanied by an awareness that the situation in the Holy Land posed serious dilemmas. On the one hand Massignon rec-ognized the legitimate claims of both Jews and Muslims to the same territory. The Jews "had taught the world that salvation comes from them and that for this salvation they had been called out of Chaldea along with Abraham and had received this country forever for him and for all his descendents."[22] The Muslim claim was founded on the night vision of Muhammad, when he was trans-ported to Jerusalem and then to heaven. In memory of this vision Muslims initially worshiped facing north, towards Jerusalem. And when this prayer direction (*qibla*) was changed to the south, to-wards Mecca, it was in memory of Abraham, the common ancestor of both Jews and Muslims.

On the other hand, Massignon considered that the faith community which should have reconciled Muslim and Jewish claims, namely the Christians, had been either prejudiced, too weak politically, or simply too greedy to act as mediators between the other two groups. The history of Christians in the Middle East was clear on this point. The Byzantine rulers had not respected the Jewish heritage; later, under the Ottoman Turks, Arab Christians were a powerless minority; and the Crusaders, attempting to mobilize those same Christians, rapidly became plunderers of booty. After the discovery of America, so-called "Christian" Europe had colonized whole areas and enriched itself, first on gold and slavery and, in the twentieth century, on oil. The foreign policy of the European colonizers, dictated solely by the desire for gain, did not hesitate to play one group against the other. In this regard Massignon had stated as early as 1922 that the British were prime examples of such a strategy:

> [Britain's] invariable policy with respect to the new nationalities of the Middle East, like the one pursued toward Western nationalities a hundred years ago, is a policy of both preserving and splitting up; don't let any of them either perish or triumph, and maintain a clientele with each of them . . . British policy in regard to the religious collectivities of the East parallels the preceding one; it is remarkable to note that *Islam remains for her an issue of external economic policy,* a way of holding on to India and the route to India.[23]

According to Massignon, Britain had inflamed hostility between Arabs and Jews in Palestine just as it had previously done between Hindus and Muslims in India; it had advocated partitioning both countries in order to protect economic interests as the empire declined. Thus, in 1948 Britain was supporting both the Arabs and the Jews in order to maintain her oil interests in the region. Unknowingly or not, both Jews and Arabs were being victimized and the conflict between them, aggravated by the colonial policy pursued by Europe generally; "But, in order to understand that they have been duped, Jews and Arabs must emancipate themselves from the European economic system to which they have been subordinated . . ."[24] The geographical proximity of Jews and Arabs in the Holy Land should unite the two groups to oppose colonial abuses. On another, deeper level the spiritual hunger that had led each to claim the Holy Land as sacred space should guide them both in a shared search for a "higher unity."

Having spoken out against partitioning Palestine and set forth what he considered the legitimate position of both Jews and Arabs, Massignon concluded that any solution which mediated between each group's claims to the land, would necessarily exact the greatest sacrifice from the Jews. This was true because they would be unable to possess for themselves alone this land, "symbol of the spiritual Israel to which the Bible and the psalms invite other races."[25] The loss would prove doubly hard because in Jewish eyes both Muslim and Christian claims in the region had little validity. Islamic assertions of having descended from Abraham were recognized by few Jews, and controversy over the virgin birth of Jesus placed Christian claims in doubt.

Massignon himself witnessed a skirmish in Jerusalem between Arabs and Jews and in several articles that summer recounted his firsthand experience of the factional violence Gandhi had combatted with *satyagraha*. On February 26, while leaving the garden of Gethsemane, "I fell into intense Judeo-Arab cross fire, carried on with great mutual hatred." The incident occurred as he was on his way to the Hebrew University and what proved to be his last visit with his long-time friend, Judah Magnes (1877–1948), its founder and first president. Years before, in 1922, Massignon had been instrumental in having the library of his mentor, Ignace Goldziher bequeathed to Hebrew University.

Like various members of the Jewish community, Judah Magnes supported the idea of Jewish-Arab coexistence in the Holy Land. A native of California, this American rabbi and Zionist had settled in Palestine after World War I. Founder of the Ihud (Unity) party, he advocated Arab-Israeli political cooperation. The ideas he put forth in 1947 to the United Nations Special Committee on Palestine corroborated those of Massignon: Palestine should be a binational state with Jews and Arabs as partners possessing equal power. In August that year Magnes had outlined to the New York press his project for a confederation between the state of Israel and the future Palestinian state. Massignon characterized him as "the conscience of Israel."[26]

However, the demand of Magnes and others for Jewish and Arab equality was ignored as the war continued throughout 1948, exacerbating the situation of the Palestinian refugees. Massignon's outrage at Israel's capture of Nazareth in July 17 increased when, on September 17, the United Nations mediatior, Count Bernadotte was assassinated by the Israeli terrorist group, Stern. Through the offices of Monteil, Massignon attempted two days later, on September 19, to bring Magnes's project of a federated Palestine to the attention of the French ministry of foreign affairs. No one paid attention. When Magnes died suddenly of a heart attack, October 28, 1948, in New York, Massignon wrote of their last conversation, the day he had encountered Arab-Israeli fire on the way to see his Jewish friend. The voice of Magnes both "grave and calm," expressed "his passionate desire for God's justice," and the demand of "equality for Islam and the Arabs."[27] The name of the Jewish peacemaker recurred in the writings of Massignon until the end of his life. In 1952, while traveling in the United States, he "encountered noble souls, who venerated the memory of Judah Magnes . . . who wanted the new State of Israel to be binational, Judaeo-Arab, *in equality*: among the sons of Abraham." He also made a point of visiting Magnes's grave in Brooklyn.[28]

Israeli military victories had expanded the territory of the new state beyond the original U.N. projections, and more persons were thereby displaced. The 1949 armistice ended the war, but the refugees remained and their numbers grew. Massignon was haunted by their plight and worked to arouse awareness in the French Catholic Church. He was particularly sensitive to the needs of Arab Christians, most of whom did not belong to the Latin rite. They were, he felt, often either ostracized by Muslims or ignored by Latin rite clergy. To that end, he persuaded Cardinal Suhard, the cardinal archbishop of Paris, to establish an episcopal commission to investigate the needs of the Palestinian refugees. Several lines in a letter to Mary Kahil summarize Massignon's impatient assessment of the Church's response: "I have been fighting for the Holy Places since May 3, when I very respectfully ordered Cardinal Suhard to do his duty; he gave in, and under the imposing patronage of a 'high society listing' for ecclesastics, they constituted a committee to protect the refugees of Bethlehem (a committee which now condescends to inscribe Ibrahim [Massignon] in the last place on the list, where I would prefer not to be found at all, given that there are exhibitionists of the genre of canon X . . .)"[29]

Nevertheless, his demands did bring results; in August 1949, Massignon participated in a fact-finding mission of the Catholic Relief Committee and traveled to Egypt, Jordan, Lebanon, and Israel. (Among its members he met a young journalist, Robert Barrat, who later became an ally in protesting French policy in North Africa.) Although ostensibly sent to investigate the plight of displaced Palestinian Christians, Massignon could not separate their situation from that of the Muslim majority and wrote about it in *Le Monde*. Whether Muslim or Christian, these refugees shared a common culture, rooted in the Middle East and far removed from that of the Israelis, supported by American money. Both groups claimed sacred places in the Holy Land, and by the thousands they were now crowded together: "As I questioned them the cry of Judah Magnes haunted me: it is inconceivable that after Central Europe the Holy Land knows the horror of displaced person camps. God, however found a host in Abraham, and these Arabs are the last witnesses of that cult of hospitality which our racisms reject."[30]

As a gesture the French Episcopate decided to "adopt" the city of Bethlehem, home to many Arab Christians. At Christmas, during his customary visit to the Holy Land, Massignon wrote his second annual letter to members of the Badaliya. He decried the conditions he found in the region:

Arab refugees, both Muslims and Christians, crowded into internment camps as Displaced Persons, where the disdainful materialism of the U.N. gives them the minimum of food and shelter, without the least consoling warmth, without the least encouragment to hope for a future, treating them as incurably lazy cowards. Ninety thousand of them are putting up with a desolate life around Hebron, the very place where through Abraham God discovered a host (at Mambre). Our disdainful racisms deny these poor Arabs, sacrificed and exiled by colonial technology, the sacred respect of the host, that divine hospitality of which Arab tribal honor is the last depository and which almost two thousand years ago the bourgeois of Bethlehem had already denied the Holy Family. Our powerless visits have at least made us pray better for them, in prayer wrung from us and thirsting for justice.[31]

Massignon visited the camps again in February 1950, and thereafter it became an annual occurrence. By 1951 he considered that life in the Jordanian camps was becoming a seedbed for violence: "I noted two months ago that their mentality is evolving, alas, from Muslim resignation to the divine will to a desire to be armed by their racial brothers in order to reconquer their lands from the Israelis."[32] The Arab desire for revenge was wreaking destruction in other ways as well:

> In the concentration camps I have just revisited, I can see with great sorrow that in the face of Israeli racism, an Arab racism is forming that is just as terrible and that is beginning to wish that the 800,000 Arab refugees might die of despair, so that the sin of Israel would *subsist*.[33]

When Massignon in 1951 reflected on his efforts for the disenfranchised over a period of thirty years, he could only think that he had failed, a judgment he would reiterate several more times in the years to come. His studies of Muslim artisans in Syria and Morocco had attempted to point out their unique cultural heritage, but even as he studied these groups, they unionized under the impetus of political pressures Massignon considered dehumanizing. The North African immigrants he had taught in night school for twenty-two years had yet to achieve an official status in France. "Finally, the Zionist refugees, on whose behalf I had worked in Palestine, have thrown out Arab laborers since 1948." The conclusion was unavoidable, "The examination of conscience I have just made before you is thus a record of failure."[34]

However, pessimistic evaluation of results never meant that Massignon simply withdrew; it spurred him to reformulate the problem, first in terms of personal responsibility and then in terms of action. Both approaches are significant not only in and of themselves but also because they reflect the twofold and increasingly radicalized direction of Massignon's life in its last decade. His usually gentle and self-effacing manner belied an iron will combined with passionate convictions. As one crisis after another rocked the Arab world, Massignon's religious commitment became the ever more profound source of energy from which he drew in order to combat the injustices he saw. The example of Gandhi provided the ongoing impetus for the "Christian examination of conscience" that guided Massignon's response:

> The one to whom I owe the most in this regard is Gandhi, whom I saw twice. He taught me to listen to the cries of the excluded, the pariahs, and the displaced persons. They are superhuman cries of separation. These cries separate us from our own, from the milieu we love, and bind us to these unfortunates who have meant nothing to us. If we understand well this cry of separation, we know we will be unable to discover a family in them either, because they are sacred guests, or they are strangers. One must not try to assimilate them, but confronted with them, we must offer ourselves to God in substitution for what they lack, because it is God who attracts us to Him by our common destitution; to them we provide the alms of hospitality which Abraham, the first displaced person, gave to God.[35]

Massignon laid down a heroic challenge for the treatment of refugees, "We must not love him as ourselves, as our neighbor. We must love this stranger more than ourselves." However, anyone demonstrating such heroism would derive few feelings of self-satisfaction, for the refugee "is the shadow of God on our life, a shadow which often appears to us as the enemy; this shadow is black, dirty, contaminated with all the epidemics, both undesirable and even unconscious of our efforts to save him." Moreover, the problem would remain insoluble no matter how heroic the service rendered, because refugees constituted a permanent element of human life on earth, a fact reflected both in the Bible and the Muslim notion of hospitality. For this reason Massignon felt the refugee to be "a sacred element which the profanation of the notion of hospitality has caused us so-called civilized people to forget, although the Bible affirmed it as a duty for the people of Israel and later for Christians."[36]

People displaced by forces beyond their control created a situation with international implications. Massignon envisaged "a kind of super-national recognition of their permanent presence" and "a second nationality, temporary and superior to the first," not only for refugees but for all those whose work took them to foreign countries: laborers, pilgrims, and academicians among others. Although he cast his prediction within the eschatological framework so dear to him, he correctly foresaw that such mass migrations of people, combined with increased means of transportation, were creating a new world, a world where nationalism would become more and more problematic: "Frankly, one must in this period of progress, of multiplying means of transportation, understand that the refugee problem raises the issue of dynamic rather than static geography, a problem of humanity's intermingling as it tends towards final unity."[37]

However, Massignon's efforts to promote such internationalization, like his work on behalf of Palestinian refugees, produced little tangible effect. Writing April 7, 1950, to Robert Schuman, then French foreign minister, Massignon asked him to use his influence so that the United Nations would implement the December 9, 1949, resolution that sought to internationalize Jerusalem and the Holy Places. However, Schuman never responded directly to this plea, and the United Nations, unable either to devise or enforce a plan agreeable to all parties, shelved the issue. The de facto divisions of the 1949 armistice remained in place until the 1967 war, four and a half years after Massignon's death.

As Massignon dealt with the apparently endless and insoluble crises of the postwar Arab world, he often seemed to be a man with his "back to the wall," an expression he sometimes repeated and elaborated upon, "It's not a bad position from which to fight."[38] Increasingly he found strength for his lonely struggle in his faith, for the intensity of Massignon's convictions concerning social justice was matched only by his faith in the God of Abraham revealed in Jesus. As his political positions evolved and became more radical in the face of deepening conflict, so too did the expression of that faith.

The excerpted letters to Mary Kahil provide a small glimpse of Massignon's interior journey and the one they shared together. From the early days of their correspondence, he had likened his conversion to the experience of being cast afloat in a bark on the high seas.[39] If the image can be found in Hallaj, it was certainly reinforced by Massignon's summers on the Atlantic coast. Sometimes it suggested peaceful acceptance of sudden vicissitude, as in this 1941 letter to another woman, immobilized temporarily by an accident: "There too, as when one is swimming in the ocean, one must, I think, 'open one's heart' to the next wave and stay on the surface, all the while gently putting one's head under the wave."[40] With the years, as the demands of faith became more radical, so did the image. In 1947 he wrote to Kahil from Brittany:

> From beyond the horizon, beneath the solemn gusts, the ocean is rising with its tide and clamor. It is going to launch the assault. No longer does the heart refuse anything to love . . . and denuded and quivering beneath the wind, the beach that covers over and spreads the sand, plays dead. The last wave is going to submerge everything. On this distant coast where I arrived forty years ago, fleeing the first relationship [Luis de Cuadra] only to fall into the strangest trap of the Badaliya, the desire for God overwhelms me mercilessly.

The siege pushes ahead without respite, pressing in ever closer. I have lost everything and wish to have nothing more.[41]

Kahil, by reason of her unique friendship with Massignon and her founding role in the Badaliya, shared both his spiritual journey and the image of the bark on the high seas that epitomized the journey. However, being of a less ascetic and more expansive temperament than her single-minded companion in faith, she sometimes flinched under the rigors of the challenge he set forth for her. In response to her sadness that maternal concern for a friend had gone unrequited, Massignon wrote in August 1948: "[God] has promised you an entire spiritual generation and you will have it, but not before crossing those great torrents of bitterness where Ibrahim has splashed in mud for forty years, awaiting a passenger who slipped into his bark more than thirteen years ago, but who continues to gaze backward and not seaward."[42] In May 1951, Massignon again summarized his role in her life with the same image, "If you climbed into my bark, it was so that I might lead you deep into the ocean, beyond any visible coast; it was so that you might disembark there."[43] This uncompromisingly austere position typified her friend, but Kahil remained steadfastly loyal and attentive until the end. Indeed, she played a key role in helping him fulfill one of his life's major aspirations.

On February 5, 1949, thanks to an indult from Pius XII, Massignon transferred his Catholic affiliation from the Latin rite of the Roman Catholic Church to the Melkite rite of the Greek Catholic Church, the rite to which Kahil and Arab Christians belonged. Some claimed that the change was sought solely because he wished to be ordained and knew that in the Greek Catholic Church marriage presented no impediment to ordination; others saw the case differently:

He felt himself to be, he wished to be an Arab Christian by adoption. He sought a change of rite first of all as a *badaliya*, in order to share from within the life of the Church in those Arab Christian communities that were so often misunderstood and even scorned. This was for him a corollary of his self-gift to Islam, an image of the call addressed by the Lord to the world of Islam and of His unending expectation.[44]

Massignon himself explained in a letter ten years later to Pope John XXIII that "His Holiness Pius XII had expressly given me to the Oriental Arabic language rite so that I might completely fulfill my vocation of *badaliya*, a vocation embraced in 1908 for a renegade whom I wanted to save."[45] He also wished to pray the official prayers of the Church in Arabic.

The 1949 shift in rite occurred as Massignon was protesting the lot of the Palestinian refugees and attempting to safeguard the integrity of Eastern rite Catholics; it undoubtedly provided him a new sense of solidarity with those he was endeavoring to help. Obviously, too, the change also opened the way to priesthood because his marriage no longer presented an obstacle to fulfilling the dream abandoned in 1914 when he had finally decided not to join Charles de Foucauld in the Sahara. The tenacity of Mary Kahil would prove instrumental in making that seemingly futile dream a reality. From 1934, when their friendship was renewed, she had reminded Massignon of his long buried wish. Well-connected with Melkite Church authorities, she shrewdly presented Massignon's case only after the November 1947 election of Maximos IV to the Greek Catholic patriarchy; his predecessor, Cyril IX, was opposed to ordaining foreigners whom, he felt, sought to compete with the native clergy.

Kahil's primary contact was Bishop Kamel Medawar, the auxiliary, who had lived in Cairo since 1940 because Cyril preferred the Egyptian city to Damascus, the patriarchal seat. Initially, conversations between Kahil, Massignon, and Medawar concerned the Badaliya; on January 6, 1947, Medawar provided the imprimatur for the group's approval by the Church. According to the bishop's account, only after the election of Maximos, in November 1947, did discussion shift to the possibility of ordination for Massignon. Because the latter came to Cairo only infrequently, it was Kahil who "began to discuss this subject, discretely but insistently, mostly with the patriarch, secondarily with me." Medawar went on to explain

that for Massignon the priesthood signified the way to "complete
the total offering of himself in the spirit of *badaliya* . . ."[46] Neither
Massignon nor Greek Catholic authorities ever conceived his priesthood as involving active ministry, such as preaching or distributing
the sacraments to the Catholic community. Its impact would be almost completely interior. Because Catholics believed that the priest
renews the self-offering of Christ through celebrating the Eucharist,
ordination would allow Massignon to express ritually his own mystical substitution for Muslims. In his own person he would thereby
witness to the fact that the Badaliya existed first and foremost as a
spiritual rather than a juridical entity.

Massignon himself visited the patriarch Maximos IV in August
1949 and asked to be ordained. The latter agreed, citing his longstanding work on behalf of Muslims and his vow of *badaliya* as suf-
ficiently serious to justify admission to the priesthood. A flurry of
correspondence shows that events then moved rapidly, as the patriarch reflected on an appropriate date. At year's end Massignon sent
a letter to Kahil stating that he was coming to Cairo for the annual
sessions of the Arabic Academy and asking about a possible date
for his ordination. She immediately wrote to Bishop Medawar in
Damascus: "Our friend Massignon is arriving the 15th (December
1949)—quite decided to consecrate himself to the Lord in the way
you know about—only *you alone* are able to grant him this unparal-
leled favor; you know it—there is only you."[47] In her letter she requested that Medawar come to Cairo from Damascus and offered
to pay any expenses involved. Massignon himself wrote him on
December 20, asking that he be ordained quickly. On Christmas eve,
which Massignon spent in Bethlehem, Kahil telegraphed the patriarch stating that Massignon urgently wished to see Medawar. On
January 6, Massignon wrote the patriarch that he would remain in
Cairo until February 2 at the latest, "and I am taking the liberty to
express to you the very profound desire I have in my heart to receive
Holy Orders before returning to France." In the same letter he
asked that Medawar officiate and that the ordination remain secret.

At the last moment, the event almost never took place because of Vatican opposition. On January 14, the same day Medawar told Massignon in writing of the affirmative decision of the patriarch, the latter wrote the Vatican to inform the Congregation of the Eastern Rite that Massignon would be ordained. Kahil received news of the forthcoming ordination from Medawar the next day, the fifteenth; she wrote back to him on the twenty-first to say he was expected in Cairo on the twenty-fourth or twenty-fifth. On the latter date, Cardinal Valeri, writing for the Congregation, restated that the Holy See opposed the ordination of married men from the Latin rite, even if they had, like Massignon, transferred into a different one. However, this letter reached the Greek-Catholic patriarch in Damascus only after the ordination had taken place.[48]

At dawn on January 28, 1950, Louis Massignon was ordained a priest of the Melkite rite by Bishop Medawar. The ceremony was witnessed only by Kahil and the pastor of Sainte Marie de la Paix, the small Byzantine rite church which owed its existence to Kahil's initiative in 1941. The next day, January 29, marked the sixteenth anniversary of the day Massignon and Kahil had met again in Cairo. For them both the ordination signified a deeper fulfillment of their vow of mystical substitution embodied in the group of Badaliya. Over the years Kahil had strongly encouraged Massignon to seek ordination, and in large measure her persistence and access to Church authorities enabled him to achieve the lifelong dream of priesthood, born of his association with Charles de Foucauld.

Even after the event, Rome evinced its dismay in a series of letters between Church authorities and Maximos IV. Finally, at year's end, while the patriarch and Medawar were in Rome, they learned from Cardinal Tisserant that the latter considered the incident closed.[49] Later Medawar visited Paris and learned that the "archdiocesan office of Paris did not attach much importance to it [the controversy over the ordination] and that 'what is done is done.' "[50]

Massignon had expressly requested that his priesthood be kept secret, and this stipulation formed part of the justification advanced by the patriarch for permitting the ordination in the first place. Nevertheless, the secret inevitably became public because it was known within Massignon's circle of friends and because he himself sometimes inadvertently revealed it by assuming that people knew when they did not. One day a woman attending his classes at the Collège de France visited him in his office:

> He didn't give me the chance to say why I wanted to have a conversation. As was his wont, he was the one who talked. But he spoke totally in allusions, so much so that I could not grasp his meaning. Not understanding, I registered: "My daughter is the one who accepts it the least." But what? Several days later, once I found out about the ordination, everything became clear; he thought I knew, hence this tone of allusion which was so disconcerting.[51]

Persons other than Massignon's daughter expressed reservations. Almost two years later, November 6, 1951, Claudel confided to his journal: "M. a priest. He has succeeded in sneaking into holy orders."[52] According to a letter Massignon wrote to Medawar, even a churchman as sympathetic as Monsignor Montini expressed surprise.[53]

For Massignon himself, such reservations mattered little, for his priesthood represented the culmination of his desire for a life of self-sacrifice. It thereby linked him to intercessors such as Hallaj and Foucauld, who had modeled such a life for him. In turn he felt closer bonds with those for whom he wished to give his life in mystical substitution. This group began with Luis de Cuadra and extended to the entire Muslim community. As if to epitomize how his priesthood allowed him to integrate the many significant spiritual aspects of his life, Massignon finally visited Tamanrasset and, as was mentioned in chapter 3, spent the night of October 19–20, 1950, praying in Foucauld's hermitage. The strength he derived from celebrating the liturgy daily at dawn in a small study of his apartment enabled him not only to continue but also to intensify his involvement in the deepening conflicts which surrounded him.

Six months after his ordination Massignon wrote Claudel a letter which suggests that he considered his new status a source of strength in his increasingly isolated struggle to right the wrongs he perceived. At this time, Claudel knew nothing about Massignon's priesthood, and the letter, dated July 29, 1950, was occasioned by a misunderstanding between the two men. Claudel's name had been afixed without his knowledge to a communique from "Le Comité international pour l'étude des questions européennes," which appeared July 11 in *Le Monde,* at the beginning of a series of articles that advocated preventive use of the atomic bomb. Like many others Massignon had written Claudel in protest, only to learn that the latter had resigned from the sponsoring group two years previously. Massignon's letter of July 29 apologized for having thought that his friend would advocate use of the atomic bomb to resolve international problems. After alluding in the first paragraph to his mistake, in the second, Massignon evokes their forty-year friendship, but he cannot resist mentioning their opposing views on Israel:

> Fraternally. We are both drawing closer to the end, which the slogans of all the Kravchenkos are working to hasten. And I feel that in order to end well, you like myself must work at making ourselves despised by "right thinkers." As for me, I am succeeding at it rather well, getting myself covered with insults I don't answer, having been to the Holy Places in February in order to sympathize with those poor Arab peasants whom you promised to deliver from their feudal oppressors thanks to Ben Gurion. Yes, they've been delivered from it because they have all been (yes, all of them now, even the ones who had rallied, the scabs, and the *concordistes*) thrown out. "Displaced Persons." Like Our Lord. I beg God to die alongside them. May Foucauld, who somehow promised me that, and who for six months now I have "rejoined" in an astonishing fashion, help me to do it. Amen.[54]

Claudel seemingly accepted the apology, but his journal comment about this letter reflects how he and many others were alternately mystified and put off by the tendency of Massignon to evoke within a single conversation, themes, personages, and events drawn from the entire range of his experience: "Response of Massignon who asks my forgiveness. He went off the track as is his wont.

Kravchenko, Ben Gurion, the hierarchy which doesn't do its duty, etc. Our paths are diverging more and more."[55] The implication in the letter that the renewed link with Foucauld referred to Massignon's priesthood necessarily escaped Claudel at this point. Foucauld had ardently wished Massignon to be ordained, and the impact and supportive function of the priesthood is clearly although indirectly present in the latter's reference to his feelings of increasing isolation, his assertive defense of the Arab refugees, and his desire to die near them. The priesthood reinforced his underlying commitment to mystical substitution and thereby gave new impetus to the compassion which had long impelled him to identify with the disadvantaged and, especially, the poorest Muslims. It provided the mainspring of his tenacious and unrelenting public presence during the last ten years of his life as the infirmities of old age began to encroach and France became ever more embroiled in disengaging itself from its colonies in North Africa.

EIGHT

The Road to Independence in Morocco

In the Middle East the French role in Syria and now the plight of the Palestinians had only confirmed Massignon's judgment about the wrongs perpetrated on Muslim peoples by the Western powers. In the Maghreb the political climate in both Morocco and Algeria was deteriorating rapidly. Although their status vis-à-vis France differed (Morocco, a protectorate, was nominally self-governing, while Algeria was an overseas department of the mainland) both countries were moving inexorably towards independence. Meanwhile the French government appeared increasingly helpless either to stem the tide by reforming their policies or to prepare for an orderly transfer of power.

Such paralysis was undoubtedly reinforced by the fact that, whatever scenario prevailed, national identity was at issue. Territory and influence beyond the mainland helped define France as a major power. The prospect of losing these represented a more serious blow than it might have, had the country not recently emerged from the chaos of war and occupation. Whole segments of the French population bitterly opposed one another as the drama of decolonialization unfolded during the 1950s and early 1960s. The tensions provoked violence in France itself, especially near the end of the Algerian conflict. By speaking out publicly during this period on behalf of Muslims living in North Africa and France, Massignon embarked on a road that involved considerable personal risk and laid himself open to charges that he was subverting national security.

Although the Arab-Israeli situation in the Middle East had never

185

distracted him from attending to rising tensions in the Maghreb, during the last decade of his life Morocco and Algeria increasingly preoccupied him, and his involvement grew in direct proportion to the suffering and chaos in the region. Whereas his was often a solitary voice in protesting the treatment of the Palestinians, a rising chorus of opposition joined him in opposing government policy in the Maghreb throughout the 1950s and until the end of the Algerian war in 1962. Among that chorus were French intellectuals of the left such as Jean-Paul Sartre and Albert Camus, and also a group of Catholic intellectuals, the best known of whom was François Mauriac. Massignon played a key role in the latter group because of his professional knowledge and experience of the region.

For him the question was less that of promoting independence than of correcting longstanding abuses resulting from French colonial practices. He found ways to protest government policies that in his eyes ignored the indigenous culture and maintained North Africans in a state of economic inferiority. When the Academy of Colonial Sciences and the Committee of the *cahiers* of Charles de Foucauld requested that Rome canonize Foucauld as the "saint of colonialism," and thus of the status quo, Massignon was outraged and in June 1949 resigned from both groups. That autumn he learned that a mosque in Algeria had been desecrated by the police during an electoral campaign; they had chosen the spot for a drunken gathering. He recounted how both he and the League for the Rights of Man denounced the action in an Algiers newspaper. The governor general then requested that he visit Algeria in order to evaluate the charges, but Massignon refused, citing his experience with military police on the Macedonian front during the First World War. He feared that group loyalty among the police would only aggravate the situation of the aggrieved Muslims.[1]

In 1951, Emmanuel Mounier, founder and editor of *Esprit*, asked Massignon, who had repeatedly written about Algeria, to summarize the existing situation. The latter had expressed reservations about France's future there as early as 1922, and his critique of French policy had become more trenchant in the essay written eight years later for the Algerian centenary.[2] Now, in 1951, the same themes recurred but with heightened urgency as demands for independence became louder amid growing evidence that the government had yet to deal effectively with the socioeconomic problems plaguing the country.

Massignon stated in *Esprit* that he remained skeptical of efforts (e.g., the statute of 1947) which attempted to address inequities between the two populations by giving Muslims a larger voice in governing their own affairs and by promoting the teaching of Arabic in schools. Although the government professed an interest in the welfare of the indigenous population, its concern seemed "an interest by command, which maintained an Islam badly provided for, at once stagnant and obsequious, of 'Beni Yes-Yes.'" Meanwhile, in spite of government pressure, the situation was worsening: "The duel is shaping up between a native population that is in the majority, growing rapidly, and making undeniable cultural gains—and a minority of absentee and wealthy colonists, with a weak birth rate, and that is using its undeniable technical superiority to defend privileges that are more and more suspect."[3]

Yet Massignon still believed that his country at its best could facilitate a better life for all of Algeria, and his belief in that possibility rested on his cherished concept of sacred hospitality. Just as he had maintained in the Arab-Israeli conflict, Massignon asserted that a solution could be found if Muslims and Frenchmen worked to accommodate one another in an effort that ultimately supposed faith in the God of their mutual father, Abraham. As a result, while the message he formulated in the *Esprit* article sought equal rights for Muslims, it stopped short of calling for Algerian independence, because that move would definitively isolate the two peoples from each other.

If Massignon's convictions about the Algerian situation were based on his religious faith in sacred hospitality, he was clearsighted enough to know that mutual respect and understanding would never be achieved unless social and material inequities were eliminated. Algeria's problems could not be resolved merely by a better industrial infrastructure which, if the past were any example, would scarcely improve the lot of the *fellahs,* the Algerians in rural areas. Concretely, the French government and the European settlers must cease using Algeria's resources and its people as a means of self-enrichment and begin promoting the economic, cultural, and religious well-being of the Muslim population. They must also express a genuine interest in the values of Islam and in the Arabic language.[4]

Just as the primacy of the Holy Places, in Massignon's eyes, figured in any solution to the Arab-Israeli conflict, so too, the "historical vocation" of France as a civilizing influence could still be invoked to save "a future of social cooperation" in Algeria. However, a hundred and twenty years of French education presented a two-edged sword, because the Muslim elite, educated in French schools and formed in French ideals of liberty, could see that their own country was not free. At the same time, because of their inferior status Muslims often conformed to French demands that were either illegal, immoral, or culturally insensitive. In so doing they were inevitably compromised and resented the colonizer who was responsible for the abuses. "They will never forgive us for having degraded them before their own consciences, and in the secret vengeance they are preparing against us, we will be able to recognize our own corrupt mark."[5]

In the face of cynically immoral practices, Massignon noted increased Muslim observance in Algeria and made a prediction which has been fulfilled far beyond the Maghreb. His *Esprit* article predicted the rise of Islamic fundamentalism and correctly foresaw that the Islamic religious revival would become a political tool to rival communism among Arab peoples seeking independence, "This religious revival of the masses . . . is focused on a desperate and revolutionary fanaticism."[6] If understanding between the two populations of Algeria did not improve immediately, he warned prophetically that what had happened in other portions of the vanishing French empire in the Middle East and Asia would also occur in Algeria:

We can prepare ourselves to evacuate soon a million brothers of our race, in conditions which, short of a few zeroes, the columns of refugees fleeing Damascus in 1945 under the amused eyes of British soldiers and the transport planes emptying Hanoi right now, can give us a foretaste.[7]

In 1951, as independence forces were gaining strength in the Maghreb, tensions between Arabs and Jews continued unabated. The 1951 Christmas letter to the Badaliya reflects how varied were the responses of Massignon to these ongoing and worsening crises. Even while proposing concrete solutions, he also crafted rituals from his own rich experience of symbol and prayer in order to sustain himself and others in the struggle. The letter begins by summarizing his own work as a member of the Paris Badaliya group. Ever preoccupied with the refugee question in the Middle East, Massignon had attended the Catholic Congress for Refugees held at Ste-Odile in Alsace. There he had argued that an international organization be maintained to protect "refugees, displaced persons and those without a country—in peacetime and so that in periods of conflict, neutral security zones be created."[8] On October 19, he and several friends had gone to pray at the mosque of Paris during the solemn Friday prayer. In response to anti-Islamic sentiment appearing in the French and Belgian press, this visit, the first of three over the next several years, "marked our respect for the insulted faith of our fellow citizens, friends, and Muslims of Africa and the whole world."[9]

However, according to Massignon's letter the most significant event for him that year had occurred September 19. On that date, coincidentally the feast of Our Lady of La Salette, Massignon visited Ephesus. This ancient city became included in his personal spiritual geography; because the saints venerated here were honored in both traditions it symbolized for him another point of reconciliation between Muslims and Christians. On this site Mary reputedly lived with the disciple John after the death and resurrection of Jesus; here Mary Magdalen was first buried; and finally the Seven Sleepers were walled alive in a cave rather than worship idols, a tale recalled by

Muslims in the sura "The Cave" and a favored topic of Massignon's courses at the Collège de France in 1935 and 1937.

Moreover, the life of the mother of Jesus at Ephesus held special significance for Massignon as he attempted to express concretely his vow of mystical substitution within the context of the shifting world around him. Just as he considered his own life as one given over to his Muslim friends, so, too, Mary had lived solely in order to form Jesus, the human image of God. When Jesus at his death confided her to John, her maternal compassion was extended first to the disciple and then to all peoples. Massignon saw in that dynamic of compassion extending from Mary to Jesus and then to the world the "spiritual direction" of the Badaliya. He and others were called on to make their own the needs and suffering of their Muslim brothers and sisters and ultimately to suffer in their stead.

However preeminent Mary was among the religious figures that both Christians and Muslims associated with Ephesus, Massignon would draw most heavily on the legend of the Seven Sleepers in his work for reconciliation between Muslims and Christians. Not only were these saints venerated in both traditions, but their "resurrection," although shortlived, pointed to the eschatological hope shared by Shi'ite Muslims and Christians alike, that one day justice would ultimately be achieved for all poor and oppressed peoples.

Coincidentally, and perhaps decisively in terms of Massignon's interest, a chapel dedicated to the martyrs was situated near Vieux Marché, a village not far from Massignon's summer home in Binic on the northern coast of Brittany. The chapel dated from 1703, but the Seven Sleepers had been venerated on the spot since the early Middle Ages because a dolmen there was thought to represent the cave of their entombment. At a nearby spring a square entrance with seven openings had been constructed in stone similar to that of the dolmen. Massignon noted the importance of the Seven Sleepers in his 1951 letter to the Badaliya and the next year commemorated their July 27 feast by having a mass celebrated in their honor in the chapel.[10] Two years later, in 1954, he organized what became an annual pilgrimage to Vieux Marché. A group of Muslims and Christians gathered with him on the Sunday following July 22 (feast of Mary Magdalen) to pray for reconciliation and mutual understanding; the service coincided with the traditional Breton "pardon," a regional devotional rite held each year to celebrate God's forgiveness. Until his death Massignon participated annually in the July pilgrimage; a photo of the 1962 event shows him three months before he died, frail and spent from his seemingly endless labors for peace.

In his efforts during this last period of his life, Massignon raised the ire both of compatriots whose political views differed from his own and of some whose cause he supported. "Why has this Orientalist, an historian of mysticism, gotten himself involved in 'politics?'" asked one critic quoted by Massignon in a 1952 article. Another responded that since mysticism was undefinable and ostensibly useless, anyone who derived "politics" from it had evidently failed to discover its reality. Another observation quoted in the same article was more trenchant. According to Massignon, the head of the reformist Ulemas of Algeria "considered that I had spent twenty years creating for myself a kind of 'mask,' that I was the worst agent of the fifth column and that it was evidently the colonialist fifth column that was operating through my mask as a mystic."[11]

Such criticism was painful, but by far the most painful criticism of all came from persons whom Massignon had mentored. It is impossible to know how often such incidents occurred, but one such case was cited in several of his articles.[12] A 1935 account has been quoted here in chapter 6, and a second, more precise version of the same incident appeared in 1952. The later one attacked Massignon's hope that substantial cooperation between the French and Algerian Muslims might yet be achieved. A past president of the North-African nationalist student organization, Muhammad ben Saï had prepared a *diplôme d'études supérieures* under Massignon's direction and wrote:

> I cannot forgive myself for having loved you because you disarmed me. You have been worse than those who burned our houses, raped our daughters or clouded the minds of our elderly. For several years

of my life, you disarmed me by letting me believe there was a possibility of reconciliation and understanding between a Frenchman who is Christian and an Arab who is Muslim.[13]

For some proponents of Algerian independence, the empathy and concern of Massignon seemed to work at cross-purposes to their goal. From their perspective, the way he himself exemplified the notion of sacred hospitality lulled people into thinking that his compatriots shared his views and that self-determination could be attained without severing all ties to France. Saddened though Massignon was by such stinging rebukes, his call for reconciliation in the Maghreb remained constant and always included prayer for mutual respect between its French and Muslim inhabitants. He conveyed his message peacefully but relentlessly until the end and relied more and more on spiritual means to promote it during his final years.

Chief among those means was fasting, whose power of witness Massignon had first learned from Gandhi and which he noted again during a three-month visit to the United States in the autumn of 1952. Invited by the University of Chicago to give the Haskell lectures in religion, he used the opportunity to visit the eastern half of the country and also Quebec. His comments in the 1952 Christmas letter to the Badaliya characterized it as yet another itinerary of pilgrimage, which differed from his many others throughout the world only because he was traveling in North America for the first and only time. The trip included not only the regions studied by his deceased son Yves in French-speaking Canada, northern New England, and New Orleans but also Arabic-speaking enclaves of Christians in Chicago and Detroit, the grave of Judah Magnes in Brooklyn, and the Ford Theater in Washington, D.C. Massignon was impressed that Lincoln had proclaimed a national day of fasting during the Civil War:

We also prayed there where Abraham Lincoln, "Father Abraham," as the Negros called him, was assassinated in Washington (1865), for having brought about the emancipation of the Negro slaves, after having declared a solemn fast ("a day of humiliation, fasting and prayer," April 30, 1863) towards this end, a gesture worthy of Gandhi, which no other U.S. president appears to have dared renew: in order to bring about justice for the oppressed, to the "mustad afin" as the Qur'an says.[14]

The call for fasting by an American president undoubtedly showed Massignon how effectively it focused attention on a cause. However, the example would have produced less impact had he not been steeped for years in the teachings of Gandhi and the latter's use of fasting as a tool of nonviolent social protest. Indeed, while still in the United States, he was invited to speak of his longstanding respect for Gandhi at a conference sponsored by a UNESCO commission and held in New Delhi, January 5–17, 1953. The conference was entitled "Gandhian Outlook and Techniques in the Solution of Tensions between and within Nations." Massignon commented that "this invitation had pursued me by cable during my university trimester in the United States." Apparently, he had hesitated to say yes. However, after recalling his early interest in Gandhi dating from 1921, their brief meeting in 1931, a trip to New Delhi in 1945 when Gandhi's imprisonment prevented another meeting, he agreed to speak at the conference. "I could not avoid going," he concluded.[15]

In fact, the trip to New Delhi constituted another pilgrimage and a profoundly significant one for Massignon. He considered that "Gandhi had helped him to find maxims for meditation and action that he had sought for fifty years."[16] The practice of nonviolence in the face of opposition and even death acquired new meaning for him as he visited places made sacred by the events of January 1948, leading to Gandhi's murder. On January 5, 1953, he meditated in the small garden of Birla House, the site of the assassination, before placing a wreath at Raj Ghat, where the Hindu's body was cremated. The next day he and two Muslim delegates to the conference followed the route of Gandhi's last pilgrimage by visiting Mehrauli, a Muslim shrine seven miles south of the city. Muslim women of Delhi who had been fasting with Gandhi had complained to him that because of Hindu violence they were unable to go alone to

Mehrauli. He offered to accompany them and did so January 27. There Gandhi promised that the shrine, vandalized by Hindus, would be repaired. Three days later he was murdered by a Hindu extremist who was angered by his overtures to Muslims. In his own pilgrimage to Mehrauli, Massignon noted a plaque stating that the shrine had been repaired in accord with Gandhi's last wish.

On the eve of a decade of violence in North Africa, this journey concretely revealed to Massignon that Gandhi's lifelong struggle to maintain unity in the face of sectarian and ethnic hatreds was linked to his own call for sacred hospitality. The significance of Mehrauli became a conscious point of reference for Massignon's own commitment to justice in North Africa, a commitment he himself clearly stated seven years later in a newsletter to the Amis de Gandhi:

> Invited by the government of India in 1953 to the Gandhian Seminar held in New Delhi, your president [Massignon] then went to Mehrauli; there, in that place he meditated on and understood the last fast, the last pilgrimage, and the last vow of nonviolence which Gandhi had lived out with the Muslim women of India. He realized then that only by transposing the Gandhian methods both to the mainland and to North Africa could the mortal tension between Muslims and Frenchmen be eased.[17]

Massignon soon made regular fasting an integral part of his own program for peace in the Maghreb, first of all in response to rising unrest in Morocco. For years Sultan Sidi Muhammad ben Youssef, the country's religious and political leader, had supported Istiqlal, the national independence party founded in 1943.[18] Massignon had longstanding ties both to the sultan and the party, and on November 19, 1946, as part of the celebration of the feast of the throne he had given a talk in Arabic about how the word *istiqlal* signified independence.[19] However, many French colonists and traditionalists of the Muslim elite adamantly opposed the sultan and any talk of ending the Protectorate. In the years that followed, violence erupted, foreshadowing the somber drama that would unfold in Algeria.

Massignon became personally involved in Morocco after an uprising in Casablanca, December 7 and 8, 1952, that had been organized to protest the murder of a union leader in Tunisia. According to eyewitness reports, the demonstrations had provoked a police ambush in the poorest part of the city, killing fifty people by official accounts and by unofficial accounts anywhere from one to two thousand. Catholic religious working in the slums where the riots occurred witnessed the bloodshed and sent back reports to the mainland; the liberal Catholic community in France reacted immediately.

François Mauriac, returning from Stockholm where he had received the Nobel Prize for literature, became a spokesman of protest, urged on by the Catholic journalist Robert Barrat, Jean-Marie Domenach, editor of *Esprit* after the death of Emmanuel Mounier, and Louis Massignon. They were joined by two of Massignon's university colleagues, Professors Charles-André Julien and Régis Blachère. The group called a meeting January 26 at the Catholic Center for French Intellectuals to explain the situation to the public. Massignon was visiting refugee camps in Jordan at the time but sent Robert Barrat a telegram of support. The meeting itself was a resounding success; four hundred fifty people crowded into the room while an equal number gathered outside.[20] Efforts to alert French public opinion to what had happened continued throughout the first half of 1953 and proved effective, much to the anger of those who justified the French action in Morocco as necessary to restore order and who equated the burgeoning independence movements throughout North Africa with the spread of world communism. Indeed, long after Morocco achieved independence, critics such as Georges Spillman, a retired general who had served there, condemned those who, like Massignon, raised their voices against the French government response to the December 1952 uprising: "In one segment of French public opinion, no longer solely among the left, but also among Catholic liberals, the myth of French guilt was given credence. It gave birth to a deplorable guilt complex."[21]

On May 21, 1953, two Moroccan religious and political figures, the pasha of Marrakech, El Glaoui, and El Kittani presented a petition to the French government asking that the sultan be removed on the grounds that he was an unfit religious leader. The accusation was ironic because both men, widely known for their doubtful morality, owed their positions to the French protectorate. El Glaoui, the only feudal lord to have survived the advent of the protectorate, had gained immense wealth by exacting money from the tribes within his area of control. It was public knowledge that for years the pasha had drawn much of his income from taxing the prostitutes in his city. El Kittani was ostensibly a holy man or marabout, the president of a spiritual confraternity that promoted intercessory prayer to saints. In fact, his position provided a lucrative livelihood.

The nucleus of opposition headed by Mauriac decided that the moment had come to organize their resistance. On June 3 the committee France-Maghreb was created for the purpose of "reinforcing the links of friendship between France, the Maghreb and the Muslim countries."[22] Composed largely of academics, intellectuals, and legislators, including François Mitterand, it lobbied to arouse public opinion and thereby exert pressure on the government. Mauriac was named president, Charles-André Julien and Massignon two of the vice-presidents. The latter's decisive influence in the group received special tribute years later from Mauriac, "What made the force of France-Maghreb was that it was a question . . . of friendship. Louis Massignon, our master and inspirer, had communicated to us all his attachment for the Maghreb."[23]

In this context of impending crisis, fueled by groups agitating for the sultan's removal, Massignon organized his first day of fasting. He described it in a communiqué of *France-Islam,* which he sent to Monsignor Montini at the Vatican: "The private fast of June 12 was observed in peace, silence, and in a spirit of fraternal substitution, of *badaliya*—for the reestablishment of a serene peace in North Africa."[24] That date had been chosen because the petition of the Moroccans in May to remove the sultan had coincided with Ramadan, the great period of Muslim fasting and recollection, and June 12 marked its end.

Massignon's efforts and those of France-Maghreb sparked the

ire of many, including General Alphonse Juin, a former résident général of Morocco. At Juin's reception into the French Academy, June 25, he attacked the Moroccan independence party:

> It has attempted quite recently and not without success, in connection with the repression of the trouble it fomented, to mobilize for its own ends what one commonly calls the religion of the heart. Christian consciences, ever quick to become moved over false reports and overly sensitive to arguments about moral and spiritual implications, have deliberately taken up its defense.[25]

The "Christian consciences" to which the general referred belonged in large part to members of France-Maghreb. However, all those opposed to French policy in Morocco were angered not only by such remarks but also by the Academy's applause for El Glaoui, who had been specially invited to attend. His presence seemingly confirmed reports that the French government chose simultaneously to ignore reports of his dubious integrity and support his maneuvers to remove the sultan on religious grounds.

Mauriac, also a member of the French Academy, had boycotted the reception of Juin, but upon hearing the general's words, he defended his friends in a famous article published in the *Figaro*, June 30. If Mauriac felt himself attacked, he pointed out that others including Massignon had likewise been targeted, "a professor at the Collège de France, Louis Massignon, that scholar and Christian who was given the grace to know and love Islam as père de Foucauld knew and loved it."[26]

June 29, the day before the Mauriac piece appeared, France-Maghreb held a press conference where Massignon resoundingly condemned the hypocrisy he saw exemplified in the Moroccan religious leaders. Because of the riveting force of his rhetoric, the power of his performance was remembered long after the issues themselves were resolved. He undertook to examine the "religious validity of the allegations" brought against the sultan by El Glaoui, the pasha of Marrakech, and El Kittani, who styled himself the president of a group of Muslim confraternities, "les confréries de l'Afrique du

Nord." Massignon was insensed that religion was being used for political gain and drew on his knowledge of Muslim theology and practice to level a biting critique against both men.

He noted El Kittani's title of "président" of the group of confraternities. The "confréries" belonged to the mystical tradition of Islam, long studied by Massignon, which taught that intimacy with God was possible. Because such teaching contradicted the Islamic dogma of a God whose transcendence precluded all possibility of intimacy, confraternities were marginal to the life of the Islamic state. Ordinarily, therefore, no member of a confraternity could claim a role in the organization of Muslim life. "The Muslim state, which does not recognize any confraternity, enjoins its members not to meddle in public affairs because they have 'renounced the world.'" Exceptions did exist, however; in instances where the state had become corrupt, then "the Muslim conscience considers that the protestation of the mystic, should be raised." Thus Massignon admitted theoretically the right of El Kittani to protest "if he estimated that the modernism of the sultan had compromised the Faith." But he wondered why in doing so El Kittani had used the "empty and absurd title of 'president' of an imaginary federation of confraternities which Muslim law ignored."[27]

On the one hand, Massignon acknowledged that the latter had "at least understood that he had to formulate on his own his personal oral testimony as a Witness of God against the sultan." Such a move complied with Muslim practice. On the other hand, "the constant rule of the Muslim community . . . is to proceed by a preliminary purification of the mouth of the witness who is going to speak."[28] On these grounds, both El Kittani and El Glaoui were tainted.

Massignon recalled that El Kittani had first allied himself with the French government in order to avenge the death of a relative, "atrociously executed" by the sultan's family forty years before. His rhetoric matched the severity of the charges. "The God which inspires his [El Kittani's] conduct is not the God of Abraham, of pity and self-sacrifice, of the 'Abdal,' of the substitute saints, it is, he believes, the God of private vengeance (which Islam has specifically abolished.)" El Kittani became progressively involved "in situations that were ever more worthy of condemnation; he deliberately became someone possessed by his pride and concupiscence, a simoniac, a ventriloquist of God." Moreover, rather than using his erudition and knowledge of Islamic law in the service of the community, El Kittani had "judged it more profitable to work at constituting an income-producing consortium from the confraternities."[29]

As for the pasha of Marrakech, El Glaoui had profited from the taxes he levied on prostitutes in his region, "taxes contrary to the Qur'an," which forbids prostitution. The French authorities had encouraged him to perfect his collection techniques, an attitude which "reveals to what administrative cynicism the Muslims in Morocco had been handed over by a mainland which obstinately neglected to suppress abuses, its essential duty overseas." The pasha's qualms of conscience had been eased by a French law passed under Vichy, which considered these establishments as businesses, thereby freeing the ruler from any legal responsibility for them. In return for his cooperation El Glaoui had "become 'the friend of France,' valuable and indispensable, whom they tried to find a place for at the coronation in London [of Elizabeth II], at the Academy and in the poor old guest book of the Municipal Council of Paris."[30]

At the end of these remarks, someone asked Massignon how Muslims could tolerate that he a non-Muslim would condemn prostitution when such a declaration disqualifies the testimony of a Muslim in favor of it. The vehemence of Massignon's response reflected his outrage at those who tolerated prostitution, knowing that it violated basic tenets of their faith, even as they invoked religion for their own ends. In spite of such examples, he asserted that the proclamation of divine truth transcended dogmatic differences; the sacred word was weakened neither by faulty messengers nor by unfaithful believers:

> In asking such a question a French Christian confesses his colonialism as a monopolizer of the truth and his moral inferiority vis-à-vis

the colonized Muslim to whom he attributes the same stance, that of a customs agent. Ignoring that there exists between men a common principle of reference, one same God of truth, the colonist is unable to suppose that a Muslim might feel validly called back by a Christian voice to the observance of a clear canonical precept. This Christian does not think that the testimony of the word could lead to mutual understanding . . . But the Muslim, who believes in the equality of origin of the three Abrahamic religions, Israel, Christ and Islam, knows that they refer to the same God of truth . . . If for the Christian this word is Jesus, for Islam, it is the uncreated Qur'an. The testimony of a Qur'anic verse, recited as authentic, carries weight, whatever intermediary does the reciting. Truth shines forth in holiness, even when it emerges from the mouth of hell.[31]

Massignon's words circulated far beyond the press conference. They were published the next day in *Le Monde* and in the September issue of *Esprit*. Three days after the press conference, Mauriac hosted a dinner party and commented on the event's success to his skeptical guests, whose political views were more akin to those of Juin. He was gleeful that anyone who had attended the press conference hoping to see the France-Maghreb group embarrassed had been roundly disappointed. Mauriac went on to describe the performance of Massignon, "Louis Massignon was particularly admirable. He suddenly let himself shift into thinking out loud and his meditation, so noble and so beautiful was profoundly moving . . ." The guests, however, were unsympathetic and pressed their host for facts and figures. Pinned down and unable to respond to their satisfaction, Mauriac exclaimed laughingly, "Help, Massignon!"[32]

United in their Catholic faith and sharing the same passion for justice, the two men collaborated well in France-Maghreb despite their radically different temperaments. The ascetic Massignon was sometimes irritated because he considered Mauriac to be attached to his "socialite" role. The latter occasionally made fun of Massignon for the importance he attributed to El Glaoui's involvement in the brothels of Morocco. Jean-Marie Domenach recalled an episode involving the two which took place in the office of *Esprit* during the height of the Moroccan crisis: "One day when we were meeting and Mauriac, probably a little tired, had stayed at his property of Vémars, I remember Massignon picking up the telephone and calling Mauriac: 'Mon Cher, don't just make believe that you're presiding.'"[33] Obediently, Mauriac returned to Paris, compelled, as Domenach observed, by the sheer spiritual force which emanated from Massignon, but the editor likewise added, "I am saying it; let's be frank: it wasn't always amusing or easy" to deal with such imperatives. Charles-André Julien, reflecting on his long association with Massignon, both as a university colleague and comrade in protest, commented in the same vein about his friend:

> Massignon hungered and thirsted for justice. He threw himself like a knight in armor into the battle against wrongs, without always measuring the adversary's forces and the effectiveness of the weapons at hand. He brought to the struggle more passion than method. To the very extent that he was sure of himself in the scientific arena, to that extent, he had a need to feel united in action with those he trusted and who sometimes had to temper his too hasty ardor. His combat in the world was a form of his combat for God.[34]

Shortly after the France-Maghreb press conference, Julien and Massignon found themselves together because of an incident that occurred on Bastille Day, 1953. The North African contingent (NORDAF) had wanted to march separately from the members of the CGT union, but the latter group had failed to communicate to NORDAF the plan cleared with the police. As a result the North Africans were not correctly positioned. In the ensuing confrontation, five North-African workers were killed at the Place de la Nation. Massignon and Julien among others went to the Paris mosque to pray over the bodies. Julien recounted how, as they came to the entrance, an Algerian approached and cried out, "Monsieur Julien, do not abandon us!"

In the face of such disarray I did not know how to respond, but Massignon, near the bodies of the victims, did it through a short prayer in Arabic. I don't know what it meant, but to see the amazed faces of the Algerians who listened to it with poignant fervor, it seemed to me that they were communing in the one same hope in God.[35]

On the first coffin Massignon placed a calligraphy of the saying of Hallaj which had drawn him in 1907, first to Hallaj and ultimately to God: "Two prosternations suffice in love, but the preliminary ablution must be made in blood." He added a copy of a verse about martyrdom from the Qur'an.

Events in Morocco followed their ineluctable course that summer, culminating in Sidi Muhammad's removal through a coup led by Muslim notables and supported by many French inhabitants of the protectorate. Both groups feared the sultan's demand for Moroccan independence. Gathered August 13 at the palace of El Glaoui in Marrakech, they declared the sultan unworthy to continue as imam of the Moroccan Muslim community and proclaimed one of his elderly relatives, Muhammad Ben Arafa, imam in his stead. On August 20, the conspirators demanded that the sultan abdicate in favor of one of his sons. After Sidi Muhammad refused to do so, they declared Ben Arafa, the new sultan. That same day the French government, explaining that it feared bloodshed if the legitimate ruler were maintained by force, exiled the deposed sultan and his family, first to Corsica and eventually to Madagascar. On August 21 the members of France-Maghreb assembled to hear Massignon proclaim, "The France-Maghreb Committee has lost a battle, it has not lost the war." Paul Claudel, at opposite ends of the political spectrum, thought differently; that same day in his last journal reference to Massignon, Claudel noted with seeming satisfaction: "The sultan of Morocco removed to Corsica and replaced by a creature of El Glaoui's, the pasha of Marrakech, to the great consternation of Mauriac, Massignon and their friends of *Témoignage chrétien*."[36] The written version of Massignon's famous June 21 press conference appeared in *Esprit* only after the sultan's overthrow. His indignation about the sultan's removal is amply revealed in the stinging rhetoric of the last paragraph, which was added after the coup:

> Like the resistance fighters of 1940, here we are, already assigned responsiblity for thousands of imprisoned people, Muslims this time; they have been punished ever since Casablanca [scene of the December 1952 riots], in the name of Glaoui and El Kittani, for having studied in France with us and hoped in us. The cup is full. Let General Eisenhower, who a short while ago was saying that he wished to save Islam "from Dakar to Mindanao" not attempt, through fear of communism, to provide security for Glaoui and Kittani; just as they have done, he would be signing a "pact" with the masked technicians of international slavery and repudiating his great predecessor, Abraham Lincoln, whom they killed at the end of the War of Secession.[37]

Besides writing and speaking out about the situation of Muslims in North Africa, Massignon continued the days of fasting he had inaugurated June 12. The second one took place August 14, in the middle of the critical events in Morocco. However, the date had also been chosen by France-Islam because of its religious significance for both Christians and Muslims, and therefore it symbolized one of those points of convergence between the two faiths, so dear to Massignon. It fell on a Friday, the day when the sura of the Cave, the story of the Seven Sleepers, was recited in the mosque. On August 14 also, Eastern rite Christians were concluding a two-week fast in preparation for the feast of the Assumption; their rite recalled that of Muslims and the June 12 fast which had coincided with the end of Ramadan. Under the aegis of France-Islam, a third day of fasting was held September 19, and again the date held significance for Massignon. It was the feast of Notre Dame de La Salette, the anniversary of Massignon's 1951 visit to Ephesus, the Muslim feast of Ashura and, that year, the Jewish feast of Yom Kippur. He had written about this fast to Martin Buber, the successor of Judah Magnes as head of the Ihud party, and the latter responded that he would participate

and pray for "Israel and her adversaries, linking them together in my
fast and my prayer . . ."[38] Finally, the first Friday of every month, beginning September 4, was designated a day of fasting for the restoration of peace in Morocco. Massignon fasted monthly for the rest of
his life.

Although the sultan was deposed and a successor named, the affair refused to die. On January 29, 1954, Sidi Muhammad and his
family were transferred to Madagascar and installed in a resort hotel
south of the capital Antananarivo or Tananarive. One of their first
French visitors was Louis Massignon, whose presence in January
1955 affirmed his support for the man he considered the legitimate
ruler of Morocco. During the two years following the sultan's overthrow, rising terrorism in Morocco clearly revealed that the attempt
to replace him had failed, and in November 1955, Sidi Muhammad
was officially restored to the throne. Returning from exile in Madagascar, the sultan publicly thanked Massignon for his support, during a stopover in Paris at the end of October. When the latter came
to Rabat, August 20, 1956, he was personally greeted by the monarch. This gratitude was reiterated several days later, on August 23,
when on Radio Tangiers the sultan recalled the fast organized by
Massignon on his behalf.[39]

In 1954, after Sidi Muhammad's overthrow but before the outbreak of the Algerian War in November, Massignon became president of the Amis de Gandhi and the *Comité pour l'amnistie aux
condamnés politiques d'outre-mer*. The latter group initially dealt
with the question of amnesty for political prisoners in Madagascar
and was seemingly far removed from his primary commitment to
Muslims in the Middle East and the Maghreb. However, at the time
the exiled sultan was living under virtual house arrest there and, as
Charles-André Julien explained:

> Because I knew of [Massignon's] passion for justice, I convinced
> him to assume the presidency of the *Comité pour l'amnistie des con-
> damnés politiques d'outre-mer*. He was less politically labeled than I
> was, and I persuaded him that he could be more effective. I had the

impression that he accepted this new responsibility as if God had marked him with his seal and forbade him to give it up.[40]

Massignon threw himself into the task of organizing both prayer and speech in support of the cause. Among other things he arranged a prayer vigil of some two hundred people, including Mauriac and his family, the evening of June 12, 1954, at Notre Dame Cathedral; the cardinal had consented to the site "on condition that it not be announced in the press."[41] The *comité* also held a huge meeting at the Mutualité on June 24 to demand that the government free political prisoners in Madagascar and the Maghreb. Massignon was joined by over two thousand people, including Jean-Paul Sartre and Albert Camus, whom he characterized among others as "Gandhians in the wider sense."[42] A manifesto was issued which expanded the appeal for clemency to include prisoners in the Maghreb. Thus, when Massignon visited Tananarive in January 1955, both the deposed sultan and the political prisoners of Madagascar preoccupied him.

The latter country had experienced its own violent drama resulting from demands for independence. Following a 1947 uprising, thirty-two Malagasy, including three deputies to the French National Assembly, were tried at Tananarive and convicted in October 1948, of having fomented the rebellion. Six, including two of the deputies were condemned to death; the third deputy was sentenced to life imprisonment. It was estimated that by 1948, there were more than 5,500 political prisoners in Madagascar. Eventually, in 1949, the six death sentences were commuted to life imprisonment on Corsica, but the question of amnesty remained for large numbers of political prisoners.

During Massignon's January 1955 trip to Madagascar he met with the families of Malagasy political prisoners and reviewed the situation. Charles-André Julien remembered the astounding impression Massignon made when he returned from Madagascar and reported on his trip:

> At the Hotel Lutetia, after his return from Madagascar, he summarized his mission. Suddenly, as if inspired, he abandoned the theme

of the prisoners and with sumptuous lyricism improvised brilliantly. When we returned to concrete facts about amnesty, they appeared to us as if bathed with a poetry and humanity that bestowed on them the stamp of eternity. Yes, that day, I became fully aware that Massignon possessed genius. [43]

By June 1955 the amnesty question had been revived in Paris, thanks to the publicity of Massignon's visit, agitation by the *comité* and the favorable results of a public-opinion poll the group conducted on the island. Not content with his efforts in January to console the families of the imprisoned senators, Massignon went in July 1955 to Corsica to visit the men imprisoned at the fortress of Calvi. In this instance success crowned his work, a rare occurrence in his persistent gestures on behalf of victims and the disenfranchised: on March 22, 1956, five Malagasy senators were liberated. Shortly thereafter many other political prisoners were freed. By the end of 1956 a state of siege had been lifted from the last areas of Madagascar.

Although his energy was increasingly directed to the political and social problems of Muslims in the Maghreb and France, Massignon continued until the end to promote causes that had long preoccupied him. One of the more curious of these involved the Ugandan convert, Charles Lwanga and his companions; they were martyred in 1886 rather than submit sexually to their nominally Muslim ruler. Massignon's concern about immoral sexual practices in male or female Christian societies and also the priesthood had first found expression years before in the "Prière sur Sodome." He felt that the example of these martyrs served as an antidote to such disorders, and at his suggestion, a group of priests celebrated a monthly Mass in their honor. Returning home from Madagascar in January 1955, Massignon himself visited Namugongo, Uganda, where the young men were killed. Their canonization in 1964, two years after his death, was hastened by his efforts to promote their cause among Church leaders, including the African bishops.[44] In the light of Church concern in recent decades about sexual misconduct among clergy, Massignon's discussion of the issue might seem to

have been prophetic; for some of his peers it was viewed as one ec-
centricity among the many exhibited by this eminent professor who
seemed increasingly caught up in religious and social causes extrane-
ous to his profession.

Yet if Massignon's involvement on behalf of the oppressed and
his ecclectic interests suggest that toward the end of his life he abandoned his scholarship altogether, such was not the case. The wide
array of topics he continued to study included eschatological themes
linked to Shi'ism, reflecting an interest begun in the 1930s; he was
consoled by the belief that an ultimate day of reckoning would
bring justice to the forgotten and disadvantaged. That hope was inseparable from the notion of mystical substitution lived out across
time by heroic persons, a theme which in turn was linked to his theory of history. All three aspects are reflected in articles written during this last period.

However, in the middle 1950s a new dimension appears which
provides insight into how Massignon interpreted his own apparently
fruitless struggles in the cause of justice. Religious figures in the history of Islam had always occupied key roles in his spiritual universe;
Abraham, Salman Pak, Hallaj, and the Seven Sleepers were variously
thought of links in the chain of intercessors, witnesses to truth
(*isnad*), mystical substitutes or *abdal,* and finally as signs of the ties
between Islam and Christianity. Their importance continued, but
his reflection began to extend to non-Islamic figures, most notably
Gandhi, and most surprisingly, Marie Antoinette. Familiar themes
focused increasingly on how individuals come to know and realize
the unique vocation which furthers God's deepest designs for them.

His discussion of Fatima, the daughter of Muhammad, who figured peripherally in the studies on Salman Pak, illustrates how his
thought had evolved. Predictably, she interested Massignon as another link between Islam and Christianity. In the ordeal (*mubahala*)
proposed to the Christian delegation from Yemen and witnessed by
Salman, she was one of the five, along with her husband Ali and two
children, whose lives were presented by Muhammad as guarantee of
the truth of Islam. Standing between her father, husband, and sons,

Fatima mediated relationships of paternity, marriage, motherhood, sonship, and brotherhood. Thus her very being constituted the Islamic parallel with Mary, the mother of Jesus, and hence another analogy between Christianity and Islam.

Beyond that obvious parallelism Massignon viewed Fatima as a suffering intercessor, a role she shared not only with Mary but with numerous other intercessors, mostly feminine figures, whose lives as *abdal* brought salvation to others. If as Ali's wife and the mother of Hasan and Husayn, Fatima was linked to the development of Shi'ism, her prayer identified her with such women and also with the Shi'ite hope for ultimate justice after life in an unjust world. As a woman, Fatima was powerless to control situations and vulnerable to abuse from others. In Muhammad's confrontation with the Christians, her presence was dictated not by choice but by reason of family relationships. Grieving her father's death and mistreated because she refused to affirm the legitimacy of the new caliph, she soon died and, according to legend, was secretly interred at night by her husband Ali and Salman Pak. To find consolation or show compassion for others, prayer was her sole recourse. Unable to obtain redress for those she loved, she could only pray that justice might ultimately be done at the end of time.

Her intercessory role was synonymous with her prayer and its distinguishing feature, eschatological hope. It was a role shaped by the strictures of her destiny but drawn forth by a call from God. Massignon alluded to her as he formulated his understanding of "vocation." Writing about Fatima and others during the middle 1950s he suggested that prayer, vow, and vocation are three indistinguishable aspects of the same reality:

> The inner drama of Islamic history, where woman has been veiled and humiliated for so long, since she is both a sign of temptation and the visitation of grace, is guided by the faithfulness of noble and unfortunate women who, beyond all the male oaths, have kept the vow linking them to the word of the Holy Book. And the very first, the most veiled, is Fatima, the favorite daughter of the prophet.[45]

Massignon's notion of "vow," here applied to Islam, was developed from many sources and owed much to Gandhi:

> In India, there is the question of vow—*vrata*. The point, I will say, having studied this word, is that you meditate before beginning to act and do not act merely by idealism. It means that you are no longer theoretical; it means that you are steadfast, that you meditate, contemplate. You try to find the inner meaning. You are fixed. You have vowed your life.[46]

Massignon associated "vow" with the feminine and "oath" or "solemn promise" with the masculine, "In prayer the vow is the arm of women just as the oath is the arm of men."[47]

However, this distinction in no way made vows the province of women. Indeed, "Each human person is essentially a vow, and his life concludes when his vocation bursts forth." The West identified vows with prayer, an adequate description provided prayer was defined according to the Semitic languages, namely as "something which comes from God." Although prayer was often envisaged "as spontaneous; to what extent is it not something wrested from us by God."[48] On the one hand this definition of vow and prayer connotes passivity in the one praying, and this stance coincided with Massignon's perception during his conversion experience that a mysterious Stranger had invaded his consciousness and turned his entire life upside down. On the other hand, the definition implies action since God's initiative elicits a response and marks the imperceptible beginnings of vocation, "The true and only story of human persons is the gradual emergence, through their public life, of a secret vow; far from degrading the vow, acting in public life purifies it."[49]

Massignon adopted Gandhi's saying that "God is the essence of the vow," or, phrased differently, "The vow is the very image of God."[50] He coined his own definition, "The vow is essentially the desire for God . . ."[51] By identifying his decades of work for Indian independence with the vows born of his religious commitment, Gandhi's autobiography gave Massignon a vocabulary for interpreting his own activity towards the end of his life. He noted that

Gandhi in explaining himself had eschewed "a grand mythology or an immense and unwieldy metaphysics, unlike so many of his compatriots . . ." His originality had consisted in the fact that "he has given us in his writings only cases of conscience lived out, where his 'inconsistencies,' as he called them, betray an ingenuous passion for an experiential truth embraced ever more closely."[52] Certainly, Massignon himself possessed a complex and often unwieldy symbol system, through which he was wont to filter the significance of his life. His encounter with Gandhi produced writing whose directness and urgency were often absent elsewhere.

The triad of prayer, vow, and vocation is set against the constraints imposed by "solemn promises" and "destiny." "Destiny is what the milieu we live in imposes on us; vocation is above it." The sense of vocation is indestructible because "there is hope in the depths of each of us, and this hope is enough to destroy the idea that destiny seals off vocation. Vocation opens to transcendence."[53] Massignon schematized this opposition by charting the life of Gandhi in a "life curve," comprising two parallel columns. The column on the right traced its objective happenings; on the left were found the "singular moments . . . corresponding to the 'inner experiences' of truth and justice" by which he resolved the dilemmas posed by the events and obligations of his milieu.[54]

The conflict between these two poles is experienced by everyone and demands resolution:

> Two elements of unequal value confront each other; the inner vocation we are unsure we will be able to fulfill but which is dearer to us than life, and on the other hand, the summons issued by the milieu, caste, race and group that says "you are committed to the milieu, you don't have to go looking for something else . . ." Someone [is] in a family where they have always been doctors or in the military, "What's gotten into you that you want something else?" Right there is the summons, "You've been prepared for this. We know the milieu. Why do you want to be something else?"[55]

The obstacles imposed by destiny include interpersonal relationships, "The solemn promises we have made to others forbid us or at the very least advise us against following our intimate, personal vocation . . ." The resulting tension, which Massignon called "knots of anguish," pits the call of vocation against the imperatives of destiny. He considered that "generally speaking a vocation is shaped in a time of tragedy or crisis," an indirect reference to the difficult situation in North Africa and his efforts to help resolve it.[56] Such a situation constitutes "the shock of an event" that intersects with the constraints imposed by the milieu and reveals that the intimate call of vocation is indeed from God.[57]

Although Massignon never explicitly said so when commenting on vocation, he undoubtedly was thinking of choices he had faced in his own "life curve," when his personal commitment to Islam confronted the political upheavals affecting its people, the Muslims to whom he had dedicated his life. By deciding to speak out publicly in defense of the peoples of the Maghreb, he had chosen to endure a kind of ridicule that neither his scholarship nor his assertive Catholicism had ever elicited. This was all the more true because ultimately his position would be criticized on all sides: by his academic peers for abandoning purely scholarly pursuits, by many French people for betraying his country, by proponents of Algerian nationalism because he never advocated independence, and by some fellow protesters who considered his support of nonviolence to be quixotic at best. Surely, Massignon was describing the confrontation between destiny and vocation in his own life when he wrote:

> The shock of the event fulfills the vow through the solemn promises which break open its secret. That's the problem of the secret, that terrible thing. Within ourselves, we have suffered terribly. We have had a call. This call, we don't know what it is. It is contradicted, and by the very fact of being contradicted, it bursts forth. We cannot act otherwise. That is what we are. We accept that they take from us everything that is not our vow. Our personality be-

comes unified through the very event that has struck us and by the oaths surrounding us which break open the secret.[58]

In the end a vocation was realized above and beyond any given action; through personal witness one stood and spoke for the truth. This idea corresponded more and more with Massignon's own perception of vocation. It provided comfort because integrity in witnessing was not measured by success or failure in any given instance, but rather by personal steadfastness, whatever the cost: "This idea of witnessing, which is closely related to vocation, seems inadequate for those who think we must accomplish actions. But in the end, is not witnessing all that Christ did?"[59] Massignon explicitly identified his work on behalf of Muslims with his own sense of vocation and explained how he prevailed during those last years of bitter controversy over the fate of Algeria:

> People will say to me: "What qualifies you to be a witness?" And then I remember a Jewish friend who used to say: "When there is no prophet one still must proclaim." The witness is bound to act just the same, whatever exterior indignities surround him or the much stronger inner unworthiness he feels.
>
> A voluntary witness, of course. Witnessing necessarily implies a move towards, a decision in favor of the demands of justice. I admit that it's what has gripped me more and more at the end of my life, and again I feel it is my vocation. But it was evident and came about only gradually because I believe that within love nothing is superior to the passion for justice.[60]

Any satisfaction Massignon felt in the mid-1950s over the outcome of his efforts in Morocco or on behalf of the Malagasy senators was tempered by the rising violence of the Algerian war. When he spoke a year before his death, in January 1961, on his many, diverse struggles for justice, Massignon was exhausted by six years of that conflict. He noted how all his efforts had been undertaken in the spirit of Gandhi and how, like his model, he had known failure.

Seen against the backdrop of the war, only his work for the *comité* constituted an unqualified success:

> A single radiant success remains in my memory, that of the *Comité pour l'amnistie aux condamnés politiques d'outre-mer*, where, from one end to the other, wonderful friends, Gandhians without knowing it, helped me liberate those whose liberty we demanded, June 24, 1954, at the Mutualité . . . Aside from that Malagasy success, which was a stratagem for dealing with the French-African problem, an ever more malevolent lack of understanding has blocked our efforts for Algeria. In union with Gandhi these have forced me to deepen the ways of making the collective demands for truth more effective.[61]

Only his faith and the example of Gandhi would allow him to endure the anguish of the years between 1954 and his death in 1962.

NINE

Algeria, the Ultimate Suffering

Although Massignon did not believe he had changed the course of events in Morocco, he had helped mobilize a segment of French public opinion which, by opposing government policy, had helped to reverse it. The rightful sultan was restored to power, and Morocco ultimately achieved independence. However, the outcome of Massignon's efforts to end the Algerian war was quite different. Whereas he had supported independence for the protectorates of Morocco and Tunisia, he hoped until the end that, in spite of the past, the Muslim and European communities of Algeria could achieve a modus vivendi acceptable to both sides. Since Algeria had formed part of France juridically for over a hundred years, he felt that both the ties and the obligations to the Muslim population were stronger than in the other French colonies of North Africa. Throughout the conflict he maintained his position unwaveringly and at great personal cost. His ideal of mutual understanding between Christians and Muslims sprang not from pro- or anticolonial ideology but from his religious faith that since both groups descended from Abraham, the practice of sacred hospitality was incumbent upon them in every area of their lives. A July 1954 article written for *Esprit* restated his persistent hope that with an understanding of the Arabic language and culture, the Muslim and French population could live side by side in peace and mutual respect, and thus ultimately fulfill what he considered to be the special vocation of France:

To maintain our colonies is impossible except on this condition. The sons and daughters of colonists must decide to study the Arabic language, without fear of becoming "shanty Arabs." We cannot silently stand by as our country forfeits its honor in North Africa. It must not repudiate its beautiful vocation overseas by permitting untruths in word and writing to go unsanctioned.[1]

In some eyes this view implied that he remained caught in the mindset of France's colonial past and that his anguish over Algeria was aggravated by inherent contradictions in his position. As one writer commented:

He never considered repudiating his youth, imbued with the grand imperial dream at the dawn of the twentieth century . . . The activity of France overseas had been seen and understood by him, not as an enterprise of spoliation, but as a gift. It was connected to an ideal of justice, and he had defined it even more as communication among men and between peoples through the respect of their usages and traditions. The Algerian tragedy tore him apart, and until the eve of his death in 1962, he remained faithful to the image of an Algeria that was an extension of France and the privileged meeting ground of two races and two cultures. And probably one can speak of the contradictions in an old man divided between his inflexibile moral principles and his lack of adaptation to the new historical conditions of his time. On a deeper level and beyond these contradictions, the example seems to reveal the ambiguity of certain values which can be called upon to promote seemingly opposed attitudes—values that for a long time had been integrated into the highest expression of French imperialism and were now claimed and absorbed by the ideology of decolonialization.[2]

Such a critique, while correctly stating that Massignon indeed hoped that France and Algeria would remain united, ignores nuances in his position. By the 1920s, he had abandoned any illusions about the beneficial results of French "imperialism." If in principle French rule overseas was a gift, Massignon saw that in fact it had become "spoliation." Algeria should not be considered an "extension" of France; rather the two cultures should be equally respected. While he advocated political and economic means for achieving this, his hopes for such mutuality ultimately rested on the spiritual ideal of hospitality, attainable only through the practice of religious faith. One could argue that such a view was naive but not that it was based on nostalgia for a colonial past.

The protracted conflict would cause Massignon deep suffering. For years he had condemned French abuses in the Maghreb; now he mourned the human losses of both sides and watched helplessly as all hope gradually disappeared that Muslims and Christians might live peacefully in the same land. Thus, his life seemed marked on all sides by loss. His efforts to bring about social, political, and economic change in Algeria appeared increasingly futile, even as his professional world was shrinking. After retiring from the Collège de France in 1954, he perceived that some colleagues, for whom he had long been an anomaly, now ignored him altogether.

The torch was passed to younger men. Henri Laoust took over his chair at the Collège de France, and scholars such as Jacques Berque concentrated on the impact of worldwide historical movements in the development of Islam rather than on its Semitic and religious roots. Always ascetic looking, Massignon began to appear more frail physically, as Berque noted when he himself was named to the Collège de France in 1956: "He was still alive, and his spirit glimmered like the wick of a votive candle about to flicker out. I saw in him at one and the same time the summation and final term of Orientalism, just as some saw in Hegel the end point of philosophy."[3]

As was customary when an eminent professor retired, Massignon's colleagues contributed a festschrift of articles in his honor, in this case, four volumes. The preface hints that his academic peers held mixed feelings about his activity in the public arena. Their reservations appear after the customary summary of the honoree's illustrious career:

Without abandoning his professional work, he threw himself into political and social movements. Over these last few years, leading the life both of a scholar and public commentator, he has worked in cooperation with the press, an effort which—like his journal articles—certainly raises criticism but likewise requires one to recognize the sincerity of their author. The ideas that inspire him are sometimes very subtle and can even appear extremist; however, they are always generous.[4]

His peers' objections notwithstanding, Massignon did possess confreres during the years of the Algerian struggle. The liberal Catholic community that was marshaled to oppose French policy in Morocco would voice increasing opposition to the war as it dragged on. France-Islam remained active, as did France-Maghreb. Moreover, Massignon never hesitated to ally himself with those whom he saw fighting for justice, whatever their religious beliefs; he marched with Sartre as well as Mauriac. Nevertheless he did stand apart because, first, his stand was based explicitly on religious faith and a total commitment to nonviolence as exemplified by Gandhi, and secondly, it stopped short of demanding independence for Algeria.

Nowhere are both his stance on the Algerian war and his ways of dealing with it more consistently revealed than in the various newsletters Massignon wrote for the Amis de Gandhi and the Badaliya from the war's beginnings in 1954 until the end of his life. In the 1954 annual letter to the Badaliya, familiar themes recurred, drawn from his personal universe of symbol and shrine. He reiterated the group's overarching goal of Muslim-Christian understanding, realized through compassion and mystical substitution. The importance he accorded to sacred places is reflected in his satisfaction that the first annual Islamo-Christian pilgrimage to the chapel of the Seven Sleepers had been a success. He recounted again how the Badaliya had originated in his prayer for the conversion of Luis de Cuadra and told how his pilgrimages of 1954 had included a visit to the

Mislata prison in Valencia, where his friend had committed suicide thirty-three years before.

In that letter Massignon also alluded to the November 1 uprising in Algeria, which in fact launched more than seven years of sustained bloodshed. The reference, in a long paragraph about political prisoners, reveals here as elsewhere that he was preoccupied by the fate of those arrested. However, there is no indication that he thought this situation to be graver than the imprisonment of the Malagasy senators or the plight of political detainees in Tunisia:

> And we pray ardently, so that in the wake of the repression of the Algerian insurgents of the Aurès [mountain range in northeastern Algeria], broad measures might liberate the Algerian political detainees imprisoned, since 1945 and 1952, under conditions that are often inhuman, discriminatory in any case, and contrary to our official promises of respect for our fellow Muslim citizens and their wives . . . Economic misery and the impossibility of expressing any grievance about their despised religion and their Arabic language, which is systematically persecuted, run the risk of driving the Algerian Muslim electorate into a general uprising, the elections [April 1948] having been openly and cynically prefabricated.[5]

The violence in question had erupted during the early morning hours of November 1, when in thirty points around Algeria, seventy different incidents of violence were recorded, causing eight deaths and substantial damage. Casualties were heaviest in the mountain region of Aurès in the department of Constantine, southeast of Algiers. Simultaneously, the Front de Libération Nationale (FLN) issued a manifesto announcing its existence and mandating a war to achieve independence for Algeria. There were swift and widespread reprisals; by the end of November 750 had been jailed in Algeria and France. The number would reach 2,000 by the end of the year.

An ultimate rupture between Algeria and France was not uppermost in people's thinking at the end of 1954 and certainly not in Massignon's. Nevertheless, the Badaliya letter and other writing during this period clearly outline the path he himself would follow for the duration of the conflict. A January 1955 article in *Esprit* asserted that the example of Gandhi's action in India could help resolve the burgeoning conflict in Algeria:

> In North Africa, where partition can still be avoided, we can, like Gandhi before 1947, persuade our compatriots, be they Christian or not, to participate unreservedly in all their [Muslim] demands for justice that are the most religious: fasting, pilgrimage, and the elimination of alcoholism and prostitution, which we regulate although it is against their faith. Gandhi went so far as a common language, and we must adopt Arabic as a second national language in Algeria if we wish to remain "at home" with those who speak it and construct with them a common future.[6]

In the course of 1955, Massignon discussed the Algerian problem at length with Monteil, who supported independence. Their contact throughout this period illustrates how, despite serious differences between them, Massignon's undeniable commitment to justice earned him not only a hearing but also profound respect. Early in 1955, Monteil was assigned to head the military cabinet of the newly named governor general of Algeria, Jacques Soustelle, and to make contact with various Algerian nationalists. He saw Massignon on each of his fourteen trips to Paris that year, and if, on the one hand, he criticized some of the latter's views on Algeria, on the other hand both men shared the same moral stance: "Certainly, his political positions on Algeria (*'francisation'*) lagged very far behind mine, but we shared an identical passion for justice—even if in my agnosticism that thirst had no religious basis."[7]

However, Monteil could only shake his head when Massignon wrote him, as he did on April 9, wondering if a possibility existed for a "voluntary redistribution of lands by serious Christian colonists," or in a letter elsewhere, asking about the status of Arabic as the second national language of Algeria.[8] Nevertheless, from his years of travel and experience in Algeria, Massignon provided Monteil with useful contacts during the latter's mission, and the two often conferred on the proper approach for obtaining the freedom of

Algerian nationalists imprisoned after the November 1 uprising.[9] A year later, after Monteil resigned his cabinet position, he together with Massignon prepared a short summary of the situation at the request of Charles de Gaulle, then removed from politics but careful to remain well-connected to information sources.

As the crisis deepened and conflict escalated in 1955, public opposition to the government's position began to crystalize, and Massignon stood at the forefront of the movement along with friends such as Jean Marie Domenach, François Mauriac, and Robert Barrat. Over the years he and his allies employed various strategies, effective in the Moroccan crisis, to voice their opposition to the war and the methods used to quell the unrest and violence in Algeria. Massignon was a tireless letter writer, and sometimes academic colleagues stood with him. On March 28 as one of a group of ethnologists, he signed an "open letter" to the head of government demanding "negotiations with the Algerian leaders of the Algerian movement."[10] On July 11 the Comité pour l'amnistie aux condamnés politiques d'outre-mer and Massignon "invited the head of state to suspend capital punishment."[11] Another important and early example of protest resulted from an episode of August 20, when two days of rioting led to severe repressions in the Aurès, the same region where fighting had begun a year earlier. Between the initial disorder and the reprisals, thousands were killed, prefiguring years of bloodshed to come.

This event precipitated Monteil's resignation from his post in Algeria and led to a fact-finding trip there by Robert Barrat. Barrat met with guerilla fighters, and the Paris press published his interviews.[12] At dawn one week later the military tribunal of Algiers had him arrested in Paris for failing to reveal his sources. The subsequent public outcry was documented September 30 in *Témoignage chrétien*, which quoted a telegram from Massignon among others. He likewise helped create a committee for Barrat's defense, which obtained his rapid release and spared the journalist from extradition to Algiers.

That same year, with increasing numbers of North Africans arrested, Massignon began visiting them at Fresnes, the Paris prison made notorious by the Gestapo during the Occupation. This move developed naturally from his teaching of night classes to North Africans for almost three decades and from having helped found Aide aux Nord-africains résidant en France, which provided social services.[13] He first visited the prison as a member of the Saint Vincent de Paul Society, but his views proved too radical for the church-affiliated society. Having demanded that these prisoners receive the legal status of conscientious objectors, a category unknown in French law, Massignon was crossed off the society's list in 1958. "These poor confreres considered that a visitor is an auxiliary of the police; that's just how far their Christian and French 'truth' extends."[14] Undaunted, he visited the prison alone thereafter.

The energy to persevere at whatever cost in such activity derived not only from a commitment to justice founded on the notion of sacred hospitality but increasingly from the example of Gandhi. Massignon was invited to join in spirit with Indian and Pakistani Muslims at Mehrauli, the Muslim shrine of Gandhi's last pilgrimage; ceremonies marking that event were to be held at the end of October. His own mode of participation linked the martyred Hindu and the Algerian War. On October 12, 1955, he was joined by members of the Amis de Gandhi along with André Peretti and Jean Scelles, fellow founders of the Comité France-Islam, on the steps of the mosque of Paris. The Fatiha, (the initial sura of the Qur'an) was prayed in Arabic for "all the victims . . . the women and children above all, fallen on both sides." Then a declaration was read which pointed out that although Algeria theoretically formed part of France, the treatment accorded Algerians proved the reality to be otherwise. Change was demanded:

> —We consider that the government of the Republic has not yet treated Muslim Algeria like Christian Auvergne and Brittany.
> —We want it henceforth to treat its children like our children, its women like our women, and its men like our men: as free men with their own destiny.[15]

Finally, the group committed itself to continue the struggle it had begun, a promise Massignon kept until the end. "Just as Gandhi did in Delhi in 1947, in front of the Muslim women with whom he had fasted for justice, we commit ourselves under oath, to pursue our efforts to maintain our pledged word and demand justice."[16]

On October 14 this declaration was submitted to Robert Schuman, then minister of justice. Such publicity brought Massignon wide attention and angered many, including right-wing extremists, whose opposition to Algerian independence included violence. He himself became a target eleven days later, October 25. He had finished speaking in Paris at the Société des savantes about Gandhi's last promise of nonviolence given at Mehrauli, and in spite of a small hostile group in the audience, the talk itself passed without incident. As people filed out Massignon and the meeting's organizers remained a few minutes to compare notes; they were then advised by a hall employee to leave by a back door. Only the next day did they learn from the press that a grenade had exploded on the sidewalk as people were exiting; three were injured.[17]

Massignon evaluated the war's first year in the 1955 annual letter to the Badaliya. Not only was the tone more somber than in previous years, but the message almost prophetically seemed to foretell the conflict's terrorist repercussions in Paris and ultimately the eviction of Europeans from Algeria:

> In North Africa, the political emancipation of Tunisia, followed by that of Morocco, has touched off in Algeria a crisis that calls into question the future of France itself; if she does not wish to accept on an equal footing the 400,000 North African Muslim workers who are more and more creating mixed families, then by an implacable rule of reciprocity, Muslim Algeria will not want to treat as brothers, the million French colonists who live there like privileged persons.[18]

His outspoken activism on behalf of North Africans and his espousal of Gandhian nonviolence made Massignon vulnerable to misinterpretation on many issues besides the war. Crises of October

1956 illustrate this well. All that month the U.N. Security Council was debating the fate of the Suez Canal, nationalized by the Egyptians and threatened by French and British military invasion; on October 23 a Moroccan plane carrying Ben Bella, a founder of the FLN, was hijacked by its French crew and taken to Algiers; a day later the Soviets crushed the Hungarian revolt. The Suez crisis prompted Massignon to special fasting above and beyond the customary monthly fast of the Badaliya, and he hammered the press with protests over the Ben Bella highjacking.[19] Predictably, he was also asked in an interview to condemn the Soviet intervention in Hungary. He wished to temper his remarks for two reasons. On the one hand, while he had no love for Soviet communism, neither did he trust its adversaries, the most powerful of which was the American government. (In his eyes America had compromised itself by supporting Israel against the Palestinians, and both superpowers were engaged in a godless struggle for world domination.) On the other hand, "I tried to show by a dual condemnation that truth does not stop at borders . . . and that in any case it must first be asserted 'intra muros' inside our city."[20] Therefore, instead of specifically condemning the Soviet invasion, he responded to the request by stating, "I am not a specialist in Magyar affairs," and asked for prayers and nonviolence in the spirit of Gandhi. However, the comment about specialization was taken out of context and appeared on the front page of the *Figaro*; the prayer request and other comments were eliminated. Massignon, furious, recounted how two accounts of the interview, the one truncated, the other falsified, made it appear in the Paris press as if Gandhi's teaching had led him "not to choose between victims and executioners and thus to betray the truth."[21] The effect was to "brazenly deny that I had condemned Budapest so as to make me appear like the sole calumniator of my country."[22] He for his part felt that truth and justice were indivisible and that the request for prayer covered the entire situation. François Mauriac attempted to explain Massignon's position in his regular column for the *Express*.[23]

The war showed no signs of abating in 1957; indeed, both sides were caught in an escalating spiral of violence. The nationalists used it not only to terrorize the Europeans and intimidate the local populations but also to settle scores with rival independence groups. As the situation worsened, the French military employed ever harsher measures in attempting to end the disorder. Such widespread and ongoing disdain for human life caused Massignon his deepest anguish because it struck at the very heart of the respect demanded by "sacred hospitality." His involvement in protest intensified. When the FLN stepped up its fight through terrorist attacks in Algiers itself, the army began using torture as an interrogation method in order to obtain information. As a security measure many Algerians were relocated in internment camps. Once these allegations reached the French press, public opposition to the conflict became more widespread, and demands to end the torture and relocation camps led to a series of silent protest demonstations. Massignon was in charge of organizing the first one, planned for the esplanade of the Invalides. He explained Gandhian nonviolence to government officials, but later the Paris prefect of police forbade the demonstration. Massignon obediently canceled it; however, unaware of the reversal, around five hundred sympathizers gathered the next day, only to be promptly arrested. Although the second demonstration, June 22, was likewise forbidden at the last minute, Massignon attended anyway, marching at its head along with Sartre and Mauriac. "They only arrested the young people, which mortified me."[24]

Specific instances of torture were revealed. Djamila Bouhired, a twenty-two-year-old member of the Algerian resistance, was tortured and condemned to death for having placed a bomb in the Algiers office of Air France. The bomb did not explode, but two others placed at the same time in popular European cafes did. Her case attracted international attention and became the subject of a book. Massignon commented about her situation:

> Pray that the French state does not execute Djamila Bouhired: France would bear a stain of infamy. Upon returning at three in the morning to the Barberoussa prison, she announced her death

sentence to the attentive prison cells by singing. I am not saying that the heroism of this child guarantees her holiness, which is the secret of God . . .[25]

In May 1957 a young Algerian, Muhammad Ben-Sadok, killed Ali Chekkal, former vice-president of the Algerian Assembly, for being a "collaborator." The murder was widely reported because it occurred in the Paris suburbs at the end of an important soccer match attended by President René Coty.[26] Massignon visited the accused in prison and filed a deposition on his behalf, thereby helping him escape the death penalty. The eleventh annual letter to the Badaliya carried this note under the heading "alms": "We prayed that attenuating circumstances might be accorded to the the young Muslim terrorists, the Algerian terrorists Ben Sadok and Djamila Bouhired, so that French honor and justice might be preserved."[27]

Some of those who supported continued French control in Algeria, among them conservative Catholics and a few army chaplains, suggested that torture could be tolerated as a last resort in order to combat the equally intolerable situation of urban terrorism initiated by the FLN in Algiers. Such tactics could be justified all the more since it was suspected by many that the violence was being fueled by international communism for its own ends. According to this view then, the Algerian war involved fighting not just for French Algeria but for the survival of the free world. Massignon, however, indignantly rejected such arguments:

> The sacristy owls continue to flap around aimlessly, claiming that as long as the Soviets haven't stopped torturing, we are allowed to torture in Algeria. That's what they call defending the honor of the Army. It's a bit much, and the hard-hitting summary which J.-P. Sartre . . . made of the terrible book of Henri Alleg has converted Gabriel Marcel, among others.[28]

For chaplains of army units engaged in torture and who, like one Père Delarue, justified their practices as "effective even though unusual,"[29] Massignon had only withering pity: "Let us sorrowfully take upon ourselves the moral deficiency of the chaplains responsible, of those who let themselves be mobilized in order to 'calm' the consciences of the officers and soldiers 'troubled' by the aforesaid methods ('skillful, for the desecration of the human body'), and who have dared to justify them."[30]

Well aware that the French who actively supported the Algerian cause were also subject to arbitrary arrest, if not to torture, Massignon added, "We prayed for the generous Christian men and women who have, in the name of sacred hospitality, voluntarily exposed themselves to endure the same brutality (contrary to the law) as their Muslim sisters and brothers in Algiers."

Massignon himself had escaped physical injury in the 1955 episode of the grenade, but at a conference he gave early in 1958 he was physically attacked. The Catholic Center of French Intellectuals invited him to give a lecture, February 17, 1958, on Charles de Foucauld. As he was about to begin, an individual approached and struck him. Massignon described the incident in a letter:

> I fell into a snare; hardly had I opened my mouth when pamphlets began to be thrown about describing me as a traitor (for having requested amnesty for "assassins of color"); the platform was taken over by force. The letters Père de Foucauld wrote me were thrown on the ground. I was struck, hit squarely beneath my right eye and only escaped a chair brandished over my head thanks to an unknown friend who fell to the ground with his face all bloodied. The police needed twenty minutes to eject the agitators. I then took over and spoke for twenty minutes.[31]

This incident reflects in a small way how volatile and potentially dangerous the French political climate had become by 1958. Indeed, the situation was verging on chaos. A no-confidence vote in April provoked the twentieth ministerial crisis since the Fourth Republic's creation in 1947. Governments had fallen successively because they were unable to achieve consensus about the fate of Algeria and thereby end the war. Many, including Massignon, had already urged that General de Gaulle return and restore order to an increasingly critical situation. Edmond Michelet, an early Gaullist and later a minister under de Gaulle, urged Massignon to concretize his support for the general; responding at the end of April, Massignon agreed to sign a document addressed to President Coty, the legislators, and de Gaulle. It requested that Coty "invite General de Gaulle to form a government, that the Assembly ratify this choice and General de Gaulle accept the mandate."[32] A letter to Monteil that July illustrates what had motivated him, "In fraternal union with you I gave my name to Charles de Gaulle on April 28, so that he might fulfill the African vocation of France by keeping the word pledged to Islam."[33] Massignon apparently hoped that the new head of state might somehow achieve his cherished notion of mutual understanding and respect between the Muslim and European communities in Algeria. Although that hope was not to be realized, until the end he characterized de Gaulle as "a noble man, pure and strong, whom no one has ever bought."[34]

On May 13, the end of the Fourth Republic and the advent to power of de Gaulle were precipitated when a committee of public safety created by the Algiers military command demanded that the general return and restore order. Almost immediately Massignon became concerned because the petition addressed to President Coty which he had signed became public; the radio broadcast it the evening of May 15, two days after the committee of public safety had demanded the general's return. Massignon wrote Michelet that under the circumstances such news only served to "heighten confusion in many minds" and cautioned that "such a government could only be formed within republican legal forms, the single guarantor of the unity of the country."[35] This position reflected his conviction that all forms of protest or witnessing to truth must occur within the parameters of the law. Such a belief was consonant with Gandhian nonviolence, but for Massignon it had originated in his veneration of Hallaj and the latter's acceptance of death at the hands of the Baghdad authorities.

Political disintegration in France was averted when de Gaulle was invested as head of state on June 1, 1958, and reorganized the nation's political structure through the constitution of the Fifth Republic. De Gaulle came to power supported by both the proponents of French Algeria and those who favored Algerian independence. His own position seemed ambiguous; in order to stay in power long enough to resolve the crisis, the general needed to mollify both sides simultaneously, at least for a time. Therefore, although his government restored national order, it brought no immediate solution either to the war or its negative effects, as Massignon noted in the 1958 annual letter to the Badaliya:

> The regime of authority France has accepted since May 13, 1958, has singularly limited nonviolent demands for truth and justice by practically abolishing silent demonstrations and public meetings which insisted that an end be put to judicial extortion of confessions (written up in advance) through physical and psychological pressure. They have maintained the decree of November 4 [*sic*], 1955, abolishing the right of asylum (that fundamental law, etched in all free hearts.) Concentration camps have reached the mainland with their methods of administrative inquisition, in order to "protect civilization against the FLN and communism." All of this only accelerates, alas, the physical and psychic uprooting of the "regrouped" Muslim populations . . . Too many believers among us are resigned to such practices, as dubious from the standpoint of social morality as of political effectiveness.[36]

If the issue of the internment camps in Algeria and France remained a central one in 1959, other matters troubled Massignon as well. He was appalled to learn that Ramadan had been celebrated in Algiers by a twenty-one-gun salute, and that afterwards the bodies of two rebels killed by police were exposed to the forced gaze of the Muslim population, "(SS style) in order to teach them that liberty can be found only beyond and through death."[37] In April, debate ensued about teaching Arabic in the lycées of Algiers. Massignon, his successor at the Collège de France, Henri Laoust, and a colleague, Régis Blachère, protested against replacing modern Arabic with "an arbitrary Maghrebin, dialectical Arabic." With such a tactic "they wish to cleanse the craniums of 837,000 people displaced in the 'resettlement' camps, in order to purge them of any Arab ideal and throw them back on French, a language of civilization, for their own good, naturally."[38]

Yet Massignon considered that sooner or later de Gaulle would end the Algerian conflict, and in the March convocation of the Badaliya, he wrote: "All eyes are fixed on France and its leader, generally judged capable of resolving the Algerian problem, because he doesn't seem disposed to perjure the word of France."[39] The rituals and pilgrimages that sustained and encouraged him continued. On July 13, in remembrance of both Gandhi and Lincoln, he summoned the Amis de Gandhi to an August day of fasting for peace. The end of July took him to the crypt of the Seven Sleepers at Vieux Marché for the annual pilgrimage. Around the world people participated in the fast day, August 14. Massignon was also heartened, first on September 16, when de Gaulle declared Algeria's right to self-determination, and then on January 29, 1960, when that promise was renewed:

> After the first fast of August 14, our second Gandhian day of fasting for peaceful reconciliation took place January 29, the very day the French head of state renewed his declaration of September 16 about the right of Algeria to self-determination. Coming in the middle of a week of Algerian insurrection, this delayed public meetings such as our January 30, 1960 meeting of the "Amis de Gandhi."[40]

Nevertheless, the internment camps continued to operate, and in 1960 Massignon became directly involved in condemning their existence. Through his years of fasting, Massignon had come in contact with Lanza del Vasto (1901–1985), "a pure Gandhian,"[41] who had formed many young people in Gandhian principles of nonviolence. One among them, Joseph Pyronnet, had gathered thirty persons to protest against the camps by prayer, fasting, and a request that they themselves be interred. In 1959 Massignon, as president of the Amis de Gandhi had signed at Pyronnet's urging a letter of protest addressed to de Gaulle. It condemned the creation of a camp at Larzac, a military facility in the Massif Central. Pyronnet then organized a silent demonstration April 30, 1960, in front of the camp at Vincennes. Invited to attend Massignon wrote to Monteil:

> I am writing today that I accept to be among the personalities who will participate in the silent demonstration of Joseph Pyronnet in front of the internment camp at Vincennes: the scandal of the internment camps is opening the eyes of younger generations, who feel that this aspect of military duty dishonors the military profession; we risk seeing the formation of clandestine networks of spiritual resistance, evidently illegal; but what we are doing in Algeria, does it conform to law?[42]

Actively participating in such a demonstration was no small matter for Massignon, now close to seventy-seven years old and in compromised health. Sporadic bouts of neuritis in his right hip had caused him increasing pain since his return from the Middle East at the end of January, and the vision in his right eye was almost gone.[43] Although the sheer intensity of his presence often deflected others' attention from his physical condition, he was well aware of it, as he explained at the end of March in letters to friends. One was to Thomas Merton, first known to him through Maritain. The latter had urged Massignon to visit the Trappist during his 1952 trip to the United States. Massignon had been unable to do so and their two-year correspondence had begun only in 1959. Here as in later letters to Merton, health concerns are mentioned: "I am 'humbled' by a *nevrite* since two months, and I can't go to the nearest post office without fits of anguish. I know it is merely the result of a vertebral displacement, not an organic illness, but I endure . . ." (original English text).[44] He ended by saying, "My wife goes to the post office, so I stop." If the neuritis made walking a source of pain, flights of stairs were more difficult yet. Thus, Massignon hesitated to take the *métro* to the demonstration site and asked Gabriel Marcel to pick him up, adding that "a car coming from you would reassure my family who find that I am giving in to extremists."[45]

The demonstration occurred as scheduled, but Marcel could not attend. Massignon managed to arrive and along with seven hundred others was arrested; twelve police vans and more than two hours were required to carry or drag away participants sitting on the grass. He recounted the scene:

> With all this my neuritis tightens up my right knee and makes it rigid. On April 30 contrary to what Domenach said (*L'Express* May 6) the policeman who wanted to "drag me by the feet" noticed this. In a reflex of fear he stood me on the aforesaid feet, an easier position for "embarking me" (after Theodore Monod whom they propelled head first into the prison van—he hit his head—and before Lanza, whose head hit the doorframe so hard that he bled freely). They promised us that the next time they'd have water canons . . .[46]

Fellow demonstrator Theodore Monod recalled his impressions of Massignon that day:

> I felt a little sorry for Massignon who was on my left. L. del Vasto, on the right was in his own element, but poor Massignon gave me the impression of a poor soaked bird, in his little raincoat of faded gabardine. I thought I learned—I didn't insist on it too much, of course—I thought I learned that he feared the welcome he would receive at home when he would have to admit this new adventure . . .[47]

Some demonstrators were taken to the police station, but a group including Massignon was driven to a cemetery on the outskirts of town where a policeman killed by Algerian terrorists was buried. Pyronnet himself had suggested this move in order to show that the demonstrators disavowed violence in all forms. Afterwards, Massignon and the others were obliged to walk a considerable distance before finding a bus to take them back to the city.[48]

Two days before the next demonstration, scheduled for May 28,

Massignon and Gabriel Marcel talked, at the request of the organizers, about their understanding of Gandhi and nonviolence. On May 28 several hundred people gathered as planned at the circle of the Champs-Elysée; this time the group including Massignon was incarcerated for the night in the prison set up in the former Beaujon hospital. His presence was not lost on those who spent that night with him, "in that cell where I spent several hours at Beaujon, some young students came to say 'We're glad there's a professor from the Collège de France here with us.'"[49] In a letter to Merton June 3, Massignon summarized the event very simply: "We have been incarcerated again (as on April 30th) on May 28th. We had gathered for nonviolence at the Rond-Point des Champs Elysées. We remained 8 hours in a cell where there was an exchange of thoughts on nonviolence. The public opinion was impressed more than on April 30th" (original English text).[50]

Massignon's public protests ended there, although he did visit Pyronnet's group June 11 during its week-long fast at Nanterre and supported Action civique non-violente, created by them in order to organize and sustain their resistance. However, the Amis de Gandhi did not join forces with the ACNV because, as Massignon had explained at his May 26 talk to the group, the participation of the former in the May 28 demonstration was based "on strictly limited social grounds: a 'no' to internment camps for suspects."[51] The reasons advanced for this decision illuminate Massignon's own understanding of Gandhi's teaching. He felt that the ACNV by reason of its very success was being pulled in two directions. Internally, the group was being drawn to the notion of a kind of "world disarmament" to be achieved through a general strike affecting all areas of civic life. In contrast "Gandhi did not desert; he remained with his brothers in order to intervene in their battles at the risk of his life."[52] Externally, the group risked being co-opted by other protest organizers who had participated in the May 28 demonstration in order to learn nonviolence as simply one strategy among others but who did not believe in it per se.

Several months later Massignon's prediction of clandestine resistance and civil disobedience was seemingly realized. The writer Francis Jeanson was accused of running an underground network providing money and shelter for members of the FLN. The opening of his trial at the beginning of September coincided with the publication of the "Manifeste des 121," declaring that those who opposed the war claimed "insubordination" as a right. It was signed by some of the era's most distinguished French intellectuals. A series of rhetorical questions outlined the conditions legitimizing that right:

> What is civic-mindedness when in certain circumstances it becomes shameful submission? Are there not cases when refusing to serve is a sacred duty, when "betrayal" signifies courageous respect for the truth? And when the army is shown to be in a state of open or latent revolt against democratic institutions, through the will of those who utilize it as an instrument of racist or ideological domination, does not a revolt against the army acquire new meaning?[53]

Massignon, however, did not sign the document because, like Gandhi, he believed that resistance must be limited to speaking the truth to one's adversaries and enduring whatever legal consequences followed from such a move. If such witness brought retaliation, then so be it. The ensuing suffering placed one in the company of both Jesus and Hallaj, killed for proclaiming the truth. He was equally adamant in denouncing any attempts to water down the truth by so-called extenuating circumstances:

> Worsening of the Algerian drama: the folly of the partisans of insubordination (which neither Socrates nor Gandhi would have admitted; the just one dies, struck down by the laws of the City)—the not lesser dementia of people who maintain that their conscience (Christian or not) can participate in torture without being violated by the devil and that it can lie indefinitely 'through patriotism.'[54]

In the few years remaining to him, Massignon, now seventy-seven, continued to oppose the war but concentrated his public activity on the annual July pilgrimages to Vieux-Marché, the monthly fasts of the Badaliya, and those he initiated periodically for the Amis de Gandhi. By his own admission he also felt increasingly alone and solitary, a perception revealed in letters of the period, "I am in a state of abandon by all my friends, who are content to collect my remains and my relics; in the end I must die alone . . ."[55] A similar sense of having been bypassed can be discerned from a June 1960 dialogue between Jacques Berque and Massignon about the future of the Arabs. The latter remarked at one point: "I think that Berque is also more in contact with the real and with people who make history than am I, who see from far off and who find myself a little bit removed, even while trying . . ." To this comment Berque responded with the courtesy and affection of a younger colleague for a mentor: "Certainly not, Sir, you are not removed. You are always in the avant-garde."[56] Yet the fact remained that in the struggle of Muslim countries for autonomy and technical equality with the West, Massignon's call for mutual understanding seemed distant to many and out of touch with the immediate concerns of emerging nations.

Moreover, Massignon's physical condition was deteriorating. Following the cardiac episode of 1927 in London, he had enjoyed excellent health in spite of his asceticism and endless travels, but his eyesight was now impaired and the neuritis continued. In two letters to Merton that summer he worried first that his legs might force him to participate "from the window of a taxi" in the annual pilgrimage to Vieux Marché. "And what is going to happen to my delegation to Moscow on August 15th [*sic*], to Marburg on September 10 and to Cairo and Jerusalem in Dec.?" Moscow was the site of the twenty-fifth international meeting of Orientalists, and as it drew closer he wrote, "I hope against hope and come back to Paris on the 4th, so as to take the plane for Moscow." He also wondered: "How shall I be able to walk between the bus and the plane at the airports, etc?"[57]

His anxiety proved well founded because a dramatic episode occurred at the Moscow meeting. Suddenly immobilized during the sessions by what he described as attacks of a *névrite aggravée*, he spent fifteen days in the Hospital of the Soviet Academy of Sciences. His Soviet colleagues at the conference, "touched with pity at these crises . . . hospitalized him almost forcibly . . . lavishing attention so as to 'stabilize' him."[58] Far from home and temporarily helpless, Massignon's thoughts turned inward to the immense reserves of an interior life nurtured over more than half a century. "I lived there from the twelfth to the twenty-seventh of August in deep spiritual solitude in the middle of that immense country . . ." As his own life gave unmistakable signs of ebbing, Massignon's thoughts returned to his early years, to the rediscovery of Mary Kahil, and beyond, to Luis de Cuadra, to the early days in Egypt, the discovery of Hallaj, and the definition of his own vocation as one of mystical substitution and compassion. On the fifteenth, he began to compose what became the fourteenth annual letter to the Badaliya, "In the hospital my meditation concentrated on a recapitulation of events in the life of our little Badaliya, above all since 1947 . . ."[59] The letter constituted in effect a kind of testament because it summarized the annual letters he had written every year following the group's official recognition in 1947.

Begun in Moscow, the letter was completed only in January 1961, because upon his return to Paris Massignon could barely move. Hospitalized September 29, 1960, he underwent surgery October 4, and although he did recover it was apparent to family and friends that his health had been definitively compromised.[60] That Massignon himself clearly realized this can be inferred from the 1960 letter to the Badaliya and other documents written in 1961 and 1962; in them he contemplates his activity over the years and assesses its significance. Since the Badaliya was born from his own spiritual drama, the letter encapsulates the itinerary he had followed since his self-offering for the salvation of Luis de Cuadra:

> And thus, above and beyond the Egyptian setting where we suddenly recognized our "Neighbor" in that soul [Cuadra] and the Face of Christ in insults, we have from year to year, thanks to other encounters with that same grace, been made to recognize our "neighbors" in other areas of age-old suffering, first in the borders common to Islam and Mediterranean Christianity, and then well

beyond, to the very limits of the planet. The absolute compassion of the Good Samaritan has carried us from a detour on the road to Jericho to ecumenical reflections about humanity in space as well as time and to explanations of it among our friends.[61]

The Amis de Gandhi also received a testament. On the thirteenth anniversery of Gandhi's assassination, January 28, 1961, Massignon reflected on his own understanding of *satyagraha,* honed and deepened through the years of his own nonviolent witness. He had maintained his position even though, except for his influence in freeing the Malagasy senators, his efforts to achieve social and political justice for Muslims had met with failure in Morocco, Algeria, and France. The example of Gandhi had taught him that the ultimate significance of such efforts lay not in success but in the articulation of the truth. He had spent years trying to discover "how to communicate our conviction about truth to the other, when the other stakes his honor on defending this truth by falsifying it through recourse to ruse or violence . . ."[62] Now, he could summarize the answer, "In the end, we do not live here below in order to conquer but to give witness and to pass on the testimony to those younger than ourselves."[63]

No stranger either to power or privilege, Massignon had used his access to both in order to fight for justice. In its seventh year by 1961, the Algerian war was entering its final phase. Tragically, each step toward peace was matched by a corresponding rise in violence both in Algeria and France. Now in the last two years of his life, with war-related terrorism evident at his very doorstep and the infirmities of old age sapping his strength to protest, only faith sustained him. His influence coincided more and more with his person, as the unwavering flame of his presence appeared in ever starker contrast with the frailty of his body. Resolutely and implacably, he continued to call readers and listeners to moral accountability.

In November 1960 Charles de Gaulle had announced that a referendum would be held in January 1961 about the reorganization of political structures in Algeria and the principle of self-determination.

De Gaulle's December 9–13 trip to Algeria occasioned violent demonstrations both for and against the country's independence; by official estimates rioting during these days killed one hundred twenty people in Algiers alone. Massignon commented to the Badaliya:

> Our 70th fast coincided with the inspection of the Algerian situation by the chief of state: his call for human understanding on an equal footing between the two communities lanced the abcess; the riots of December 11 and 12 broke out, showing French extremists that the time for "Arab bashing" was past, and to Muslim extremists that the time for revenge seeking was over. What remains is to make them accept the perspective of a new future to construct and live together.[64]

Several days after the general's trip, *Le Monde* published, at Massignon's request, a text from *France-Islam*. Along with requesting a week-long truce at Christmas, it mourned those who had died in the riots and stated that the case of Algeria "was not a question of a war between Christians and Muslims but of a drama tied to world evolution." Finally, with an eye to the approaching referendum, the text reiterated Massignon's fundamental themes of mutual respect and hospitality, declaring: "prior to consulting the people, counter-demonstrations with their simplistic slogans cannot substitute for the dialog necessary to explore the juridical forms which best guarantee Algeria's future along with the rights of the community's diverse elements and all this within a spirit of hospitality and mutual respect."[65]

The results of the referendum January 8, 1961, ratified de Gaulle's policy of self-determination for Algeria, and the country's independence became only a matter of time. However, violence not only continued unabated, it increased both in France and Algeria. The FLN was responsible on one side, and on the other, a new extremist element, the OAS (Organisation Armée Secrète), created in February by various military officers in order to forestall independence. That same month Massignon noted:

Decolonialization still leaves in its wake too many impure and insatiable hatreds on both sides. Why? Because the existence of sadism and torturers attests to it—our laicized societies find themselves face to face with the sin of sacrilege, the abuse of sacred Hospitality, whether it be on the body of young men or on the psyche submitted to the slavery of interrogations.[66]

The announcement by de Gaulle on March 17 that he would begin negotiations with the FLN was followed April 11 by a press conference where he first spoke of "a sovereign Algerian state." These moves provoked a series of terrorist episodes claimed by the OAS in Paris and elsewhere in France and an unsuccessful coup in April, masterminded by several generals in order to set up a counter-government. Massignon invited the Badaliya to its monthly fast in May and observed that "this serene peace can only be achieved, the events of April 22–25 have proven it, through two prior steps: the restoration of mutual, fraternal respect of Christians for each other and of Muslims for each other, steps that are prior to a sincere, social agreement between Christianity and Islam."[67]

After the French government opened negotiations with the FLN at Evian on May 20, Massignon wrote the Badaliya: "We are led to meditate on our knees before the confrontation of Evian . . ."[68] Mystical substitution and nonviolent witness again dictated his response. He reiterated his belief that the "unity of the human race" could not be achieved as some imagined, by "racial hatred" and practices of "bestial torture" promoted by politicians and even sometimes by the Church. Rather, "the history of the world is guided and illumined, through the worst crises . . . by pure testimony and the heroic nonviolence of witnesses whose apparent defeat, wrapped in the imperial purple of martyrdom, begins the kingdom of God deep in all souls of goodwill."[69]

In spite of the negotiations the conflict continued to drag on and manifest itself in random terrorism. During this period, as it became clearer that only time lay between Algeria and independence, violence instigated by the OAS and FLN escalated. In France, especially in Paris, not a day passed without a press report of yet another attack, scattering damage and death in its wake. Under constant threat, the Parisian police found itself engaged in a stalemated "battle of Paris," which, as their losses steadily increased, heightened racial tension and fear within their ranks. After de Gaulle escaped an assassination attempt on September 9, the police began arresting North African suspects in large numbers. On October 4 an 8 P.M. curfew was imposed on the Muslim population.

Powerless to halt the spiraling urban terrorism, Massignon suffered intensely during the summer and autumn, and his health was visibly declining. In August he wrote:

> Humanly speaking the situation is atrocious, and there is no perceptible glimmer of daylight. My health has sounded an alarm, and I am trying to thin out my correspondence and finish several articles . . . I am refusing requests, somewhat because of fatigue and mostly because of a need for silence and darkness. I am becoming ever closer to Gandhi.[70]

Finally, bloody events of October 17 and 18 broke the cycle of terrorism and reprisal. They evoked from Massignon a response which both typified and summed up the convictions of an entire lifetime. The North African inhabitants of the Paris region planned a demonstration to protest the October 4 curfew. Early in the evening of October 17, over twenty thousand of them, including whole families, peacefully emerged from various *métro* stations in the center of the city and spilled into the streets. Police reaction was immediate and brutal, resulting in one hundred deaths, eleven thousand arrests, and one thousand deportations. The dead included a night school student known to Massignon from his classes at Gennevilliers. On October 24 he went to the morgue, paid for the right to remove the body, and then accompanied it to the cemetery. The experience was wrenching, as he wrote the next day:

> As for religious resistance, yesterday I had to pay 20,000 francs at the morgue, which was asking the ANARF [Association des Nord-

Africains Résidant en France] 46,000 F to give them the body of a Kabyl Christian killed five days ago by the authorities (others were drowned at Saint-Denis); we saved him from being dissected by medical students, and he will be decently interred (the White Fathers have naturally not budged).[71]

That same day, October 25, a small news item in *Le Monde* told of Algerian corpses being pulled from the Seine, immediately southwest of Paris. A day later one was reported near the Pont Neuf in the heart of the city. By November 8 over sixty bodies had been discovered in the river and in underbrush around the forests of the region.[72] Massignon had already written the Badaliya demanding "a truce of God, in order to bury the dead . . . Not only in Algeria but also on the mainland, the bodies of the murdered enemy disappear, incinerated or drowned. We have seen it these last days [October 17], to our shame."[73] He was speaking literally because he and other members of the Badaliya had themselves attempted that month to rescue bodies from the river, only to be rebuffed by police.

The revulsion Massignon felt at the indignity inflicted on human bodies purchased at the morgue or floating in the Seine coalesced in a plea he addressed as president of the Amis de Gandhi to "the compassionate conscience of our race." In a statement published in *Le Monde*, November 9, he called such a conscience Antigone, "she who went out at the cost of her life to bury her brother, the 'traitor' cut down on the edge of the city; she who was born to share not hatred but love." The issue now concerned the bodies of Muslims killed "secretly in the name of order and the nation." He demanded that the authorities stop disposing of these bodies either by burning or submerging them, a practice long known in Algeria and illustrated by "the latest incidents of the mainland." He cited the example of having gone to claim the body of his student and proposed a plan to deal with the situation: "M. Massignon asks that these dead receive from the nation a decent Islamic burial, at the Bobigny cemetery for example; and he suggests that a 'curator general' be named, who could be the director of the Paris mosque, in order to identify, gather up, and inter these bodies."[74]

The tragic events of October had revealed the precarious situation of North Africans in France and prompted Massignon, who had long since desisted from demonstrating, to counsel firmly against any such participation by the Amis de Gandhi. His concern for their safety would be a recurring theme in the last year of his life:

> The problems of Algerians in France are becoming more and more difficult, and I beg you not to participate, either by your presence or your signature, in any of the nonviolent protests we are presently bombarded with. People don't understand that these little demonstrations of muscle-flexing are completely ill-timed and that there are only two ways for confronting these killers: either (and this is forbidden us as proponents of nonviolence) to eliminate them or else silently to receive their blows until the very end; convinced as I am of the power ultimately of the spirit, especially when this spirit (worth more than the whole world since it shattered the atom) is as Saint John of the Cross said, worthy of God alone.[75]

In the 1961 Christmas letter to the Badaliya, his last, Massignon compared his act of providing burial for his student to that of Tobit in the Bible and termed it an act of "supreme hospitality."[76] His diminishing strength is evident in the very brevity of this 1961 letter, only four pages long, begun at Christmas and completed the following Easter. It was organized according to the five pillars of Muslim life in community: "witness, prayer, fasting, almsgiving, and pilgrimage." He had used the same categories in the third and final division of the long "testament" of 1960. Here the headings of the 1961 letter organize the entire text and seem a fitting summary for the preoccupations of Massignon's entire life. The comment about the burial occurs under the rubric "almsgiving."

Stating under "witness" that "it is essentially a question of witnessing to faith in the Last Judgment," he implies that the suffering which inevitably results from standing up for the truth will finally bear fruit for the oppressed at the end of time. This notion, reinforced by his longstanding interest in Shi'ite themes, had sustained him throughout the years of the war, when his work for peace seemed futile, his life more alone, and his strength diminished. In such a context of powerlessness, the ultimate gift comes from the substance of one's own life, as he notes under "almsgiving": "the fundamental alms is that of one's self, that is to say, Hospitality, which is a synthesis of the works of mercy."[77] By burying his student, Massignon had literally practiced this injunction that, according to the Gospel, forms the basis of the last judgment.

Aside from mentioning that gesture, Massignon does not refer to war-related events in Algeria or France in this letter. Indeed, by Easter, 1962, when he completed it, the war had ended; March 18 the two sides had signed an agreement at Evian, and a cease-fire was declared the following day. However, in the monthly convocations of the Badaliya during this period, he remained preoccupied with the safety of Algerians in France because of the October 17 violence and the ongoing terrorism of both the FLN and the OAS. In February, for instance, he wrote:

> it is not in Algeria alone that through violence the international colonialist consortium propels disadvantaged Muslims towards communism, but also here in France. Because it is the true guarantee for maintaining the security and dignity of our million compatriots in Algeria, the presence of half a million Algerian Muslim workers must be respected, respected not only in their work life, but at their burial. As we recalled in connection with the painful events of October 17 in Paris, hospitality toward foreign guests extends to interring them with the prayers of their faith.[78]

His words sounded an almost prophetic warning. For example, on February 8, an anti-OAS rally resulted in eight deaths at the Charonne *métro* station in Paris when police suspected to be in league with the OAS charged the demonstrators. And even after the Evian peace agreement was signed, fanatics in the FLN and OAS refused to disarm. Europeans and Muslim supporters of French rule began a mass exodus from Algeria. Reprisals continued even after independence was declared July 3, so that amidst continuing terrorism and under fire, most of the remaining Europeans left the country. Thus, any immediate joy Massignon felt at the war's end was soon muted because peace at the conference table did not efface the violence. Several weeks after the cease-fire, April 6, he spoke optimistically about "these days when the pledged word, founded on the link of sacred hospitality between the children of Abraham, finally honored, has begun to bear fruit . . ."[79] However, by June 1, with daily accounts of atrocities in the Paris newspapers, he entreated the members of the Badaliya: "Let us not grow weary of repeating that we must pray 'together' as Christians, Jews and Muslims, for the coming of that Peace, so much desired and which has delayed so long."[80]

In this last year of his life, Massignon continued his usual activities to the degree allowed by his health. During his annual vacation in Brittany, he went to the ninth pilgrimage of the Seven Sleepers. He continued fast days for peace in North Africa; at his death they numbered ninety-two. A collection of his essays was forthcoming under the title *Parole donnée*. Massignon had agreed to the project the year before, chosen the articles to be included, and was now preoccupied with the introduction. Although a photograph taken at the July pilgrimage reveals someone worn by suffering, the account of his relationship to this book reflects how, until the end, he remained involved in issues that mattered to him.

Monteil was charged with writing the introduction and choosing titles under which articles were grouped. He began working on the book, and at first Massignon made only minor corrections, but that soon changed. Reviewing their correspondence, Monteil realized that although "reticent at the outset about the very object of our common enterprise, he ended up by considering my 'introduction' as . . . his own." Between the summers of 1961 and 1962 (July 4, 1961, and August 28, 1962), Monteil recalled receiving a total of twenty-seven letters about the project, "The very content of my text was challenged, at first 'touched-up,' then turned completely topsy-turvy, to the point of becoming almost unrecognizable. All told, more than half of the definitive pages published in 1962, are not mine but literally from the hand of Louis Massignon."[81]

The modifications often either attenuated the prose or eliminated personal information; Monteil found such changes curious, since Massignon himself possessed a unique prose style and the details he eliminated were inoffensive. Endlessly voluble in conversation about his personal life and history, he perhaps felt that the written word somehow defined and revealed him in a way the years of oral "testimony" did not. Knowing that his own death was near undoubtedly conferred on such definition a weight it otherwise might not have had. Whatever the case, he was still making corrections on the galley proofs in July; it was only on October 9, less than three weeks before Massignon died, that Monteil "was able to obtain his definitive agreement (8 corrections and 22 deletions), finally allowing the publisher to bring out the book December 1, 1962." Death came October 31.[82]

Indeed Massignon had no illusions about his health. While still working on *Parole donnée* with Monteil, he ended a letter, August 25, with the straightforward comment: "Right now it's not only my spinal column that is complaining; it's this heart that I used to label 'the insensible muscle' . . . all the same I want to go to Kabul."[83] In spite of his physical state, he still relished travel and had received an official invitation to a celebration of the 900th anniversary of death of the Afghan mystic Ansari. However, letters from his summer home in Brittany show that he knew the Afghanistan trip was doubtful. On August 28 he wrote, "Gripped with pain on both sides at once, I wonder how to answer the invitation of the Afghans. Through the grace of God."[84] Early in September he expressed hope that his doctors might permit him to go, "Pray that I can have the 'passport' for Kabul from my doctors. About twelve days from now I will go to Paris to see about that."[85] However, the doctors said no, and in September Massignon returned from Brittany to Paris for the last time. Those who saw him the month before he died described a "face etched by suffering,"[86] and a man absolutely worn out. This struck Monteil on his own last visit, when he obtained final approval for the publication of *Parole donnée*: "On the ninth, I found him alone, riveted to an armchair in his empty dining room, without a book, a little bell at his side. He had what he used to call a 'ravaged face.'"[87]

Yet for all that, Massignon remained committed both to his scholarship and his social involvements until the end. In June he had arranged for a successor to head the Amis de Gandhi. Mary Kahil and others were contacted about the future of the Badaliya. In mid-October Camille Drevet received a note thanking her for her work on the Bulletin of the Amis de Gandhi. "Thank you for your letter and for the bulletin, which is perfect. Enclosed is an advance on my membership. With my affectionate friendship."[88] Several days before his death he arranged the monthly liturgy of the Badaliya for November 9 and invited members to pray for the success of the Vatican Council which had opened October 11; however, the fate of Algeria remained his central concern:

> Several members would have liked us in preceding convocations to rejoice at the Peace achieved in Algeria in March '62. We remain very preoccupied, not so much with the lack of comprehension among Christians who have left and regret the failure of an outdated 'colonial' Latinization, but about the liberal illusions of French teachers and managers. They are very generously returning to Algeria to continue a task of educational and social formation for which they will receive a standard of living much higher than that of the Muslim population whose progress they wish to assure.[89]

All his life he had condemned the social inequities between Europeans and Muslims in Algeria. He worried now that such well-meaning efforts would fail because the discrepancy in living standards would ignite jealousy among Algerian colleagues whose salaries were not subsidized. That would jeopardize the promotion of Muslim civilization and culture. For the same reasons he had supported teaching Arabic in Algerian *lycées*, so now, as the country faced its own future, he encouraged Muslim rather than French teachers as the better course for instructing the local population.

And having always considered that Western technology had both trampled indigenous Muslim culture and exacerbated inequities, he fired one last volley at "technocrats":

> In the period of general austerity which the Muslim population of Algeria is entering, it is clear that the generous French who are coming to help them should hold themselves to their standard of living; but that is obviously unthinkable for technicians; it would perhaps be wiser to reduce their number while increasing the recruitment of directors of studies, educators of trained groups of Muslim teachers.[90]

On October 31, Massignon was writing an article to celebrate the 1,200th anniversary of the founding of Baghdad when he suffered what proved to be a fatal heart attack. Entitled "The Medieval Symbolism of the Destiny of Baghdad," the unfinished article was eventually published, thanks to the efforts of his colleague Régis Blachère, who partially deciphered his friend's miniscule and almost illegible handwriting.[91] Baghdad had witnessed Massignon's conversion more than a half century before, and this ultimate fragment of his thought alludes to cherished symbols of a lifetime, to the sura of the Seven Sleepers and the mysterious coming of the Shi'ite Mahdi or "just one" at the end of time. The unfinished article itself provides what he would have called an "intersign," suggesting that his personal universe of sacred symbol and place accompanied him until the end. He died around ten o'clock the evening of October 31. More surprising to friends was how he had almost realized his wish, often stated, of dying on November 1, All Saints Day, the feast of holy ones throughout the ages who offer their lives to God for others.

However, in a paradox reminiscent of others in his existence, friends did not immediately learn that Massignon had died. In life although his travels had spanned the globe, his daily existence had alternated between the seventh *arrondissement* of Paris and the northern coast of Brittany. His imperious need for self-revelation had cohabited with deep shyness. Now, in death the public Massignon, whose friendships spanned not only the globe but cultures and class distinctions as well, was reclaimed by his family as their own. Shielded from the clamor that surrounded the public Massignon, they accompanied his body to Brittany, to Pordic, where he had spent summers as a child and young man. After a small funeral November 6 in the parish church, Massignon was interred in the family burial vault built by Fernand Massignon years before and located in the cemetery behind the church.

Only after the funeral did friends and colleagues learn that Massignon had died. The Wednesday, November 7 edition of *Le Monde* contained a short article that incorrectly stated his death had "occurred during the night of Saturday to Sunday" or November 3 and noted that it was "surrounded by an extreme discretion."[92] On November 8 a front-page eulogy in *Le Monde* began an outpouring of tributes from around the world. Although the date of death was accurately reported that day in the paper's death notices, its inconspicuous position made it pass largely unnoticed. Therefore Massignon's son felt obliged to print a correction the day before a November 15 memorial Mass sponsored by the Amis de Gandhi; he stated that "his father had died October 31 at 10:45 P.M. and not November third as most of the press had announced."[93]

Thus, Louis Massignon, a man passionately present to both his friends and enemies, had disappeared from their midst unnoticed. On November 6 one of them, François Mauriac, himself an old man, expressed not only his sorrow at the loss but also wistful regret that he had learned of Massignon's death only that day, upon returning from the funeral of another friend:

> I could not perform the same duty for Louis Massignon, or even accompany him from afar with a prayer, not having been alerted about his death. Stating that the erudition of this celebrated Islamist is no dead letter is to state the obvious. I know no more striking example of knowledge transformed into love. Massignon next to my fireplace in 1911 or 1912, recounting the story of his miraculous conversion; Massignon, the friend of père de Foucauld, the Massignon of Al Hallaj and the Seven Sleepers; Massignon se-

cretly ordained; irreplaceable Massignon! He was an Arab story-teller who had to recount his life. At least he received the grace of seeing the last colonial war end and the dawn of the [Vatican] Council emerge. Now he will intercede for us.[94]

The young Massignon, whose seeming self-absorption in his conversion had so irritated Mauriac almost a half-century before, had been transformed in the course of a lifetime. On one level he stood out because the dramatic events of his life were matched by the power of his rhetoric to evoke them. He was remarkable because the depth and breadth of his learning enabled him to create a highly original universe of sign and symbol. Ultimately Massignon was unique because his life, prodigious learning, and creativity were fused with a passionate commitment to justice that compelled him to risk his very self in the struggles he undertook against ethnic and religious hatreds. And the very years of struggle forged his legacy, a life unforgettable for its intensity and sheer range of activity, a life pursued without compromise and consumed by the pursuit of truth.

Notes

1. Beginnings

1. Louis Massignon, "Labbeville, sa vie paroissiale," *Opera Minora*, ed. Youakim Moubarec, vol. 3 (Paris: Presses Universitaires de France, 1969), 331–332. "Meditation of a Passerby on His Visit to the Sacred Woods of Ise," *Testimonies and Reflections, Essays of Louis Massignon*, introd. Herbert Mason (Notre Dame, Ind.: University of Notre Dame Press, 1989), 165–166. (*Opera Minora* will hereafter be cited as *OM.*)
2. "Meditation," *Testimonies*, 166; Massignon wrote this essay in English.
3. Vincent Monteil, "Entretiens," in L. Massignon, *Parole donnée* (Paris: Seuil, 1983), 13n (hereafter *PD*).
4. L. Massignon, "Meditation," *Testimonies*, 167; Pierre Roche, *Catalogue de guerre des médailles, médaillons, plaquettes, jetons et gypsographies de Pierre Roche* (Paris: Canule, 1918), 21; Roche, *Exposition de l'art du fer forgé, du cuivre, et de l'étain au musée Galliera, mai-septembre 1905, rapport de Roche au nom du jury* (Paris: Librairies-Imprimeries Réunies, 1905), 6.
5. Roche, *Exposition*, 6.
6. Daniel Massignon, "Louis Massignon et le dialogue des cultures," *Horizons Maghrebin*, no. 14/15 (1989): 162.
7. "Toute une vie avec un frère parti au désert," *PD*, 65; letter 54, 28 Feb. 1911, *Paul Claudel, Louis Massignon, (1908–1914)*, ed. Michel Malicet (Paris: Desclée, 1973), 111 (hereafter *Claudel-Massignon*); Pierre Rondot, "L. Massignon et le Docteur Quesnoy," in *Cahiers de l'Herne*, no. 13, ed. Jean-François Six (Paris: Ed. de l'Herne, 1970), 374 (hereafter *L'Herne*); D. Massignon, "Chronologie," *L'Herne*, 13–14.

8. "Toute une vie," *PD*, 65.

9. L. Massignon, letter, 25 Feb. 1901, "Louis Massignon à Henri Maspero," *L'Herne*, 25 (hereafter "Massignon-Maspero").

10. Monteil, "Entretiens," *PD*, 56.

11. "Massignon-Maspero," *L'Herne*, 27.

12. Herbert Mason, Biographical Foreword, in Louis Massignon, *The Passion of al-Hallaj, Mystic and Martyr of Islam*, trans. Herbert Mason, vol. 1: *The Life of al-Hallaj* (Princeton: Princeton University Press, 1982), xxi (hereafter, *Passion*, Mason trans.); Monteil, "Entretiens," *PD*, 56.

13. Letter, 25 Feb. 1901, "Massignon-Maspero," *L'Herne*, 27.

14. Mason, Foreword, *Passion* 1: xxi.

15. "Meditation," *Testimonies*, 166.

16. Ibid., 172n3; *Pierre Roche, Estampes modelées et églomisations, un catalogue de ses oeuvres*, introd. Louis Massignon (Paris: Ed. de la Nouvelle Revue Critique, 1935). *Eglomisations* originally involved painting on a glass backed with gold leaf. Instead Roche superimposed paper-thin metallic leaf cut in various shapes and varnished. He substituted mica, paper, and parchment for glass.

17. Monteil, "Entretiens," *PD*, 37.

18. "L'honneur des camarades de travail et la parole de vérité," *OM* 3: 841; Frederick Winslow Taylor (1856–1915) an American, pioneered efficiency engineering and sought through scientific study to streamline factory production and management. *Dictionary of American Biography* (New York: Scribner's, 1936), 323–324.

19. Letter 54, 28 Feb. 1911, *Claudel-Massignon*, 111.

20. Monteil, "Entretiens," *PD*, 20–21.

21. Ibid., *PD*, 37. There the trip is dated 1899, and Massignon would have been sixteen. Daniel Massignon states that his father was fourteen at the time, "Dialogue," 162.

22. Louis Massignon, "Notes sur ma conversion," an unpublished account of his conversion, written in April 1922, and quoted extensively as "Notes LM" in Daniel Massignon, "Le Voyage en Mésopotamie et la conversion de Louis Massignon en 1908," *Islamochristiana* 14 (1988): 131, 148n75.

23. Robert Baldick, *The Life of J.-K. Huysmans* (Oxford: Clarendon, 1955), 275, 276, 286.

24. Lucienne Portier, "Louis Massignon et Charles de Foucauld," *L'Herne*, 349.

25. Gustave Boucher was "a rather shady character who combined the

occupation of bookseller with the more lucrative profession of police spy." Baldick, 175.

26. Letter 46, 26 Dec. 1910, *Claudel-Massignon*, 100.

27. "L'Arabie et le problème arabe," *OM* 3: 452.

28. "L'apostolat de la souffrance et de la compassion réparatrice au xiiie siècle: l'exemple de Sainte Christine l'Admirable," *OM* 3: 640.

29. Pierre Rocalve, "Place et rôle de l'Islam et de l'islamologie dans la vie et l'oeuvre de Louis Massignon" (diss., Sorbonne, 1990), 99n78bis.

30. Honoré d'Urfé, *L'Astrée*, vol. 2 (Geneva: Slatkine Rpts., 1966), 386–387.

31. Letter, 1 Dec. 1902, "Massignon-Maspero," *L'Herne*, 31.

32. "L'amitié de Jean-Richard Bloch," *OM* 3: 554–555.

33. Roger Martin du Gard, letter to Pierre Abraham, in *Europe*, special edition, "Hommage à Jean-Richard Bloch," 19–20, quoted in Claude Sicard, "Roger Martin du Gard: les années d'apprentissage littéraire" (diss., Université de Lille, 1976), 126.

34. Sicard, "Roger Martin du Gard," 141.

35. Letter, 7 Dec. 1902, "Massignon-Maspero," *L'Herne*, 32.

36. Vincent Monteil, *Le Linceul de feu* (Paris: Vegapress, 1987), 24 (hereafter *Linceul*). The quote is an excerpt suppressed by Massignon from a draft for the introduction to *Parole donnée*.

37. *En Route* and *La Cathédrale* comprise the other two novels of the trilogy. *L'Herne*, 33.

38. Letter, 25 Dec. 1903, "Massignon-Maspero," *L'Herne*, 35.

39. Louis Massignon, *Tableau géographique du Maroc dans les quinze premières années du XVI siècle d'après Léon l'Africain* (Algiers: Jourdain, 1906), ix.

40. Letter 54, 28 Feb. 1911, *Claudel-Massignon*, 111.

41. "Toute une vie," *PD*, 66; Mason, Foreword, *Passion* 1: xxii; Monteil, "Entretiens," *PD*, 11; D. Massignon, "Le Voyage," 151n93.

42. Ibid., 182.

43. "Les modes de stylisation littéraire," *OM* 2: 372.

44. "A year ago at the end of autumn, I was leaving for Baghdad on an archeological mission, and I talked one last time with my late teacher Hartwig Derenbourg about the thesis I was preparing—a subject he had been willing to announce himself in the *Annuaire de l'Ecole pratique des Hautes Etudes* (1908, p. 73)—on the doctrine, trial, and execution of a mystic, al-Halladj . . ." "La Passion d'Al Halladj," *OM* 2: 11.

45. Charles de Foucauld, *Voyage au Maroc: compte rendu de la Société de Géographie de Paris* (Paris, 1884); *Positions déterminées dans le Maroc*, extracts in *Comptes rendus des séances de la Société de Géographie et de la commission centrale* (Paris, 1885), 296–297nn9–10; "Itinéraires au Maroc" in *Bulletin de la Société de Géographie de Paris*, ser. 7, vol. 8 (1887): 118–125; *Reconnaissance au Maroc* (Paris, 1885).

46. "L'honneur," *OM* 3: 840.

47. Jean-François Six, ed., *L'Aventure de l'amour de Dieu, 80 lettres inédites de Charles de Foucauld à Louis Massignon* (Paris: Seuil, 1993), 27.

48. "Toute une vie," *PD*, 66.

49. "Textes musulmans pouvant concerner la nuit de l'esprit," *OM* 2: 398n1. The Arabic expression "night of power," refers to the night when the Qur'an descended into the soul of Muhammad.

50. Henri de Castries, *Islam, impressions et études* (Paris: Colin, 1896), 5.

51. Ibid., 6.

52. "La Cité des morts au Caire," *OM* 3: 233.

53. Monteil, "Entretiens," *PD*, 30.

54. L. Massignon, unpublished journal, Nov. 22, 1906, quoted in D. Massignon, "Le Voyage," 189n140.

55. Monteil, *Linceul*, 30.

56. "La Cité des morts au Caire," *OM* 3: 285.

57. "Toute une vie," *PD*, 66.

58. "L'honneur," *OM* 3: 841.

59. D. Massignon, "Dialogue," 163; Letter 10, 25 Feb. 1934, *L'Hospitalité sacrée*, ed. Jacques Keryell (Paris: Nouvelle Cité, 1987), 180 (hereafter *HS*).

60. Louis Massignon, "Les Maîtres qui ont guidé ma vie," *Horizons Maghrebins*, no. 14/15 (1989): 157.

61. L. Massignon, Preface to the New Edition, *Passion*, Mason trans., vol. 1: liv.

62. Attar Fariduddin (1140–1220?) supposedly wrote between 100,000 and 200,000 verses.

63. Monteil, "Entretiens," *PD*, 30; Louis Massignon, *La Passion de Hallaj*, vol. 1: *La vie de Hallaj* (Paris: Gallimard, 1975), 30. My translation differs somewhat from that of Mason in the English edition, 1: lxvi.

64. Letter 112, 29 Aug. 1912, *Claudel-Massignon*, 195.

65. "Etude sur une courbe personnelle de vie: le cas de Hallaj, martyr mystique," *OM* 2: 173.
66. *Passion* (Mason trans.), 1: 126.
67. "L'expérience mystique et les modes de stylisation littéraire," *OM* 2: 370.
68. Letter of Louis Massignon to Fernand Massignon, 29 Apr. 1907, quoted in D. Massignon, "Chronologie," *L'Herne*, 14.

2. Conversion

1. Monteil, "Entretiens," *PD*, 21.
2. L. Massignon, *Passion* (French ed.) 4: 148.
3. Letter, 5 Jan. 1908, "Massignon-Maspero," *L'Herne*, 36.
4. L. Massignon, "Les Maîtres," 158.
5. Ibid., 159.
6. "Notes LM," quoted in D. Massignon, "Le Voyage," 189–190n142.
7. L. Massignon, "Les Maîtres," 159.
8. "Voyelles sémitiques et sémantique musicale," *PD*, 345.
9. Letter of Beylié, 15 Feb. 1908, to Mme Gaston Maspero, quoted in "Massignon-Maspero," *L'Herne*, 36.
10. D. Massignon, "Le Voyage," 137.
11. Louis Massignon, *Mission en Mésopotamie (1907–1908)* (Cairo: L'Institut français d'archéologie, 1910), vol. 1, iii, quoted in D. Massignon, "Le Voyage," 139.
12. Monteil, "Entretiens," *PD*, 22; "L'honneur," *OM* 3: 842.
13. On this site supporters of the Umayyads killed Husayn, the son of 'Ali and Fatima and grandson of Muhammad, along with his family.
14. Suppressed by Massignon from a draft for the introduction of *Parole donnée* and quoted in Monteil, *Linceul*, 24.
15. Letter of L. Massignon, 3 April 1908, quoted in D. Massignon, "Le Voyage," 140–141.
16. Location of the tomb of 'Ali, fourth caliph and son-in-law of Muhammad. The city is located immediately south of Kufah.
17. A *kaimakam* was an assistant administrator of a subdivision in one of the three Mesopotamia provinces.
18. Letter of Gustave Rouet, quoted in D. Massignon, "Le Voyage," 141.
19. Unpublished letter, 22 Apr. 1908.
20. "Notes LM," quoted in D. Massignon, "Le Voyage," 143.

21. Ibid.
22. Letter, 1 May 1908 of the kaimakam of Kut to Ra'uf Chadirchi, quoted in D. Massignon, "Le Voyage," 156.
23. *Mission en Mésopotamie* 1: v, quoted in D. Massignon, "Le Voyage," 140.
24. "La Syrie et le problème des contacts culturels entre Orient et Occident," *OM* 1: 171.
25. "Notes LM," quoted in D. Massignon, "Le Voyage," 144.
26. "L'involution sémantique du symbole," *OM* 2: 629.
27. "Notes LM," quoted in D. Massignon, "Le Voyage," 145.
28. Letter 54, 28 Feb. 1911, *Claudel-Massignon*, 111.
29. "L'involution semantique du symbole," *OM* 2: 628–629.
30. "Notes LM," quoted in D. Massignon, "Le Voyage," 145.
31. Report of Doctor Assad Efendi.
32. "Notes LM," quoted in D. Massignon, "Le Voyage," 146.
33. Ibid.
34. Ibid.
35. Ibid., 175.
36. "L'idée de Dieu," *OM* 3: 831–833.
37. "Notes LM," quoted in D. Massignon, "Le Voyage," 147.
38. Paul Claudel, unpublished journal, 3 Nov. 1909, quoted in Jacques Keryell, *Jardin donnée* (Paris: Ed. St-Paul, 1993), 113 (hereafter *JD*).
39. Letter 5, 31 Oct. 1908, *Claudel-Massignon*, 53.
40. Letter 54, *Claudel-Massignon*, 111.
41. "Notes LM," quoted in D. Massignon, "Le Voyage," 147.
42. Ibid.
43. Ibid., 148.
44. Ibid.
45. Quoted in D. Massignon, "Le Voyage," 179.
46. Letter 74, 16 Aug. 1911, *Claudel-Massignon*, 132; text deleted by the editor.
47. "Notes LM," quoted in D. Massignon, "Le Voyage," 148–149.
48. Ibid., 149; "Voyelles sémitiques et sémantique musicale," *PD*, 345–346.
49. D. Massignon, "Le Voyage," 151n89.
50. "Notes LM," quoted in D. Massignon, "Le Voyage," 151; Claudel, unpublished journal entry, 3 Nov. 1909, quoted in Keryell, *JD*, 114.
51. D. Massignon, "Le Voyage," 152n94.
52. "Notes LM," quoted in D. Massignon, "Le Voyage," 192.

53. Claudel journal, 3 Nov. 1909, quoted in Keryell, *JD*, 114.
54. "Notes LM," quoted in D. Massignon, "Le Voyage," 192–193.
55. Canon law was in the process of being codified for the first time. In 1908 it comprised a series of norms that had been handed down over centuries and which the Council of Trent had updated. The 1918 code specified, in Canons 2357.1–2, that persons *legally convicted* of crimes of fornication must have recourse to the bishop. Such was not Massignon's case, but undoubtedly his homosexual relationships prompted Anastase's response. See T. Lincoln Bouscaran et al., *Canon Law: A Text and Commentary*, 4th ed. (Milwaukee: Bruce, 1963), 930.
56. Letter 5, 31 Oct. 1908, *Claudel-Massignon*, 52–53.
57. D. Massignon, "Le Voyage," 193n149.
58. Ibid., 182–183.
59. Fernand Massignon, unpublished letter, 27 Sept. 1908.
60. "Les modes de stylisation littéraire," *OM* 2: 371–372.
61. "Les saints musulmans à Bagdad," *OM* 3: 94–101.
62. Youakim Moubarec, ed., *L'Oeuvre de Louis Massignon*, vol. 1 (Beirut: Ed. du Cénacle libanais, 1972), 9.
63. Letter, 14 June 1909, quoted in D. Massignon, "Le Voyage," 184.

3. The Search for Commitment

1. Baldick, 155; Guy Harpigny, *Islam et Christianisme selon Louis Massignon* (Louvain: 1981), 53; "Huysmans devant la 'confession de Boullan,'" *OM* 3: 735–742.
2. "L'idée de Dieu," *OM* 3: 831.
3. Letter 1, 8 Aug. 1908, *Claudel-Massignon*, 45.
4. Letter 111, 29 Aug. 1912, ibid., 194.
5. Letter 112, 29 Aug. 1912, ibid., 195–196.
6. "Toute une vie," *PD*, 67.
7. Ibid., 67–68.
8. Harpigny, 61.
9. Letter 6, 22 May 1909, Six, ed., *L'Aventure*, 58.
10. Letter 8, 8 Sept. 1909, ibid., 61–64.
11. Monteil, *Linceul*, 48n54; 278.
12. *La Correspondance entre Max van Berchem et Louis Massignon, 1907–1919*, ed. Werner Vycichl (Leiden: Brill, 1980).
13. François Mauriac, *Le Journal de Clichy*, 130, quoted in Jean Lacouture, *François Mauriac* (Paris: Seuil, 1980), 97.

14. Monteil, "Entretiens," *PD*, 30.
15. Keryell, *HS*, 162n27; Harpigny, 59; Monteil, *Linceul*, 247.
16. Letter, 3 Aug. 1909, "Massignon-Maspero," *L'Herne*, 37.
17. Keryell, *JD*, 111–116.
18. Jean-Jacques Waardenburg, *L'Islam dans le miroir de l'occident* (Paris: La Haye, 1963), 137.
19. Letter 10, 3 Dec. 1909, Six, ed., *L'Aventure*, 69.
20. Letter 23, 7 Jan. 1910, *Claudel-Massignon*, 77–78.
21. Letter 11, 13 Jan. 1910; Six, ed., *L'Aventure*, 71–72.
22. Letter 24, 20 Jan. 1910, *Claudel-Massignon*, 79.
23. Letter 25, 9 Feb. 1910, ibid., 79. The next paragraph is deleted in the text.
24. Letter 26, 19 Feb. 1910, ibid., 80.
25. Letter 35, 21 July, 1910, ibid., 86.
26. Letter 46, 26 Dec. 1910, ibid., 100.
27. Letter 47, 5 Feb. 1911, ibid., 101.
28. Letter 54, 28 Feb. 1911, ibid., 112.
29. Letter 55, 4 Mar. 1911, ibid., 113–114.
30. Letter 56, 23 Mar. 1911, ibid., 114.
31. Letters 20–21, 19 April, 12 May 1911, Six, ed., *L'Aventure*, 96–101, 102–103.
32. Letter 57, 21 Apr. 1911, *Claudel-Massignon*, 115.
33. Letter, 4 Aug. 1911, Vycichl, ed., 43.
34. Malicet, ed., *Claudel-Massignon*, 120n.
35. Six, ed., *L'Aventure*, 105.
36. Letter, 4 Aug. 1911, Vycichl, ed., 43.
37. Letter 67, 4 July, 1911, *Claudel-Massignon*, 122; Harpigny, 63.
38. Letter 73, 13 Aug. 1911, *Claudel-Massignon*, 131.
39. Letter 74, 16 Aug. 1911, ibid., 132.
40. Letter of Foucauld, 19 Sept. 1911, quoted in Monteil, *Linceul*, 50.
41. Letter 77, 13 Oct. 1911, *Claudel-Massignon*, 135–136.
42. Letter, 17 Oct. 1911, Vycichl, ed., 47; Phil. 1:23–24: "I feel myself caught between these alternatives; on the one hand I desire to go and be with Christ, which would be by far preferable; but on the other hand to remain in the flesh is more urgent for your good."
43. Letter, 7 Nov. 1911, Vycichl, ed., 48.
44. Letter, 9 Nov. 1911, ibid.
45. Letter 86, 29 Dec. 1911, *Claudel-Massignon*, 147.
46. Monteil, *Linceul*, 42.
47. Letter 84, 25 Dec. 1911, *Claudel-Massignon*, 143–144.

48. "Notre Dame de la Salette et la conversion de J. K. Huysmans," *OM* 3: 749–751.

49. "L'Amitié et la présence mariale dans nos vies," *OM* 3: 767; the other friend was Henri Massis.

50. Letter 29, 10 March, 1912, Six, ed., *L'Aventure*, 125.

51. Harpigny, 72.

52. Letter 107, 10 Aug. 1912, *Claudel-Massignon*, 188; Harpigny, 64.

53. Letter 108, 12 Aug. 1912, *Claudel-Massignon*, 190; the list of "exotic dangers" is deleted in the text.

54. Letter, 21 Jan. 1913, excerpted outside the series, ibid., 204.

55. Malicet, introd., *Claudel-Massignon*, 25.

56. "Foucauld au désert devant le Dieu d'Abraham, Agar et Ismael," *OM* 3: 773.

57. Letter 118, 28 Jan. 1913, *Claudel-Massignon*, 205; omissions of the editor.

58. Keryell, "Notice biographique de Mary Kahil," *HS*, 94. Included in the "notice" are excerpts from Kahil's reminiscences which the author taped and transcribed.

59. Some confusion exists about the date. Harpigny, 64, cites 7 Feb. 1913, while Keryell, *HS*, 162n27, and Monteil, *Linceul*, 247, cite Feb. 2. The latter date may have been chosen because letter 119, 12 Feb. 1913, *Claudel-Massignon*, 206, states, "for ten days my friend has been a prey to one of the most violent forms of typhus . . ."

60. Harpigny, 64; Keryell, ed., *HS*, 162n27; Monteil, *Linceul*, 247.

61. Letter 119, 12 Feb. 1913, *Claudel-Massignon*, 206; see also Monteil, *Linceul*, 247, 292n44, where the "censorship" of Malicet, ed., *Claudel-Massignon* is deplored.

62. Harpigny, 64; Monteil, *Linceul*, 247n43.

63. Keryell, "Notice: Kahil," *HS*, 94.

64. Ibid., 162n28.

65. Letter, 5 Jan. 1914, "Massignon-Maspero," *L'Herne*, 40.

66. Charles de Foucauld, *Directoire* (Paris: Seuil, 1961), 164; Six, ed., *L'Aventure*, 142; letter 38, 21 June 1913, ibid., 147–148; "Toute une vie," *PD*, 68.

67. Marion Mill Preminger, *The Sands of Tamanrasset: the Story of Charles de Foucauld* (New York: Hawthorn, 1961), 219; "Toute une vie," *PD*, 68.

68. Letter 126, 16 Sept. 1913, *Claudel-Massignon*, 212.

69. Letters 43, 45; 16, 30 Sept. 1913, Six, ed., *L'Aventure*, 150, 153–154.

70. "Toute une vie," *PD*, 65.

71. Portier, "Massignon, un homme de réconciliation," in D. Massignon, ed., *Présence de Louis Massignon: hommages et témoignages* (Paris: Maisonneuve et Larose, 1987), 197 (hereafter *Présence*).

72. "L'Amitié et la présence mariale dans nos vies," *OM:* 3, 767.

73. Letter of Daniel Fontaine, 30 Dec. 1913, quoted in Harpigny, 73; letter, 5 Jan. 1914, "Massignon-Maspero," *L'Herne*, 40.

74. Letter 131, 18 Dec. 1913, *Claudel-Massignon*, 216.

75. "Toute une vie," *PD*, 69.

76. Letter 74, 1 June 1916, Six, ed., *L'Aventure*, 204.

77. Letter 79, 1 Dec. 1916, ibid., 214.

78. "Toute une vie," *PD*, 69.

79. Ibid., 64; "L'honneur," *OM* 3: 842.

80. "L'honneur," *OM* 3: 840.

81. "Toute une vie," *PD*: 64.

82. Ibid., 65.

83. "L'honneur," *OM* 3: 842.

84. "Toute une vie," *PD*: 71.

85. L. Massignon, "Les Maîtres," 160.

4. Military and Diplomatic Service

1. Baldick, 297.

2. Six, ed., *L'Aventure*, 183.

3. Harpigny, 65–66; "Toute une vie," *PD*, 69; Monteil, *Linceul*, 50; Monteil, "Entretiens," *PD*, 30.

4. Portier, "Conditionnement et liberté dans la pensée de Massignon concernant l'Algérie," *L'Herne*, 291.

5. George Antonius, *The Arab Awakening: the Story of the Arab National Movement* (Beirut: Librairie du Liban, 1969), 251.

6. "Note sur Faysal, Ier" (trans. of an Arabic text for a 1946 memorial of the Hachemites), *OM* 3: 415.

7. Ibid.

8. "Mes rapports avec Lawrence en 1917," *OM* 3: 424.

9. Ibid., 424–425.

10. Ibid., 425.

11. Jukka Nevakivi, *Britain, France and the Arab Middle East, 1914–1920* (London: Athlone Press, 1969), 66n2.
12. "Note sur Faysal," *OM* 3: 415.
13. "Mes rapports," *OM* 3: 425.
14. Ibid., 426–427.
15. Ibid., 427.
16. "Toute une vie," *PD*, 71.
17. "Note sur Faysal," *OM* 3: 416.
18. "L'Occident devant l'Orient: primauté d'une solution culturelle," *OM* 1: 212.
19. "Note sur Faysal," *OM* 3: 416.
20. Ibid.
21. Ibid.
22. "In Memoriam. Sir Mark Sykes," *OM* 3: 420; English text.
23. "L'Islam et la politique des alliés," *OM* 3: 428.
24. "L'Arabie et le problème arabe," *OM* 3: 433.
25. Ibid., 434.
26. Ibid., 442.
27. Ibid.
28. Ibid., 445.
29. Ibid.
30. Ibid., 447.
31. Ibid., 450.
32. Ibid., 451.
33. Ibid., 451–452.
34. "Le sort du Proche-Orient et le rôle de la France en Syrie," *OM* 3: 455.
35. Ibid.
36. Ibid., 458.
37. Ibid., 459.
38. Ibid., 460.
39. Portier, "Conditionnement," *L'Herne*, 291.

5. *Hallaj, Abraham, and the Scholar of Islam*

1. Yves Laporte, "Arrivée de Louis Massignon au Collège de France," in *Présence*, 22.
2. Harpigny, 66–67; Monteil, *Linceul*, 247–248; "La Cité des morts au Caire," *OM* 3: 285 (Addenda III to intro.).

3. "Le tombeau de J.-K.Huysmans," *OM* 3: 733.

4. Monteil, *Linceul*, 293n46.

5. "Foucauld au désert," *OM* 3: 774.

6. "Mes rapports," *OM* 3: 424; "Foucauld au désert," *OM* 3: 774n1.

7. "Toute une vie," *PD*, 66.

8. Monteil, *Linceul*, 77.

9. L. Massignon, Preface to the New Edition, Mason trans., *Passion*, 1: lxv.

10. Rocalve, 80.

11. L. Massignon, *La Doctrine de Hallaj*, vol. 3, *Passion* (French ed.), 90.

12. *Essai sur les origines du lexique technique de la mystique musulmane*, 2nd ed. (Paris: Vrin, 1954), 63–64.

13. Ibid., 104.

14. Ibid., 12.

15. Ibid., 15.

16. Ibid., 14.

17. Ibid., 13.

18. Ibid., 309.

19. Ibid.

20. Ibid., 314.

21. L. Massignon, "1914 Foreword," *Passion*, Mason trans.1: li.

22. "Les modes de stylisation littéraire," *OM* 2: 385.

23. *Mélanges: Institut Dominicain d'Etudes Orientales*, 1954, 189, quoted in Rocalve, 220.

24. Edward Said, *Orientalism* (New York: Vintage, 1979), 272.

25. Rocalve, 22; Waardenburg, 357.

26. "Les trois prières d'Abraham, *PD*, 266, 267.

27. Robert Caspar, "La vision de L'Islam chez Louis Massignon et son influence sur l'Eglise," *L'Herne*, 139.

28. "Trois prières," *PD*, 263.

29. L. Massignon, Preface to the New Edition, Mason trans., *Passion*, 1: lxii–lxiii.

30. Letter of L. Massignon, n.d., in Keryell, *HS*, 61. References to the death of his son Yves place it after 1935.

31. "La Mubahala de Médine et l'hyperdulie de Fatima," *OM* 1: 561.

32. "Salman Pak et les prémices spirituelles de l'Islam iranien," *PD*, 122.

33. Monteil, "Entretiens," *PD*, 25.

34. "Allocution à l'occasion du 13e anniversaire de la mort de Gandhi," *OM* 3: 379.
35. "Les résultats sociaux de notre politique indigène en Algérie," *OM* 3: 561.
36. Ibid., 564.
37. "Gandhian Outlook and Techniques," English text, *OM* 3: 366.
38. Ibid., 367.
39. Ibid.

6. The Vocation Renewed and Tested

1. Rached Hamzaoui, *L'Académie de langue arabe du Caire: histoire et oeuvre* (Tunis: Publications de l'Université de Tunis, 1975), 104.
2. Keryell, "Notice: Kahil," *HS*, 85–86, 97.
3. Unpublished letter to Thomas Merton, 31 Dec. 1960. Fourteen short letters (3 Sept. 1959 to 26 Apr. 1961) from L. Massignon to Merton are in the Thomas Merton Center at Bellarmine College, Louisville, Kentucky.
4. Keryell, "Notice: Kahil," *HS*, 98.
5. Ibid.
6. Ibid.
7. Keryell, "Introduction," *HS*, 12; "Correspondances," ibid., 324.
8. Letter 4, 10 Feb. 1934, in Keryell, ed., *HS*, 175.
9. Letter 15, 20 Mar. 1934, ibid., 183.
10. L. Massignon, *Passion* (French ed.) 1: 127.
11. Keryell, "Notice: Kahil," *HS*, 101.
12. Letter 31, 18 July 1934, ibid., 193.
13. "Al-Badaliya," in ibid., 376.
14. Harpigny, 115, places this conversation in 1913, when Kahil and Massignon first knew each other; it is cited by Kahil in Keryell, "Notice: Kahil," *HS*, 98, as occurring after their friendship was renewed.
15. "Explication du plan de Kufa," *OM* 3: 35.
16. Letter 19, 2 Apr. 1934, *HS*, 185–186.
17. Letter 21, 10 Apr. 1934, ibid., 187.
18. Letter 30, 27 June 1934, ibid., 193.
19. Letter 33, 8 Dec.1934, ibid., 195.
20. "Salman Pak," *PD*, 98–129.
21. Paul Claudel, 12–15 Apr. 1934, *Journal*, 2 vols. (Paris: Pléiade, Gallimard, 1968), 2: 157.

22. Claudel, 31 May 1925, *Journal* 1: 675.
23. Ibid., Holy Saturday, April 1925, 1: 668.
24. Ibid., 14–18 Nov. 1925, 1: 696.
25. Letter of L. Massignon, 27 Aug. 1934, *Claudel-Massignon*, 46–47.
26. "Sortes claudelianae," *OM* 3: 732.
27. Letter 19, 12 Oct. 1909, *Claudel-Massignon*, 72–73.
28. Letter 37, 27 July 1910, *ibid.*, 88.
29. "Sortes claudelianae," *PD*, 389.
30. "Tu Vertex et Apex," *OM* 3: 789.
31. "Le culte liturgique et populaire des sept dormants d'Ephèse," *OM* 3: 143.
32. Unpublished letter to Jean de Menasce, 30 Oct. 1935.
33. "La Haute-Vallée du Saint-Jean Acadien," *PD*, 252.
34. Ibid., 253.
35. Louis Massignon, "Colonisation et conscience chrétienne," *Esprit* 4, no. 39 (1935): 431.
36. Ibid., 432.
37. Claudel, 17 Oct. 1937, *Journal* 2: 207. The letter of the Spanish bishops appeared 1 July 1937. Claudel supported their position in *Le Figaro*, 27 Aug. 1937.
38. Ibid., 16 November 1937, 209.
39. "L'amitié de Jean-Richard Bloch," *OM* 3: 554.
40. "Déclaration du comité pour la paix civile et religieuse en Espagne," *Esprit* 5, no. 58 (1937): 651–652.
41. Jacques Maritain, *Oeuvres complètes,* vol. 5 (Paris: Ed. St. Paul, 1982), 1249–1251.
42. Lacouture, *François Mauriac*, 333.
43. Letter 48, 20 Feb. 1938, *HS*, 202.
44. Monteil, "Entretiens," *PD* 10.
45. Letter 64, 11 Oct. 1938, *HS*, 211.
46. Letter 66, 5 Nov. 1938, ibid., 212–213.
47. André Gide, *Journal, 1939–1949, souvenirs* (Paris: Pléiade, Gallimard, 1954), 1050–1051.
48. Solange Lemaître, "Louis Massignon," *L'Herne*, 443.
49. Monteil, *Linceul* 12; Rocalve, 283, state that he was mobilized in March 1940. However, D. Massignon, "Chronologie," *L'Herne*, 16, cites Sept. 1939; a section ultimately omitted from the introduction to *PD* cites 1939, quoted in Monteil, *Linceul*, 64.
50. Monteil, "Entretiens," *PD*, 12.
51. Monteil, *Linceul*, 156.

52. "Mentioned (here) will be only one final and decisive interior event, the shattering of his military life, June 28, 1940, at Mont-de-Marsan: prelude to his option for nonviolence," quoted in ibid., 64.

53. Quoted in ibid., 65.

54. Claudel, 5 Oct. 1942, *Journal* 2: 417.

55. Monteil, *Linceul*, 65.

56. Letter 73, 10 Nov. 1944, *HS*, 216–217.

7. Conflict in the Middle East

1. Harpigny, 116.

2. Marie-Madeleine Davy, "L'Homme 'en qui Dieu verdoie,' " *Question de*, no. 90 (Paris: Albin Michel, 1992), 220; Maurice de Gandillac, "Jean Danielou et 'Dieu vivant,' " in *Jean Danielou, 1905–1974* (Paris: Cerf, 1975), 139; letter 223, 5 June 1955, Jules Monchanin, *Abbé Monchanin: lettres à sa mère 1913–1957* (Paris: Cerf, 1989), 520.

3. Marcel Moré, *Dieu vivant* 1 (1945): 5.

4. Ibid., 16 (1950): 11.

5. "Hallaj, martyr mystique de l'Islam," 4 (1945); "Notre Dame de La Salette," 7 (1946); "La Palestine et la paix dans la justice," 12 (1948); "Les trois prières d'Abraham," 13 (1949); (with Paul Claudel and Jean Daniélou) "Sur l'exégèse biblique," 14 (1949).

6. Letter of Massignon, 14 Feb. 1949, *Claudel-Massignon*, 36.

7. Harpigny, 242.

8. Monteil, "Entretiens," *PD*, 12.

9. *Témoignage chrétien*, no. 156, 27 June 1947, quoted in Christiane Lacour, "Rencontres avec Louis Massignon," *L'Herne*, 285. The group initially called the Comité chrétien pour l'entente France-Islam was soon referred to as simply "France-Islam."

10. "Allocution," *OM* 3: 379.

11. Ibid.

12. Monteil, *Linceul*, 189.

13. "Le problème des Réfugiés Arabes de Palestine," *OM* 3: 518.

14. "Situation internationale de l'Islam," *OM* 1: 55.

15. Gabriel Marcel, "A Louis Massignon dans l'invisible," *L'Herne*, 450.

16. André Chouraqui, "Revendiquez la paix de Jérusalem," *L'Herne*, 234.

17. Lacour, *L'Herne*, 285.
18. "La Palestine et la paix dans la justice," *OM* 3: 462.
19. Ibid., 463.
20. Ibid.
21. Ibid., 464.
22. Ibid.
23. "Le sort du Proche-Orient," *OM* 3: 456.
24. Ibid., 457.
25. Ibid., 458.
26. Monteil, *Linceul*, 194.
27. "La mort de Judah Leib Magnes (1948)" *OM* 3: 494.
28. Badaliya annual letter, no. 6, Dec. 1952, 6. Mimeographed copies were circulated annually to the membership, 1947–1961, but the letters have never been published.
29. Letter 150, 23 May 1949, *HS*, 259.
30. "Les lieux saints," *Le Monde*, 2 Nov. 1949, 3.
31. Badaliya annual letter, no. 3, Dec. 1949, 1.
32. "Réfugiés et condamnés politiques," *OM* 3: 552.
33. "Le problème des Réfugiés " *OM* 3: 527.
34. "Réfugiés européens et migrations internationales," *OM* 3: 535.
35. Ibid., 535–536.
36. Ibid., 536.
37. Ibid., 538.
38. Quoted in Monteil, *Linceul*, 75.
39. Letter 27, 8 May 1934, *HS*, 191.
40. Lemaître, *L'Herne*, 443.
41. Letter 112, 31 Jan. 1947, *HS*, 237.
42. Letter 143, 27 Aug. 1948, ibid., 253.
43. Letter 168, 20 May 1951, ibid., 271.
44. Louis Gardet, "A Propos du sacerdoce de Louis Massignon," in *Présence*, 194.
45. Letter 228, 16–17 Feb. 1959, *HS*, 308.
46. Kamel Medawar, in Harpigny, 127n271, 129.
47. Letter of Kahil to Medawar, 3 Dec. 1949, quoted in Harpigny, 131n280.
48. Harpigny , 131.
49. Ibid., 133.
50. Ibid., 134.
51. Portier, "Massignon, un homme de réconciliation," in *Présence*, 198.

52. Claudel, 6 Nov. 1951, *Journal* 2: 789.
53. Harpigny, 137n303.
54. Letter of Massignon, 29 July 1950, *Claudel-Massignon*, 38.
55. Claudel, 1 Aug. 1950, *Journal* 2: 740.

8. The Road to Independence in Morocco

1. "Allocution," *OM* 3: 379–380. The Paris press reported the resignation only two years later, in 1951; Massignon cited *L'Aube*, 16 Feb. 1951; *Le Monde*, 17 Feb. 1951; letter 151, 4 June 1949, *HS*, 260.
2. "Les résultats sociaux de notre politique en Algérie," *OM* 3: 559–568.
3. "La situation sociale en Algérie," *OM* 3: 579.
4. Ibid., 583.
5. Ibid., 581.
6. Ibid., 583.
7. Ibid., 579.
8. Badaliya annual letter, no. 5, Dec. 1951, 1–2; "Réfugiés," *OM* 3: 535–538.
9. Badaliya annual letter, no. 5, Dec. 1951, 1.
10. Badaliya annual letter, no. 6, Dec. 1952, 4.
11. "L'Occident devant l'Orient," *OM* 1: 208.
12. L. Massignon, "Colonisation et conscience chrétienne," *Esprit* 4, no. 39 (1935): 431.
13. "L'Occident devant l'Orient," *OM* 1: 208–209.
14. Badaliya annual letter, no. 6, Dec. 1952, 6.
15. "La signification spirituelle du dernier pèlerinage de Gandhi," *OM* 3: 339.
16. "Allocution," *OM* 3: 376.
17. *Bulletin des Amis de Gandhi*, no. 4, June-July 1960, quoted in Camille Drevet, "L. Massignon et les amis de Gandhi," *L'Herne*, 394.
18. Harpigny, 213; "Allocution," *OM* 3: 380.
19. Charles-André Julien, *Le Maroc face aux impérialismes, 1415–1956* (Paris: Ed. Jeune Afrique, 1978), 196.
20. Robert Barrat, *Justice pour le Maroc* (Paris: Seuil, 1953), 27; Julien, *La France*, 266n81.

21. Georges Spillmann, *Du protectorat à l'indépendance, Maroc 1912–1955* (Paris: Plon, 1967), 161.

22. Lacouture, *François Mauriac*, 471.

23. François Mauriac, *Nouveaux mémoires intérieurs* (Paris: Flammarion, coll. folio, 1965), 356–357.

24. "Communiqué," Comité France-Islam, 22 July 1953, quoted in *HS*, 281.

25. General Juin as quoted in *Le Monde*, 26 June 1953, 2.

26. Lacouture, 469.

27. "L'Islam et le témoignage du croyant," *OM* 3: 587.

28. Ibid., 587–588.

29. Ibid., 591.

30. Ibid., 591–592.

31. Ibid., 593.

32. Claude Mauriac, *Et comme l'espérance est violente,* vol. 3 of *Le Temps immobile* (Paris: Grasset, 1976), 511–512.

33. Jean-Marie Domenach, "L'actualité de Louis Massignon," in *Présence*, 277.

34. Charles–André Julien, "Massignon, paladin de la foi et de la justice," *L'Herne*, 301.

35. Ibid.

36. Claudel, 21 Aug. 1953, *Journal* 2: 843.

37. "L'Islam," *OM* 3: 595.

38. Letter 187, 16 Sept. 1953, *HS*, 284–285.

39. "Allocution," *OM* 3: 381.

40. Julien, *L'Herne*, 302.

41. Claude Mauriac, *Les Espaces imaginares*, vol. 2 of *Le Temps immobile* (Paris: Grasset, 1975), 417.

42. "Allocution" *OM* 3: 376.

43. Julien, *L'Herne*, 302.

44. Harpigny, 84.

45. "La notion du voeu et la dévotion musulmane à Fâtima," *OM* 1: 585.

46. "Gandhian outlook and techniques," *OM* 3: 363.

47. "La notion du voeu," *OM* 1: 573.

48. "Le voeu et le destin," *OM* 3: 688.

49. "Un voeu et un destin: Marie-Antoinette," *OM* 3: 654.

50. "L'Exemplarité singulière de la vie de Gandhi," *OM* 3: 355; "Le voeu et le destin," *OM* 3: 696.

51. "L'Exemplarité," *OM* 3: 357.

52. Ibid., 356.
53. "Le voeu et le destin," *OM* 3: 689.
54. "L'exemplarité," *OM* 3: 359.
55. "Le voeu et le destin," *OM* 3: 695.
56. Ibid., 696.
57. Ibid., 697.
58. Ibid.
59. Ibid., 689.
60. Ibid., 689–690.
61. "Allocution," *OM* 3: 376.

9. Algeria, the Ultimate Suffering

1. L. Massignon, "La 'renaissance arabe' et notre avenir nord-africain," *Esprit* 22 (1954): 56.
2. Raoul Girardet, *L'Idée coloniale en France, 1871–1962* (Paris: La Table Ronde, 1972), 224–225; Portier, *L'Herne*, 299.
3. Jacques Berque, *Arabies* (Paris: Stock, 1980), 176.
4. Henri Massé, intro., *Mélanges Louis Massignon*, vol. 1 (Damascus: Institut français de Damas, 1956), xii.
5. Badaliya annual letter, no. 8, Dec. 1954, 3. The 1947 statutes had mandated the election of an Algerian National assembly, but because of stuffed ballot boxes and voter fraud, independence candidates achieved only marginal representation.
6. "L'exemplarité," *OM* 3: 361.
7. Monteil, *Linceul*: 89.
8. Ibid., 94.
9. Ibid., 91–92.
10. *La Guerre d'Algérie et les Français*, ed. J.-P. Rioux (Paris: Fayard, 1990), 119.
11. Ibid., 67.
12. Robert Barrat, "Un Journaliste français chez les 'hors-la-loi' algériens," *France-Observateur*, 15 Sept. 1955, 36–37.
13. Jean Scelles, "Un retour à Dieu par l'Islam: L. Massignon," *L'Herne*, 185.
14. "Allocution," *OM* 3: 380.
15. "Communiqué C.C.E. France-Islam," *OM* 3: 603.
16. Ibid.; Camille Drevet, *Massignon et Gandhi: la contagion de la vérité* (Paris: Cerf, 1967), 151.

17. Drevet, *L'Herne*, 386.

18. Badaliya annual letter, no. 9, Dec. 1955, 1.

19. Badaliya annual letter, no. 10, Dec. 1956, 26; Monteil, *Linceul* 102.

20. "Allocution," *OM* 3: 378; "Colloque universitaire du 2 juin, 1957 sur le problème algérien," *OM* 3: 608.

21. "Allocution," *OM* 3: 378; Monteil, *Linceul*, 105.

22. "Colloque," *OM* 3: 608.

23. *L'Express*, 30 Nov. 1956, 21.

24. "Allocution," *OM* 3: 381; Monteil, *Linceul*: 108.

25. Badaliya convocation, 6 Dec. 1957, quoted in Monteil, *Linceul*, 110–111; G. Arnaud and Jacques Vergès, *Pour Djamila Bouhired* (Paris: Ed. de Minuit, 1957). Bouhired's sentence was commuted and she was transferred to France.

26. Bernard Droz and Evelyne Lever, *Histoire de la guerre d'Algérie*, 2nd ed. (Paris: Seuil, 1982), 130n3; Monteil, *Linceul*, 115–116.

27. Badaliya annual letter, no. 11, Dec. 1957, 6.

28. Massignon letter, 11 Mar. 1958, in Monteil, *Linceul*, 113–114. Henri Alleg, editor of the communist newspaper *Alger républicain*, authored *La Question*, detailing the month of torture he endured in May 1957. The Sartre article introduces the English edition of Alleg's book (New York: Braziller, 1958).

29. Patrick Eveno and Jean Planchais, eds., *La Guerre d'Algérie* (Paris: La Découverte/Le Monde, 1989), 129.

30. Badaliya convocation, 6 Dec. 1957, quoted in Monteil, *Linceul*, 115.

31. Unpublished letter to Bernard Guyon, 25 Feb. 1958; Harpigny, 186n398.

32. Unpublished letter to Edmond Michelet, 16 May 1958.

33. Massignon letter, 2 July 1958, quoted in Monteil, *Linceul*, 122.

34. Monteil, *Linceul*, 125.

35. Massignon letter to Michelet, 16 May 1958.

36. Badaliya annual letter, no. 12, Sept. 1958–June 1959, 7.

37. Massignon letter, 13 Mar. 1959, quoted in Monteil, *Linceul*, 128.

38. Massignon letter, 29 Apr. 1959, quoted in Monteil, *Linceul*, 129.

39. Badaliya convocation, 6 Mar. 1959, quoted in Monteil, *Linceul*, 128.

40. *Bulletin des Amis de Gandhi*, no. 1 (Jan. 1960) quoted in Drevet, *L'Herne*, 394.

41. "Allocution," *OM* 3: 381.

42. Massignon letter, 13 Apr. 1960, quoted in Monteil, *Linceul*, 133.

43. Herbert Mason, *Memoir of a Friend* (Notre Dame, Ind.: University of Notre Dame Press, 1988), 106.

44. Unpublished letters: to Jean de Menasce, 31 March 1960; to Thomas Merton, 31 March 1960.

45. Unpublished letter to Gabriel Marcel, 4 Apr. 1960.

46. Unpublished letter to Jean de Menasce, 7 May 1960.

47. "Proceedings," Louis Massignon Colloquium, 11–18 Aug. 1990, ed., Jean Moncelon, 157.

48. *Le Monde*, 3 May 1960; Georges Loire, "Connaissez-vous Louis Massignon," in *Présence*, 259.

49. "Dialogue sur 'les Arabes,'" *Esprit* 28 (1960): 1518.

50. Unpublished letter to Thomas Merton, 3 June 1960.

51. *Bulletin des Amis de Gandhi*, 4, June–July 1960, quoted in Drevet, *L'Herne*, 395.

52. Ibid.

53. Patrick Eveno and Jean Planchais, eds., *La Guerre d'Algérie*, 289.

54. Monteil, *Linceul*, 134.

55. Letter 241, 24 June 1960, *HS*, 317.

56. "Dialogue sur 'les Arabes,'" *Esprit* 28: 1519.

57. Unpublished letters to Thomas Merton, 19 July, 4 Aug. 1960.

58. Badaliya convocation, 7 Oct. 1960, quoted in *HS*, 444.

59. Badaliya annual letter, no. 14, Aug. 1960–Jan. 1961, 1.

60. Monteil, *Linceul*, 15.

61. Badaliya annual letter, no. 14, 2.

62. "Allocution," *OM* 3: 378.

63. Ibid., 382.

64. Badaliya convocation, 6 Jan. 1961, quoted in *HS*, 445.

65. *Le Monde*, 18–19 Dec. 1960, 2.

66. Badaliya convocation, 3 Feb. 1961, quoted in *HS*, 447.

67. Badaliya convocation, 5 May 1961, quoted in *HS*, 448.

68. Badaliya convocation, 2 June 1961, in *HS*, 450.

69. Ibid.

70. Massignon letter to Drevet, n.d., quoted in Drevet, *Massignon et Gandhi*, 50.

71. Massignon letter, 25 Oct. 1961, quoted in Monteil, *Linceul*, 139–140.

72. (Two were found near Argenteuil 23 Oct.) *Le Monde*, 25 Oct. 1961: 6; (three near the bridge of Bezons, one near the Pont Neuf) ibid., 26 Oct.: 4; (one near Argenteuil) ibid., 28 Oct.: 6; 8 Nov.: 4.

73. Badaliya convocation, 3 Nov. 1961, quoted in Monteil, *Linceul*, 139.
74. *Le Monde*, 9 Nov. 1961, 9.
75. Letter to Drevet, 25 Oct. 1961, quoted in Drevet, *Massignon et Gandhi*, 162.
76. Badaliya annual letter, no.15, Dec. 1961–Easter 1962, 4. Exiled to Nineveh, Tobit buried the bodies of Israelites killed by Sennacherib's retreat from Judea, *Tobit* 1:18–20.
77. Badaliya annual letter, no. 15, 2–3.
78. Badaliya convocation, 2 Feb. 1962, quoted in *HS*, 454.
79. Badaliya convocation, 6 Apr. 1962, quoted in *HS*, 456.
80. Badaliya convocation, 1 June 1962, quoted in *HS*, 458.
81. Monteil, *Linceul*, 19.
82. Ibid., 28.
83. Ibid., 27–28.
84. Letter, quoted in Drevet, *Massignon et Gandhi*, 51.
85. Letter to Serge de Beaurecueil, quoted in *Mémorial Louis Massignon* (Cairo: L'Institut français d'archéologie, 1963), 21.
86. Drevet, *Massignon et Gandhi*, 81.
87. Monteil, *Linceul*, 16.
88. Letter to Drevet, n.d. quoted in Drevet, *L'Herne*, 399.
89. Badaliya convocation, n.d. (Oct. 1962), quoted in *HS*, 460.
90. Ibid.
91. "Le symbole médiéval de la destinée de Bagdad," *Arabica*, special number (Leiden: E. J. Brill, 1962), 249–251.
92. *Le Monde*, 7 Nov. 1962, 8.
93. *Le Monde*, 14 Nov. 1962, 13.
94. François Mauriac, *Le nouveau bloc-notes 1961–1964*, 6 Nov. 1962 (Paris: Flammarion, 1968), 207.

Bibliography

I. Works by Louis Massignon

An asterisk indicates the edition used in the text.

BOOKS

Tableau géographique du Maroc dans les quinze premières années du XVI siècle d'après Léon l'Africain. Algiers: Jourdain, 1906.

Mission en Mésopotamie. 2 vols. Cairo: Institut Français d'Archeologie, 1910; 1912.

La Passion de Hallaj, martyr mystique de l'Islam. 1st ed., 2 vols. Paris: Geuthner, 1922. *2nd ed., 4 vols. Paris: Gallimard, 1975.

*The Passion of al-Hallaj, mystic and martyr of Islam. Trans. Herbert Mason. 4 vols. Princeton: Princeton University Press, 1982.

Essai sur les origines du lexique technique de la mystique musulmane. 1st ed. Paris: Geuthner, 1922. *2nd ed. Paris: Vrin, 1954. 3rd ed. Paris: Vrin, 1968.

The Origins of the Technical Language of Islamic Mysticism. Trans. Benjamin Clark. Notre Dame, Ind.: University of Notre Dame Press, 1996.

COLLECTED ARTICLES

Youakim Moubarek provides the most complete bibliography of articles by Louis Massignon in: *L'Oeuvre de Louis Massignon.* Vol. 1. Beirut: Ed. du Cénacle Libanais, 1972.

Parole donnée. Introd. Vincent Monteil. 1st ed., Paris: Julliard, 1962. 2nd ed., Paris: Coll. de poche, 10/18.

*3rd ed., Paris: Seuil, 1983. Contains 31 articles. Articles cited in the text are listed.

"La Haute-Vallée du Saint-Jean Acadien," 250–253.
"Salman Pak et les prémices spirituelles de l'Islam iranien," 98–129.
"Sortes claudelianae," 389–390.
"Les trois prières d'Abraham," 257–272.
"Toute une vie avec un frère parti au désert," 63–72.
"Voyelles sémitiques et sémantique musicale," 342–346.

Opera Minora. Ed. Youakim Moubarek. 3 vols. Paris: Presses universitaires de France, 1969. Contains 205 articles. Articles cited in the text are listed.

Volume 1

"La Mubahala de Médine et l'hyperdulie de Fatima," 550–572.
"La notion du voeu et la dévotion musulmane à Fatima," 573–591.
"L'Occident devant l'Orient: primauté d'une solution culturelle," 208–223.
"Situation internationale de l'Islam," 53–56.
"La Syrie et le problème des contacts culturels entre Orient et Occident," 162–171.

Volume 2

"Etude sur une courbe personnelle de vie: le cas de Hallaj, martyr mystique de l'Islam," 167–190.
"L'expérience mystique et les modes de stylisation littéraire," 371–387.
"L'involution sémantique du symbole dans les cultures sémitiques," 626–637.
"Les modes de stylisation littéraire," 371–387.
"La Passion d'Al Halladj et l'ordre des Halladjiyyah—Mélanges Hartwig Derenbourg (1844–1908)," 9–17.
"Textes musulmans pouvant concerner la nuit de l'esprit," 397–402.

Volume 3

"Allocution à l'occasion du 13e anniversaire de la mort de Gandhi," 376–383.
"L'amitié de Jean–Richard Bloch," 554–555.
"L'amitié et la présence mariale dans nos vies," 767–769.

"L'apostolat de la souffrance et de la compassion réparatrice au xiiie siècle: l'exemple de Sainte Christine l'Admirable," 627–641.

"L'Arabie et le problème arabe," 433–453.

"La Cité des Morts au Caire," 233–285.

"Colloque universitaire du 2 juin 1957 sur le problème algérien," 607–609.

"Communiqué C.C.E. France-Islam," 603.

"Le culte liturgique et populaire des VII dormants d'Ephèse," 119–180.

"L'exemplarité singulière de la vie de Gandhi," 354–362.

"Explication du plan de Kufa (Irak)," 35–60.

"Foucauld au désert devant le Dieu d'Abraham, Agar et Ismael," 772–784.

"Gandhian Outlook and Techniques," 363–375.

"L'honneur des camarades de travail et la parole de vérité," 840–843.

"Huysmans devant la confession de Boullan," 735–742.

"L'Idée de Dieu," 831–833.

"In Memoriam. Sir Mark Sykes. Remarks about the Present Disruption of British Policy in the Near East," 418–422.

"L'Islam et la politique des alliés," 428–432.

"L'Islam et le témoignage du croyant," 585–595.

"Labbeville, sa vie paroissiale, de la ferme abbatiale du Bec à la dernière lettre d'Altamura," 318–338.

"Mes rapports avec Lawrence en 1917," 423–426.

"La mort de Judah Leib Magnes (1948)," 494.

"Note sur Faysal," 415–417.

"Notre Dame de la Salette et la conversion de J. K. Huysmans," 749–751.

"La Palestine et la paix dans la justice," 461–470.

"Le Pèlerinage," 817–822.

"Le problème des Réfugiés Arabes de Palestine," 526–528.

"Réfugiés européens et migrations internationales," 535–538.

"Le respect de la personne humaine en Islam, et la priorité du droit d'asile sur le devoir de juste guerre," 539–553.

"Les résultats sociaux de notre politique indigène en Algérie," 559–568.

"Les saints musulmans enterrés à Bagdad," 94–101.

"La signification spirituelle du dernier pèlerinage de Gandhi," 339–353.

"La situation sociale en Algérie," 578–584.
"Le sort du Proche Orient et le rôle de la France en Syrie," 454–460.
"Sortes claudelianae," 732.
"Le tombeau de J.-K. Huysmans," 733–734.
"Tu Vertex et Apex," 787–789.
"Le voeu et le destin," 688–700.
"Un voeu et un destin: Marie-Antoinette," 654–684.

Testimonies and Reflections, Essays of Louis Massignon. Introd. and trans. Herbert Mason. Notre Dame, Ind.: University of Notre Dame Press, 1989. Contains 19 articles from *Parole donnée* and *Opera Minora.*

"Meditation of a Passerby on His Visit to the Sacred Woods of Ise," 165–172.

OTHER ARTICLES BY LOUIS MASSIGNON

"Une amitié: Henri Maspero: note sur Henri Maspero adolescent, pour Mlle Dr. Rosa Katz." *Cahiers de l'Herne.* Ed. Jean-François Six. Paris: Ed. de l'Herne, 1970. 21–22.
"Colonisation et conscience chrétienne." *Esprit* 4, no. 39 (1935): 431–432.
"Dialogue sur 'les Arabes.'" With Jacques Berque. *Esprit* 28, no. 10 (1960): 1505–1519.
"Les lieux saints." *Le Monde,* 12 Nov. 1949, 3.
"Louis Massignon à Henri Maspero." Ed. Hélène Maspero. *L'Herne,* 1970: 27–42.
"Les Maîtres qui ont guidé ma vie." *Horizons Maghrebins* nos. 14/15 (1989): 156–160.
"La 'renaissance arabe' et notre avenir nord-africain," *Esprit* 22, no. 7 (1954): 55–59.
"Le symbole médiéval de la destinée de Bagdad." *Arabica,* special number, 249–251. Leiden: E. J. Brill, 1962.

II. Collections of Articles about Louis Massignon

Articles cited in the text are listed.

Cahiers de l'Herne. Ed. Jean-François Six. Paris: Ed. de l'Herne, 1970.

Caspar, Robert. "La vision de l'Islam chez Louis Massignon et son influence sur l'Eglise," 126–147.

Chouraqui, André. "Revendiquez la paix de Jérusalem," 231–235.

Drevet, Camille. "Louis Massignon et les amis de Gandhi," 381–404.

Julien, Charles-André. "Massignon, paladin de la foi et de la justice," 300–303.

Lacour, Christiane. "Rencontres avec Louis Massignon," 282–287.

LeMaître, Solange. "Louis Massignon," 442–447.

Marcel, Gabriel. "A Louis Massignon dans l'invisible," 449–450.

Massignon, Daniel. "Chronologie," 11–17.

Portier, Lucienne. "Conditionnement et liberté dans la pensée de Louis Massignon concernant l'Algérie," 288–299.

_____. "Louis Massignon et Charles de Foucauld," 349–358.

Rondot, Pierre. "Louis Massignon et le Docteur Quesnoy," 374–380.

Scelles, Jean. "Un retour à Dieu par l'Islam: Louis Massignon," 182–187.

Présence de Louis Massignon: hommages et témoignages. Ed. Daniel Massignon. Paris: Maisonneuve et Larose, 1987.

Domenach, Jean-Marie. "L'actualité de Louis Massignon," 275–281.

Gardet, Louis. "A Propos du sacerdoce de Louis Massignon," 192–195.

Loire, Georges. "Connaissez-vous Louis Massignon?" 256–259.

Laporte Yves. "Arrivée de Louis Massignon au Collège de France," 21–22.

Portier, Lucienne. "Massignon, un homme de réconciliation," 196–200.

III. Other Works Cited

Antonius, George. *The Arab Awakening: the Story of the Arab National Movement.* Beirut: Librairie du Liban, 1969.

Arnaud, G., and Jacques Vergès. *Pour Djamila Bouhired.* Paris: Ed. de Minuit, 1957.

Baldick, Robert. *The Life of J.-K. Huysmans.* Oxford: Clarendon, 1955.

Barrat, Robert. *Justice pour le Maroc.* Paris: Seuil, 1953.

_____. "Un Journaliste français chez les 'hors-la-loi' algériens." *France-Observateur,* 15 Sept. 1955, 36–37.

Berchem, Max van. *La Correspondance entre Max van Berchem et Louis Massignon, 1907–1919*. Ed. Werner Vycichl. Leiden: Brill, 1980.

Berque, Jacques. *Arabies*. Stock, 1980.

Castries, Henri de. *Islam, impressions et études*. Paris: Colin, 1896.

Claudel, Paul. *Journal*. 2 vols. Paris: Pléiade, Gallimard, 1968.

————. *Paul Claudel, Louis Massignon: 1908–1914*. Ed. and introd. Michel Malicet. Coll. Les grandes correspondances. Paris: Desclée, 1973.

Davy, Marie-Madeleine. Interview. "L'homme 'en qui Dieu verdoie.'" *Question de*, no. 90, 218–223. Paris: Albin Michel, 1992.

"Déclaration du Comité pour la paix civile et religieuse en Espagne." *Esprit* 5, no. 58 (1937): 651–652.

Drevet, Camille. *Massignon et Gandhi: la contagion de la vérité*. Paris: Cerf, 1967.

Droz, Bernard, and Evelyne Lever. *Histoire de la guerre d'Algérie*. 2nd ed. Paris: Seuil, 1982.

d'Urfé, Honoré. *L'Astrée*. Vol. 2. Geneva: Slatkine Rpts., 1966.

Eveno, Patrick, and Jean Planchais, eds. *La Guerre d'Algérie*. Paris: La Découverte/Le Monde, 1989.

Foucauld, Charles de. *Directoire*. Paris: Seuil, 1961.

————. "Itinéraires au Maroc." *Bulletin de la Société de Géographie de Paris*, ser. 7, vol. 8, 118–125. Paris, 1887.

————. "Positions déterminées dans le Maroc." In *Comptes rendus des séances de la Société de Géographie et de la commission centrale*. Paris, 1885.

————. *Reconnaissance au Maroc*. Paris, 1885.

————. *Voyage au Maroc: compte rendu de la Société de Géographie de Paris*. Paris, 1884.

Gandillac, Maurice de. "Jean Danielou et 'Dieu vivant.'" In *Jean Danielou, 1905–1974.*, 137–142. Paris: Cerf, 1975.

Gide, André. *Journal, 1939–1949: souvenirs*. Paris: Pléiade, Gallimard, 1954.

Girardet, Raoul. *L'Idée coloniale en France, 1871–1962*. Paris: La Table Ronde, 1972.

Hamzaoui, Rached. *L'Académie de langue arabe du Caire: histoire et oeuvre*. Tunis: l'Université de Tunis, 1975.

Harpigny, Guy. *Islam et Christianisme selon Louis Massignon*. Louvain, 1981.

Julien, Charles-André. *Le Maroc face aux impérialismes, 1915–1956*. Paris: Ed. Jeune Afrique, 1978.

Keryell, Jacques. *Jardin donnée*. Paris: Ed. St-Paul, 1993.

————, ed. and introd. *L'Hospitalité sacrée*. Paris: Nouvelle Cité, 1987.

Lacouture, Jean. *François Mauriac*. Paris: Seuil, 1980.

Malicet, Michel, ed. and introd. *Paul Claudel, Louis Massignon: 1908–1914*. Paris: Desclée, 1973.

Maritain, Jacques. *Oeuvres complètes*. Vol. 5. Paris: Ed. St-Paul, 1982.

Mason, Herbert. *Memoir of a Friend*. Notre Dame, Ind.: University of Notre Dame Press, 1988.

Massé, Henri, intro. *Mélanges Louis Massignon*. Vol. 1. Damascus: Institut français de Damas, 1956.

Massignon, Daniel. "Louis Massignon et le dialogue des cultures." *Horizons Maghrebins*, nos. 14/15 (1989): 162–n170.

————. "Le voyage en Mésopotamie et la conversion de Louis Massignon en 1908." *Islamochristiana* 14 (1988): 127–199.

Mauriac, Claude. *Et comme l'espérance est violente*. Paris: Grasset, 1976. Vol. 3 of *Le Temps immobile* (10 vols.).

————. *Les espaces imaginaires*. Paris: Grasset, 1975. Vol. 2 of *Le Temps immobile* (10 vols.).

Mauriac, François. *Le nouveau bloc-notes 1961–1964*. Paris: Flammarion, 1968.

————. *Nouveaux mémoires intérieurs*. Paris: Flammarion, Folio, 1965.

Moncelon, Jean, ed. "Proceedings." Louis Massignon Colloquium, 11–18 Aug. 1990.

Monchanin, Jules. *Abbé Monchanin: lettres à sa mère 1913–1957*. Paris: Cerf, 1989.

Monteil, Vincent-Mansour. "Entretiens." In Louis Massignon, *Parole donnée*. 3rd ed. Paris: Seuil, 1983.

————. *Le Linceul de feu*. Paris: Vegapress, 1987.

Moré, Marcel. "Liminaire." *Dieu Vivant* 1 (1945): 7–11.

————. "Liminaire." *Dieu Vivant* 16 (1950): 7–15.

Moubarac, Youakim, ed. *Mémorial Louis Massignon*. Cairo: l'Institut français d'archéologie, 1963.

Nevakivi, Jukka. *Britain, France and the Arab Middle East, 1914–1920*. London: Athlone, 1969.

Pierre Roche, Estampes modelées et églomisations, un catalogue de ses oeuvres, introd. Louis Massignon. Paris: NRF, 1935.

Preminger, Marion Mill. *The Sands of Tamanrasset: The Story of Charles de Foucauld*. New York: Hawthorn, 1961.

Rioux, J.-P., ed. *La Guerre d'Algérie et les Français.* Paris: Fayard, 1990.

Rocalve, Pierre. "Place et rôle de l'Islam et de l'Islamologie dans la vie et l'oeuvre de Louis Massignon." Diss., Sorbonne, 1990. Published as *Louis Massignon et l'Islam.* Damascus: Institut français de Damas, 1993. Page numbers in the notes refer to the dissertation.

Roche, Pierre. *Catalogue de guerre des médailles, médaillons, plaquettes, jetons, et gypsographies de Pierre Roche.* Paris: Canule, 1918.

_____. *Exposition de l'art du fer forgé, du cuivre, et de l'étain au musée Galliera, mai-septembre 1905, rapport de Roche au nom du jury.* Paris: Librairies-Imprimeries Réunies, 1905.

Said, Edward. *Orientalism.* New York: Vintage, 1979.

Sicard, Claude. "Roger Martin du Gard: les années d'apprentissage littéraire." Diss., Université de Lille, 1976.

Six, Jean-François, introd. et ed. *L'Aventure de l'amour de Dieu, 80 lettres inédites de Charles de Foucauld à Louis Massignon.* Paris: Seuil, 1993.

Spillman, Georges. *Du protectorat à l'indépendance, Maroc 1912–1955.* Paris: Plon, 1967.

Vycichl, Werner, ed. *La Correspondance entre Max van Berchem et Louis Massignon, 1907–1919.* Leiden: Brill, 1980.

Waardenburg, Jean-Jacques. *L'Islam dans le miroir de l'Occident.* Paris: LaHaye, 1963.

A biography of Massignon containing an important bibliography was published after the completion of this manuscript:

Destremau, Christian, and Jean Moncelon. *Louis Massignon.* Paris: Plon, 1994.

Index